Visual culture

MANCHESTER
UNIVERSITY PRESS

Visual culture

An introduction John A. Walker & Sarah Chaplin

Manchester University Press
MANCHESTER & NEW YORK

distributed exclusively in the USA by Palgrave

Copyright © John A. Walker and Sarah Chaplin 1997

Published by Manchester University Press
Oxford Road, Manchester M13 9NR, UK
and Room 400, 175 Fifth Avenue, New York, NY 10010, USA
www.manchesteruniversitypress.co.uk

Distributed exclusively in the USA by
Palgrave, 175 Fifth Avenue, New York,
NY 10010, USA

Distributed exclusively in Canada by
UBC Press, University of British Columbia, 2029 West Mall,
Vancouver, BC, Canada V6T 1Z2

British Library Cataloguing-in-Publication Data
A catalogue record is available from the British Library

Library of Congress Cataloging-in-Publication Data
Walker, John A.
    Visual culture : an introduction / John A. Walker and Sarah
    Chaplin.
        p. cm.
    ISBN 0-7190-5019-7 (cloth). – ISBN 0-7190-5020-0 (pbk.)
    1. Arts. Modern – 20th century.   2. Popular culture.   3. Visual
    communication   4. Ut pictura poesis (Aesthetics)   I. Chaplin,
    Sarah.   II. Title.
    NX458.W36   1997
    700'.1'03–dc21   97-12983

ISBN 0 7190 5019 7 *hardback*
ISBN 0 7190 5020 0 *paperback*

First published 1997

05 04   10 9 8 7 6 5 4

Printed in Great Britain by
CPI Bath.

Contents

Preface

THIS BOOK is a *material object* made from paper and printing ink. You can hold it in your hands or use it as a doorstop. If people who cannot read the Roman alphabet/the English language opened its pages all they would see are *signifiers* – horizontal lines of black marks on a white ground – but they would not be able to grasp their *signifieds* – mental concepts – consequently they would not understand the meaning of the linguistic *signs*, the combination of signifiers and signifieds, which in this instance we call words and sentences. However, since you can read these printed signs, you realise that the book is more than a physical thing, that it is also an intellectual 'object' or *mentefact*, containing ideas and information *encoded* in English-language signs. As you read, acts of *decoding* and *communication* occur.

Book production and selling involve a lengthy process of labour on the part of authors, editors, designers, publishers, printers, distributors and bookshops. In exchange for an advance and future royalties, the authors entered into a legal contract with the publishers and sold their mental *labour power* for many months. The publishers' aim is to make a profit so that they can continue and expand their business. Indeed, both parties are subject to economic imperatives; they need to make a living in order to 'reproduce' themselves.

Tens of thousands of new titles enter the marketplace every year; consequently this book had to compete against all the others for the attention of booksellers, reviewers working for the press and other media, and potential purchasers. The book was advertised and offered for sale to the public (or more precisely a defined segment of the public), consequently it was a *commodity*. The fact that you bought or borrowed this book indicates that you thought it would be useful, hence it has a *use-value*. If you take this copy to a second-hand bookshop you may discover it still has an *exchange-value*.

Although you may own the book you are now holding, in a sense other people do too because many exact duplicates were manufactured at the same time. In other words, the book is not a unique, hand-made work of art or craft but one of an edition (batch production); therefore it is a consequence of the ages of printing, industry and *mechanical reproduction*. Some theorists maintain that, for these reasons, mass-produced, cheap, cultural products are more democratic than expensive, one-off, hand-made artefacts.

You are using your eyes to read this sentence but the book was not primarily conceived as a *visual* experience. For example, the appearance of the typeface is not especially significant – many other typefaces could have been used instead. We expected readers to be interested in the *content* rather than the *form* of the book; consequently all that was required of the typeface was legibility and unobtrusiveness. As far as the communication of its content was concerned, the book could equally well have been read aloud, recorded on tape and issued as an audio-cassette. Jacques Derrida, the French, *deconstructionist* philosopher, would disagree with this view on the grounds that writing/print always contains *graphic* characteristics not found in speech.

Of course, the inclusion of illustrations means that certain parts of the book are more visual than other parts. In the case of other kinds of books – volumes of poetry (especially concrete poetry) for instance – layout and typeface are more crucial. Books can also be works of art in their own right – illuminated manuscripts and modern examples of 'book art', for instance – and many publishers issue lavishly illustrated volumes designed to ravish the sight of readers. Academic texts, in contrast, appeal more to the intellect than the eyes.

Although we believe this book contains some original ideas, we are very conscious of our debt to earlier scholars. As readers we have been influenced, and we in turn hope to influence our readers. We acknowledge our sources via notes and references. Most writings quote or make reference to other texts, consequently they exhibit *intertextuality*.

Both authors are lecturers in British universities. Such institutions have been deemed, by the French Marxist philosopher Louis Althusser, to be *Ideological State Apparatuses*, whose function is to assist in the reproduction and development of bourgeois society. While we recognise this to be true – universities would not be funded by the state or by private enterprise at all if they did not perform this basic social function – we also believe that they offer some space for pure research and critical thinking that may transcend the reproductive function.

The preface you are now reading belongs to a category of texts called *paratexts*, that is, ancillary items such as titles, dedications, bookjacket blurbs, etc., which surround the central core of a book. Whenever a text draws attention to itself, self-reference or reflexivity occurs. As three American academics have noted, 'The penchant for *reflexivity* must be seen as symptomatic of the methodological self-scrutiny typical of contemporary thought, its tendency to examine its own terms and procedures'.[1] Although this preface exhibits reflexivity, it does not fundamentally question the role of prefaces in books. Derrida, in contrast, has analysed prefaces and noted their paradoxical nature: they are both inside and outside, before and after 'the book'.[2]

Notes and further reading

1 Robert Stam and others, *New Vocabularies in Film Semiotics: Structuralism, Post-Structuralism and Beyond*, (London & New York, Routledge, 1992), p. 200.

2 The first chapter of Derrida's *Dissemination* – 'Outwork, Prefacing' – is a preface about prefaces. As Barbara Johnson, Derrida's translator, observes, his 'preface at once prefaces *and* deconstructs the preface' (p. xxxii). See: *Dissemination*, (Chicago, University of Chicago Press/London, The Athlone Press, 1981), pp. 1-59.

Acknowledgements

WE WOULD LIKE TO THANK Katharine Reeve, who originally commissioned this book, and Matthew Frost and Rebecca Crum of Manchester University Press, for their encouragement. We are also grateful to Richard Andrews, Colin Cina, Barry Curtis, Nick de Ville, Paul Overy, Pam Simpson, John Taylor, and to students and colleagues at Middlesex University for information supplied and helpful comments on certain chapters. Thanks also to David Evans and Kent Fine Art, New York (figure 10) , the artists Stelarc (figure 15; photo: S. Hunter) and Jamie Wagg (figure 9) for supplying photographs and information, plus Amnesty International (figure 1), the Henry Moore Foundation (figure 8; photo: Brassaï), the Crafts Council, the National Gallery (figure 11), the Royal Academy (figure 5), the *South Wales Echo* (figure 14; photo: Glen Edwards), the Victoria Miro Gallery (figure 12) and UNESCO for providing images and documents. Figure 6 is reproduced from John A. Walker's *Design History and the History of Design* (London, Pluto Press, 1989), p. 70. Margaret Wagstaff and other librarians at Middlesex University were diligent in obtaining the many books and articles we requested.

Introduction

> Among the revolutions in higher education in the last twenty-five years has been an explosion of interest in visual culture . . . The point of a course in visual culture . . . would be to provide students with a set of critical tools for the investigation of human visuality, not to transmit a specific body of information and values. (W. J. T. Mitchell)[1]

IN RECENT years a new field of research called 'visual culture' has begun to be studied and taught in colleges and universities in the developed nations of the world. Also, the expression 'visual culture' is increasingly being used by writers and publishers.[2]

For the sake of clarity it is necessary to distinguish an academic discipline from that which it studies (hence Musicology/music; Art History/the history of art). The expression 'visual culture' may be a source of confusion because it can refer to both a discipline and an object of study. For this reason, in this book, the idea of discipline will be conveyed by the expression 'Visual Culture Studies' and its field or object of study by the expression 'visual culture'. However, it is perhaps premature to call Visual Culture Studies 'a discipline' because it is so eclectic. Rather than being a single discipline, Visual Culture Studies is a hybrid, an inter- or multi-disciplinary enterprise formed as a consequence of a convergence of, or borrowings from, a variety of disciplines and methodologies, as listed in figure 1.

While the multi-disciplinarity of Visual Culture Studies is intellectually exhilarating, there is a danger of incoherence and internal contradiction because the concepts and methods derived from one discipline may be incompatible with those borrowed from another. At least one writer on disciplines and inter-disciplinarity – Nicholas de Ville – believes the latter threatens the very existence of the former.[3] To overcome the implied requirement that academics become expert in a range of disciplines, it has been proposed that scholars from different disciplines should teach in teams. Unfortunately, given the financial crises experienced by universities at present, this possibility becomes more and more remote. However, it is still feasible for anthologies of articles to be published which exemplify various approaches to the study of visual culture.

What is meant by 'the visual' and 'culture' will be examined in detail shortly but for the moment visual culture can be roughly defined as those material artefacts, buildings and images, plus time-based media and performances, produced by human labour and imagination, which serve aesthetic, symbolic, ritualistic or ideological-political ends, and/or practical functions, and which address the sense of sight to a significant extent.

The importance of attending to the *visual characteristics* of the visual arts and mass media can be made clear by considering the following example. Novels, paintings and feature films are three distinct kinds of communication, yet they can overlap in certain respects. For instance, all three can depict fictional characters and tell stories. It is possible for someone to describe the characters and plot to a person unfamiliar with the original without disclosing what medium they were embodied in. (This is a common weakness of student essays about movies.) Paying attention to the visual characteristics of paintings and films is crucial, otherwise the organisation of the works in terms of visual elements – shapes, forms, tones, colours, lighting, two- and three-dimensional composition, framing, camera movement, montage, etc. – in terms of the specific characteristics of the medium of representation in question, will be overlooked. This is the central justification for the presence of the adjective 'visual' in the expression 'visual culture'. It is this emphasis which, in the main, distinguishes Visual Culture Studies from Media and Cultural Studies.

Clearly, by qualifying the term 'culture', the adjective 'visual' serves to limit the object of study: it would seem to exclude poetry, literature, music and radio – the arts based on hearing; and cookery – the art based on taste. It would also exclude perfumes and any works of art appealing to the sense of smell. However, matters are not quite so straightforward because many so-called 'visual' types of communication actually involve one or more of the other four senses. This topic is discussed further in Chapter 2.

Art historians such as Michael Baxandall and Svetlana Alpers have used the expression 'visual culture' in another, somewhat different sense: as an attribute of a whole society or a social strata. Baxandall, for example, contended that those ruling groups in Renaissance Italy who funded and enjoyed the art of painting developed particular visual and cognitive skills that facilitated their appreciation of pictures.[4] Alpers, an authority on Dutch seventeenth-century painting, characterises it as 'an art of describing'. Dutch painters developed acute skills of observation and also craft skills that enabled them to produce the very detailed, realistic pictures for which they are now celebrated, but the public too was especially conscious of the visual. Alpers writes: 'In Holland the visual culture was central to the life of society. One might say that the eye was a central means of self-representation and visual experience a central mode of self-consciousness'.[5]

Some attention needs to be paid to visual culture in this second sense because there is clearly a reciprocal relationship between the cultures of those who make and those who appreciate images – visual artists are likely to flourish in a society which has a highly developed visual culture – but it seems to us that a survey or history of visual cultures would be a social-history project, a 'history-of-mentalities' type project, rather than a Visual Culture Studies project.

The aim of this book is to provide a basic introduction to this new field for the benefit of undergraduates. Visual culture is now so important in terms of the economy, business and new technology, and such a vital part of virtually everyone's daily experience, that both producers and consumers would benefit from studying it in an objective manner. We all consume and enjoy visual culture but its systematic study within a university setting indicates that a critical understanding of its character, power and social functions and effects is the goal rather than mere appreciation. As we shall discover, analysis focuses even upon the pleasures supplied by visual culture.

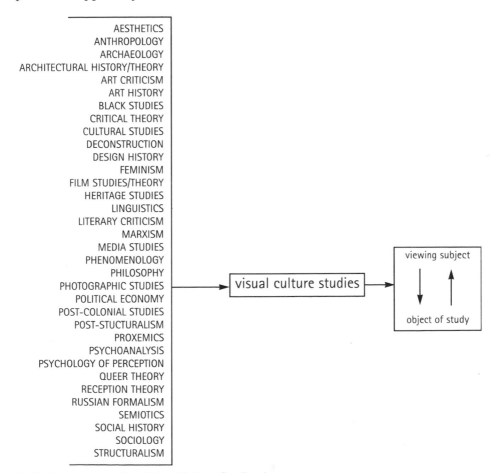

AESTHETICS
ANTHROPOLOGY
ARCHAEOLOGY
ARCHITECTURAL HISTORY/THEORY
ART CRITICISM
ART HISTORY
BLACK STUDIES
CRITICAL THEORY
CULTURAL STUDIES
DECONSTRUCTION
DESIGN HISTORY
FEMINISM
FILM STUDIES/THEORY
HERITAGE STUDIES
LINGUISTICS
LITERARY CRITICISM
MARXISM
MEDIA STUDIES
PHENOMENOLOGY
PHILOSOPHY
PHOTOGRAPHIC STUDIES
POLITICAL ECONOMY
POST-COLONIAL STUDIES
POST-STUCTURALISM
PROXEMICS
PSYCHOANALYSIS
PSYCHOLOGY OF PERCEPTION
QUEER THEORY
RECEPTION THEORY
RUSSIAN FORMALISM
SEMIOTICS
SOCIAL HISTORY
SOCIOLOGY
STRUCTURALISM

visual culture studies

viewing subject

object of study

1 Disciplines upon which Visual Culture Studies draws.

Our use of the term 'critical' implies a process of evaluation and judgement. In the view of many commentators, much visual culture is politically reactionary and anti-social, therefore the study and analysis of it associated with education is seen as one of the ways in which its negative effects can be countered. The goal of critical understanding is reached in part by the application of various modes of analysis; we describe some of them, though necessarily in a summary fashion, in Chapters 8 and 9. Students new to the subject will find that there are many texts devoted to any one – for example, the semiotic – of these approaches.

Critical understanding is also reached via the study of concrete examples in specific historical and social contexts – hence the importance of students learning as much as they can about the way societies past and present were/are organised and work. Every artefact is the result of multiple determinants or factors – economic, political, cultural, institutional, technological, human need, creative will or desire, etc. – consequently the amount of information that could be relevant to an explanation is enormous. A production, distribution and consumption model of a system or cycle of visual culture as it exists (relatively autonomously) within contemporary society is provided in Chapter 5 in order to clarify its internal relations and functioning. Chapter 6 is devoted to institutions because of their vital role in facilitating and controlling visual culture. The economic dimension of cultural production is explored to some degree in Chapter 12, focusing upon gifts, commodities and commodification.

Anyone studying contemporary visual culture confronts a moving, ever-mutating target. This is especially evident in the way technology constantly becomes obsolete, evolves and expands. This is why our final Chapter 13 is devoted to a consideration of new technologies and their impact on visual culture, designers, artists and viewers.

The contents of chapters are thematic and their sequential arrangement roughly follows an objective-to-subjective trajectory. Visual culture exists both outside and within us; thus we need to study its external material existence and also its optical, cognitive and emotional impacts: hence the chapters already cited and the later ones about looks, the gaze and pleasure. In recent years, the issue of quality has become highly contentious; therefore we thought it prudent to include a discussion of ranking and evaluation processes.

Another reason why such an introduction is needed is the flood of books and articles about the arts, design and mass media that have appeared in recent decades. A wide range of literature has been surveyed, references have been provided to numerous relevant texts, and notes and further reading have been provided at the end of each chapter.

An account of the scope and origins of the new field can be found in Chapter 3; therefore only a summary will be given here. In several instances Art History departments in universities renamed themselves

'Schools' or 'Departments of Visual Culture' because, in the face of a changing world and demands for a new curriculum, the traditional title was proving too narrow. Today, lecturers and students are as likely to discuss and research advertisements, computer graphics, designed goods, fashion, films, graffiti, photography, rock/pop performances, television and virtual reality as they are the traditional arts of architecture, painting and sculpture. So, the adoption of the umbrella heading 'visual culture' was a logical response to greatly expanded subject matter. (Most Art History departments also taught architecture and design but, as more and more subjects were added, the department title became longer and longer, and so a broader title became necessary.) Apart from the qualification 'visual', the expression 'visual culture' is unspecific as to which kind of culture is meant, but this has the advantage that many types and levels of culture can be encompassed.

Of course, there is a danger of homogenisation in assembling so many disparate activities under one heading. We should remember that each art form and medium has its particular characteristics and history. However, today's culture is increasingly hybrid; interactions and fusions between the various arts and media mean that boundary lines are becoming harder to discern. Two exhibitions held in 1996 were a demonstration of this, namely, *Spellbound: Art and Film* (Hayward Gallery, London) and *Art and Film since 1945: Hall of Mirrors* (Museum of Contemporary Art, Los Angeles), both of which explored the interface and overlap between the fine arts and the medium of film.

One significant aspect of the expansion of subject matter was the addition of more mass culture material. (Of course, the mass media had already been studied for many decades by scholars working in other disciplines such as Media and Cultural Studies.) The addition of mass culture had several consequences: first, visual aspects of mass culture began to be analysed in a serious and scholarly manner; second, the specialness of art diminished as theorists noted that all forms of visual culture possessed aesthetic qualities; third, the boundaries and interrelationships between the fine arts and mass media, plus their comparative values, became subjects of research and theoretical analysis.[6]

Another reason for the change of name was that academics became concerned with *theories* of arts, design and media, in addition to *histories* of those subjects. They were responding to the veritable explosion of theorising that occurred in a variety of disciplines from the 1960s onwards. A brief history of these developments is provided in Chapter 3, and Chapter 4 on coping with theory has also been included in order to alert students to the challenges and problems associated with reading theoretical texts and coming to terms with theories which may be hard to grasp and agree with.

How the subject of visual culture is actually taught in universities is likely to be of interest to potential and new students. For this reason, a brief account of the modular system used by so many universities is given in an appendix.

We will begin by exploring the various meanings and connotations of the words/concepts 'culture' and 'the visual'.

Notes and further reading

1   W. J. T. Mitchell, 'What is Visual Culture?', *Meaning in the Visual Arts: Views from the Outside: A Centennial Commemoration of Erwin Panofsky (1892–1968)*, ed. I. Lavin (Princeton, NJ, Institute for Advanced Study, 1995), p. 207, p. 210.

2   For more on visual culture see: N. Bryson, M. A. Holly and K. Moxey, (eds), *Visual Culture: Images and Interpretations*, (Hanover, NH, University Press of New England, 1994); Chris Jenks (ed.), *Visual Culture*, (London & New York, Routledge, 1995); *Block*, editors of, *The Block Reader in Visual Culture*, (London & New York, Routledge, 1996). A thoughtful and useful discussion is W. J. T. Mitchell's paper 'What is Visual Culture?' (note 1). To our knowledge, the first book to use the term 'visual culture' was Caleb Gattegno's *Towards a Visual Culture: Educating through Television*, (New York, Outerbridge & Dienstfrey, 1969). See also the replies to the 'Questionnaire on Visual Culture', *October*, 77 (Summer 1996), 25–70.

3   Nicholas de Ville, 'The Inter-disciplinary Field of Fine Art', *The Artist and the Academy: Issues in Fine Art Education and the Wider Cultural Context*, eds N. de Ville and S. Foster, (Southampton, John Hansard Gallery, 1994), pp. 77–103.

4   M. Baxandall, *Painting and Experience in Fifteenth Century Italy: A Primer in the Social History of Pictorial Style*, (London, Oxford & New York, Oxford University Press, 1972).

5   S. Alpers, *The Art of Describing: Dutch Art in the Seventeenth Century*, (Chicago, University of Chicago Press/London, John Murray, 1983), p. xxv.

6   For a discussion of the interaction between the fine arts and mass media see: John A. Walker's *Art in the Age of Mass Media*, (London, Pluto Press, 2nd edn 1994).

1   Concepts of 'culture'

Culture is one of the two or three most complicated words in the English language. (Raymond Williams)[1]

The study of culture concerns itself with what is most distinctive about humanity, if not with what is most crucial to its survival and well-being. Culture can be defined in one sense as that which is surplus, excessive, beyond the strict material measure; but that capacity for self-transgression and self-transcendence is precisely the measure of our humanity. (Terry Eagleton)[2]

When I hear anyone talk of culture, I reach for my revolver. (Nazi leader Hermann Goering, 1930s)

THIS CHAPTER surveys the various meanings of the term 'culture' and looks at its relations with other words such as 'nature' and 'civilisation', and its connections to social structure, class, barbarism and human conflict.

Culture and nature

'Culture' is frequently juxtaposed against the term 'nature', the implication being that the two are rivals and opposites. Culture is thereby defined as what human beings have done to, or added to, nature by means of their inventiveness and labour. (The word itself derives from the cultivation of land – agri*culture*.) The artefacts, technologies and cities that humans have made over the centuries are clearly cultural rather than natural phenomena. Even the countrysides of modern nations have been transformed by human labour to such an extent that there is little wilderness left on planet Earth. (Many animal species have been destroyed in the process.) However, this does not mean that nature and natural forces can be forgotten.

Some thinkers regard the economy as 'determinant in the last instance' but in fact nature is still the final arbiter. Although humanity has striven to understand and subjugate nature, the control we exercise over it is far from complete. Furthermore, humans remain part of nature: we are still subject to the laws of physics and evolution, to biological inheritance, urges and degeneration. It follows that culture cannot be regarded as completely different from, completely opposite to nature. When studying examples of human culture, therefore, we should always remember that they are constructed on a natural foundation.[3]

Base and superstructure

Some thinkers consider that the way societies are organised can best be explained via an architectural metaphor: a base upon which a superstructure is erected. In this instance, the base consists of material resources, productive forces (labour power, industries, machines, technologies), the economy, while the superstructure consists of 'spiritual' phenomena such as ideology, art, religion, science and philosophy. The inference is that the base is primary and determining, while the superstructure is secondary and determined. (For societies to afford culture they must first generate significant surpluses to fund, say, priests and temples.) If the base falters – as in a recession – then the superstructure begins to collapse.

As a general description of how societies normally function, this model has its uses, but it needs qualifying: first, as already explained, nature is the ultimate determinant; second, cultural activities such as fashion and pop music are businesses with their own economies (stylistic innovation and impact are essential to their survival; consequently the superstructure has a feedback effect upon the base); and third, there are exceptional times when humans disregard economic logic, when the superstructure overrides the base (for example, when humans wage wars about religious and ethnic differences even though this causes massive casualties and destruction of property).

Culture and civilisation

'Civilisation' is another word with which 'culture' has close relations; indeed, the two words are often used as synonyms. Civilisation is probably a broader concept than culture and it has an evaluative connotation: a civilised society is one that is sophisticated, enlightened, orderly, polite, humane and progressive; it has achieved high levels in terms of manners, art, science, religion and government. (Given the brutal behaviour of some self-proclaimed civilisations, we are tempted to conclude that civilisation is an ideal condition humanity has yet to attain. Furthermore, the more scientifically and technologically advanced the 'civilisation', the greater its capacity for destruction by military means and by environmental pollution.) Forms of culture, in contrast, can be found in both civilised and so-called barbaric (or savage, or primitive) societies. According to Sigmund Freud, civilisation requires the repression of certain instincts and desires. It could be argued that visual culture, in contrast, gratifies instincts and desires by providing optical and other pleasures.

Cultural capital

'Culture' too has been used in an evaluative sense, that is, when regarded as a quality possessed by a few, fortunate individuals: those deemed to be 'cultured' or 'cultivated'. Such people have the money and leisure to educate themselves, develop manners and tastes, travel, read and appreciate the arts. For them culture is the pursuit of spiritual perfection, the fostering of the best qualities and faculties of humanity. (A paradox pointed out by T. S. Eliot is that there are some individuals who contribute to culture who are not themselves cultured: for example, the naive artists who have enriched modern art and inspired many professional modern artists.) Those excluded from this category – the majority of the population – are thus judged to be rude barbarians or philistines.

Few contemporary thinkers would accept this schema because they believe everyone is cultured, and has access to culture, to some degree. However, it is the case that cultural competence (visual literacy, for example) and what the French sociologist Pierre Bourdieu calls 'cultural capital' – a quantitative rather than a qualitative concept – does vary from person to person, and from social group to social group, just like actual capital. It is also the case that today a considerable number of people are employed in what have been called 'the culture industries': journalists, critics, film editors and so on. These professionals, plus those in education, constitute the intelligentsia (or 'the chattering classes'). They generally possess more cultural capital than the rest of society. A wealthy collector like Charles Saatchi, who purchases contemporary art in bulk with money derived from an advertising agency, thereby raising its monetary value instantly, is even more fortunate because the culture he owns is a form of capital.

Culture and class

Even when culture is regarded as pervading the whole of society, various levels or types of culture are often distinguished, for instance, high, middle-brow and low. Culture with a capital C is often a synonym for 'high culture'. The latter refers to long-established forms such as painting, ballet and opera, produced by professional rather than amateur artists, which are supported and appreciated by an elite, wealthy strata of society. This kind of culture is regarded as improving and elevating; it is one of the major signs of a civilised society. Its opposite is 'low' culture or kitsch – a vulgar form of culture or entertainment associated with commercial producers and consumption by passive, undiscriminating masses. The layer of culture in between is often referred to as 'middle-brow'. It encompasses 'easy listening' music, detective novels, costume drama movies and television series of middling quality that appeal to large audiences of middle-income people. Photography, according to Bourdieu, is a middle-brow art form.

Clearly, what has just been described is a hierarchical conception of culture that is, arguably, homologous to the class structure of advanced nations:

- high culture: royalty, aristocracy, upper middle class;
- middle-brow culture: bourgeoisie or middle class, plus petit bourgeoisie or lower middle class;
- low culture: proletariat or working classes, plus lumpenproletariat or underclass.

Although this model, to our minds, is still broadly accurate (it was more accurate in the past), it is very crude. It does not do justice to the complexity of contemporary society. (Where do subcultures and avant-garde and counter-cultures fit?) What is also problematic about it is that it is static rather than dynamic: in reality classes struggle for dominance or hegemony. Even within societies stratified in terms of class, social mobility in both upwards and downwards directions occurs. Furthermore, some members of one class can and do share or appreciate the culture of other classes. For instance, kitsch is enjoyed by those with a camp sensibility even though they know it is in bad taste; a king and a peasant may both practise the same religion and watch some of the same movies.

The model is also atemporal: it does not take account of historical evolution and changes in the size and power of different classes.

Another distinction that needs to be made is that between folk and mass culture. The former is generally associated with rural, peasant societies of the past where it is assumed virtually everyone contributed to a common culture via folklore, costume, festive rituals and so forth. Mass culture, in contrast, is associated with modernity, industrialisation and mass communication systems such as television. It is produced by a cadre of professional artists and designers on behalf of the urban and rural masses. In developed nations folk culture is generally assumed to have been obliterated by mass culture although some theorists see it persisting in such phenomena as carnivals, fairground art, circuses, tattooing and subway graffiti. When New York subway graffiti appears as part of the setting for a Blondie Pop music video transmitted on MTV, then it has been appropriated by mass culture. When that same graffiti is sprayed on to panels and sold by a New York gallery, then it has been appropriated by fine art/high culture.

A further terminological complication arises from the fact that the expressions 'mass culture' and 'popular culture' are often used interchangeably. However, the latter term is also employed to indicate culture made *by* the people *for* the people. (The word 'popular' derives from the Latin 'popularis' meaning 'belonging to the people'.) 'People' here means 'the common people' not simply all the inhabitants of a particular nation.

Anthropology and sociology

Culture is a subject which has preoccupied anthropologists and sociologists besides art historians.[4] There are even subfields of the former disciplines entitled 'visual sociology' and 'visual anthropology'.[5] According to Talcott Parsons, a leading sociologist, culture is essentially about meaning and therefore depends upon symbolism; he also insisted that culture is shared, learned and transmitted. Anthropologists have tended to adopt a non-hierarchical view of culture, defining it as 'the whole way of life' of a tribe, community or nation. Thus habits, customs and rituals would be included besides so-called material culture, that is, fabricated items such as clothing, tools, carvings and shelters. Visual culture academics have been attracted to this attitude because it has enabled them to broaden the scope of their enquiries and to consider the whole range of cultural production in a society rather than the restricted quantity of 'high-quality' artefacts. (The analysis of even poor-quality movies can reveal much about the character, concerns and issues of a particular society.) Today, one can find books about manhole covers, car dashboards and the design of credit cards, besides books about Greek temples and Michelangelo's sculptures. The sheer quantity of potential material opened up by the expanded notion of culture, however, generates its own problems: no scholar can become expert in all fields; it is impossible to 'cover' the totality of visual culture via a survey course.

Many anthropologists and sociologists employ the method of participant observation in an attempt to understand the culture of another social group. This generally requires them to put aside their own artistic tastes, preferences and values in an effort to share the experience of those who make and use the cultural products in question. Again visual culture academics have found this approach liberating. They can give a lecture about a youth subculture that sprays graffiti without necessarily endorsing or condemning the practice. However, an objective and plural approach to culture does not mean that hierarchies of class and culture have been abolished – they remain part of the social structure and so need to be explicated. Also, when scholars discuss forms of culture which they share with others, they cannot leave themselves out of the equation, nor – in the end – can they avoid ethical judgements. Similarly, questions of aesthetic quality and ranking cannot be deferred for ever. These topics will be discussed further in Chapter 11.

Cultures in the plural

Given the fact that during the history of humanity many different civilisations and societies have existed (and, despite ever-increasing globalisation, there is still a wide variety of societies in the world today), we should speak of 'cultures' in the plural rather than 'culture' in the singular. 'Local' or 'regional cultures' can thus be distinguished from 'national cultures' and 'global culture'.

Robert Hewison has stressed the role of culture in achieving consensus and identity within a nation state:

> A society's culture – which is an active process, not an inert collection of objects – supplies the medium for the interaction between the real and the imaginary, the historical and the mythical, the achieved and desired, that constitutes the daily management of the social consensus. Culture shapes the context in which other social practices such as economic activity, politics and litigation take place. A country's culture is the means both of expressing national identity and maintaining – or challenging – political consensus.[6]

But even within a single nation there are normally smaller, minority cultures – 'subcultures' – which have a relative autonomy vis-à-vis the majority culture. In the world's largest cosmopolitan cities a range of races, ethnic and religious groups live. In certain inner city schools as many as twenty languages are spoken by pupils; hence the emergence of the term 'multicultural'. Scholars who compare cultures, perhaps in order to find common or universal elements, are said to be engaging in 'trans-' or 'cross-cultural' studies, while those interested in the way cultures interact are said to be engaged in 'intercultural' studies.[7]

However, a plurality of cultures does not mean that they are all equal because cultural groups vary in their sizes, power and influence: some are dominant while others are subordinate. Some cultures are official/approved/central and some are unofficial/dissident/marginal. The law of uneven development also applies: some are more advanced than others; some are growing and expanding, while others are declining. (Raymond Williams used the terms 'emergent' and 'residual'.)

Cultures in conflict

While it is possible for individuals, tribes, races and nations to live in harmony and mutual respect, it is also possible for them to be in conflict or even at war with one another. Cultures are not exempt from the human propensity for aggression – they can also be in contention. Regrettably, the values of one culture may be incompatible with those of another (see figure 2).

When different cultures meet there are often violent clashes – battles for supremacy. Military conquest usually results in the suppression of the religion, language and culture of the defeated people and the imposition of the religion, language and culture of the victors. A war is not always necessary for this to happen: a culture can be destroyed, undermined or transformed by a foreign culture emanating from a nation of greater economic and cultural strength. The way American mass culture is exported around the globe is an obvious example. In some instances resistance against Americanisation is orchestrated by the rulers of the victim state; as, for example, in Iran; and in France where the French language is policed and quota systems are imposed on the import of American cultural goods.

Culture and barbarism

According to received wisdom, culture is one of the positive achievements of our species. Certainly, some of the finest achievements of humankind have been cultural in character (the Taj Mahal, the Book of Kells, etc.). From the perspective of the social group that produces and consumes the culture in question, this is almost invariably the case. But from the standpoint of an atheist, religions may well seem oppressive to non-believers and even inimical to the best interests of cult-members: the Aztecs ripped the hearts out of living victims as part of their religious rituals. (We may admire Aztec art and architecture but if their civilisation had survived until today would its cruel religious practices still be tolerated by the United Nations?) While Nazi visual culture satisfied the Nazis themselves and was extremely powerful in terms of its visual impact, it caused fear and terror in other groups who were the targets of Nazi racism. In these cases we can see that culture and cruelty were inseparable.

For these reasons, many lecturers in visual culture adopt a critical attitude towards culture (but this does not mean they don't enjoy and value much of it); they are suspicious of the purely celebratory approach associated with art historians like Sir Ernst Gombrich, author of *The Story of Art* (Oxford, Phaidon Press, 16th edn, 1995) and Lord Clark, presenter of the famous television series *Civilisation* (BBC–2, 1969). They keep in mind Walter Benjamin's dictum: 'There is no document of human culture which is not at the same time a document of barbarism'.[8] After all, the glories of ancient Rome were based on the military conquest of other tribes, a system of slavery and forms of public entertainment in which captives and animals were slaughtered in huge numbers. The latter took place in amphitheatres such as the Colosseum in Rome which tourists now admire as ancient monuments.[9]

Benjamin's statement also implies that culture is part of the surplus value any economically successful society produces, and that surplus is usually the result of the exploitation of the labour of millions of workers who do not reap the full benefits of the wealth and culture their toil makes possible.[10]

Multiculturalism

Western universities increasingly recruit students from around the globe and from local ethnic minorities, and so they become more multicultural in character. As a result, white European academics become more aware of the predominantly Euro-centric bias of their teaching. Clearly, this problem could be solved by developing new modules or by employing staff from other nations and cultures.[11] (But given ever-declining staff numbers, this is less and less likely to happen.) Some American universities require students to take courses designed to raise their awareness of other races and cultures.

Academics also become more conscious of their own situation within a Western culture whose values may well be at odds with the cultures of their students. For instance, an atheist academic who supports the freedom of writers like Salman Rushdie to criticise religion faces an ethical dilemma when lecturing to a class that includes Islamic fundamentalist students from either Britain or abroad who believe such writers should be censored and assassinated. Student unions have been forced to ban certain student groups because of their aggressive and intolerant behaviour.

---

2 [facing page] Newspaper advertisement appealing for funds for Amnesty International, 1995.

As this 'good cause' advertisement demonstrates, not all advertising is driven by commercial motives. The extended caption accompanying the photograph is an example of what Roland Barthes termed 'relay': it expands on the limited information provided by the image. The linguistic injunction 'forget me not' is literally illustrated by the flowers with that name. This is an example of the overdetermination (the same message is delivered more than once in different forms) typical of so much advertising.

The murder of Katia Bengana is a tragic example of a clash of cultures/values: secularism versus religion; feminism versus patriarchy; individualism versus collectivism; modernity versus tradition; fashion versus costume; public display of female beauty versus veiling such beauty from the public's eyes.

From the point of view of the male Islamic killer, Katia posed a triple threat: to the power of religion; to the power of men; to the solidarity of traditional culture. Conformity to established customs and rules is clearly crucial to the survival of a traditional, religious culture. The Islamic extremist knew that if individuals were permitted to defy the rules and customs then this could result in the slow death of his culture; consequently, the murder of Katia was justified as far as he was concerned.

France has a Muslim population of several million and so the clash of cultures manifests itself there too. The French authorities pursue a policy of assimilation and secularism in schools: consequently they banned the wearing of ostentatious religious symbols. As a result Muslim schoolgirls who attended school wearing *chadors* that cover their heads and bodies were suspended. Some Muslim women are happy to submit to the Islamic rule regarding modest dress. In France, therefore, they were not free to wear what they wanted in school. In Minneapolis in 1994 a Muslim woman, dressed in black from head to toe, was arrested by the police because she was considered to be violating a state law against concealing one's identity in public! Clearly, clothes are not simply a matter of cut and style.

In Britain similar cultural conflicts occur despite a policy of multiculturalism. Islam forbids the artistic representation of the human body, therefore schoolchildren of Asian origin who hope to study art, especially sculpture, have been threatened by Muslim militants and told the study of modern, Western art is 'evil'.

Forget-
Me-
Not

Sixteen year old Katia was killed because she refused to cover her head with a veil. How much longer before you join us?

Katia Bengana was not the only young woman in Algiers who didn't want to wear the hijab, the Islamic veil, but she was one who spoke out.

She told the world about the bullies who, more than once, had warned that unless she dressed the way they wanted, they would kill her.

Factions in Algeria, calling themselves 'armed Islamic groups' have repeatedly threatened women not to go out in public without first covering their heads. They have also threatened girls who go to mixed schools and any female who goes to mixed swimming pools.

Just over a year ago, Katia was walking home from school with a friend, who was veiled. The two young women were stopped by a gunman. He signalled Katia's friend to stand aside and then shot Katia dead.

Her sorrowing family told how Katia had refused to be intimidated by the threats.

Katia's father, desperately worried for her safety, had asked her to put on the veil, even though he himself supported her right not to wear it. But Katia refused, saying she would decide for herself who she should be, and how she should dress.

'She was adamant', says her sister, 'Even if she had to die, she would not wear the veil.'

Sadly in Algeria it's not only armed groups who fail to respect human rights. The very people who have sworn to protect human rights, whose duty it is to *protect the people* - the security forces - are themselves implicated in the torture, killing and 'disappearances' of thousands. Can you even begin to imagine what it's like to be terrorised out of your most basic freedom?

Would you have the guts to speak out against men with guns? Wouldn't you pray for strong friends to stop the intimidation and the killing?

Amnesty International works tirelessly all over the world to safeguard people's basic human rights. At any given moment, we speak out on behalf of hundreds of people who are in danger of torture, 'disappearance' or death. Over the years, we have helped thousands.

We are not always successful, but the more supporters we have, the more successful we'll be.

For the sake of children like Katia, who need our help and yours, please join us.

Please join us today, because for someone somewhere, tomorrow will always be too late. Please pick up your pen. Do it now.

If 'campus wars' of the kind that have taken place in the United States are to be avoided in Europe, the best course of action for an institution of learning to take is surely to bring these conflicts out into the open, to discuss and debate them, and to involve students in finding answers to such questions as: 'How can we solve by peaceful means cultural differences and conflicts of value? Should toleration be extended to creeds that are themselves intolerant?' (It would seem the ethnic cleansers of the former Yugoslavia cannot bear to live in a multicultural society.) The 'Mission, Vision and Values' statements issued by so many universities could well provide the starting point for such a debate. Another could be the 1996 film *Higher Learning* (Columbia Pictures, directed by John Singleton) because it is a fictional dramatisation of campus battles inside an American university.

Summary

This chapter has attempted to situate the concept of culture in relation to its other, which at certain times in history has been portrayed as nature, and sometimes as barbarism. The location of culture within the Marxist diagram of base and superstructure shows the extent to which culture is a determined category, inextricably interlinked with the prevailing economy.

Theorists such as Bourdieu have combined the notion of capital with culture, to form the concept 'cultural capital', and have tried to map preferences (such as folk culture and kitsch) within any given socio-economic milieu.

Whilst the use of the term *culture* once referred to the pursuits of the privileged cognoscenti, imbuing it with class distinction, more recently culture has been used to refer to any aspect of daily life which relates to a social context. It has become a more inclusive term, and when conjoined with various prefixes, like *multi-* or *inter-*, it acquires new meanings to help explain and characterise changes that are taking place in the late twentieth century.

Notes and further reading

1　Raymond Williams, *Keywords: A Vocabulary of Culture and Society*, (London: Fontana/Croom Helm, 1976), p. 76.

2　Terry Eagleton, 'The Crisis of Contemporary Culture', *Random Access: On Crisis and its Metaphors*, eds Pavel Büchler and Nikos Papastergiadis (London, Rivers Oram Press, 1995), p. 21.

3　Sebastiano Timpanaro was an Italian theorist whose book *On Materialism*, (London, New Left Books, 1975), stressed the continuing priority of nature over mind and emphasised the physical and biological bases of culture (manifested in such things as bodily rhythms in music and dance, colours and shapes in painting and sculpture). These bases were considered to explain the trans-historical appeal of great art. His views influenced the thinking of Raymond Williams (see *Problems in Materialism and Culture: Selected Essays* (London, New Left Books, 1980)) and Peter Fuller (see *Art and Psychoanalysis* (London, Writers and Readers, 1980)).

Ernst Gombrich also believes that, despite the diversity of humanity, there are common, universal factors: 'I am convinced that the visual arts . . . rest . . . on biological foundations. Like the disposition for rhythmical orders which here manifests itself in the decorative art of all peoples, so pleasure in light and splendour is common to us all', *Topics of Our Time: Twentieth-Century Issues in Learning and in Art*, (London, Phaidon Press, 1991), p. 44. A scientific study of the biological and evolutionary sources of aesthetic experience is John D. Barrow's *The Artful Universe*, (Oxford, Oxford University Press, 1995).

4   For a survey of sociologists' views of culture see: Chris Jenks, *Culture*, (London & New York, Routledge, 1993). See also: T. S. Eliot, *Notes Towards the Definition of Culture*, (London, Faber, 2nd edn 1962); Raymond Williams, *Keywords: A Vocabulary of Culture and Society*, (London, Fontana, 2nd edn 1983); and Raymond Williams, *Culture*, (London, Fontana, 1981).

5   Many anthropologists and ethnographers have availed themselves of visual media – photography, film and video – in order to record the appearance and behaviour of the people they were studying. They have also used these media as educational aids. For a substantial survey of this topic see: Paul Hockings, (ed.), *Principles of Visual Anthropology*, (The Hague & Paris, Mouton, 1975). See also E. Edwards (ed.), *Anthropology and Photography 1860–1920*, (New Haven & London, Yale University Press, 1992); Lucien Taylor (ed.), *Visualizing Theory. Selected Essays from V.A.R. [Visual Anthropology Review] 1990–94*, (London, Routledge, 1994); and issues of the journal *Visual Anthropology Review*.

In 1986 the journal *Current Sociology* devoted a special issue (34:3) to 'Theory and Practice of Visual Sociology'. It reported that another journal entitled *Videosociology* appeared from 1972 to 1974 and that, since 1982, an International Visual Sociology Association has existed which publishes the *International Journal of Visual Sociology*. Visual sociologists have also taken and used photographs, films and videos as a means of documentation, empirical research and as teaching aids. See also Elizabeth Chaplin's detailed survey *Sociology and Visual Representation*, (London & New York, Routledge, 1994).

6   R. Hewison, *Culture and Consensus: England, Art and Politics since 1940*, (London, Methuen, 1995), pp. xvii–xviii.

7   For an examination of the concepts and problems of intercultural communication see: Ron and Suzi Wong Scollon's *Intercultural Communication: A Discourse Approach*, (Oxford & Cambridge, MA, Blackwell, 1994). Some rather shallow examples of cross-cultural graphic design are reproduced in Henry Steiner's and Alan Grant's *Cross-Cultural Design: Communicating in the Global Marketplace*, (London, Thames & Hudson, 1995).

8   W. Benjamin, 'Theses on the Philosophy of History' (1940), *Illuminations*, (London, J. Cape, 1970), pp. 255–66.

9   A chilling account of the slaughter that went on for hundreds of years in the Colosseum was given in the television programme 'The Story of the Roman Arena', *Timewatch* (a history series), BBC-2, 15 September 1993.

10   A vivid, photographic record of manual labour around the world can be found in Sebastiao Salgado's *Workers: An Archaeology of the Industrial Age*, (Oxford, Phaidon Press, 1993).

11   For more on multiculturalism and education see: Rachel Mason, *Art Education and Multiculturalism*, (London, Croom Helm, 1988), and John Arthur and Amy Shapiro (eds), *Campus Wars: Multiculturalism and the Politics of Difference*, (Boulder, CO, Westview Press, 1994). On Euro-centrism see: Ella Shohat and Robert Stam, *Unthinking Eurocentrism: Multiculturalism and the Media*, (London & New York, Routledge, 1994).

2 The concept of 'the visual'

THE MEANING of the word 'visual' may appear self-evident and thus hardly worthy of comment. Yet, as we shall discover, complicated issues are raised by this concept and related terms such as 'visuality', 'scopic regimes' and 'ocularcentrism'.[1]

Vision

All those studying visual culture need to learn the basic facts about the physiognomy of the eyes and the psychology of visual perception, not only because such knowledge is pertinent to the subject in general, but also because many artists have acquired and made use of such knowledge. In British art schools during the 1950s and 1960s, for example, departments of 'Visual Research' were founded and tutors often referred art students to the scientific findings of the psychology of visual perception as reported in texts by Rudolf Arnheim, James J. Gibson, Richard Gregory and others, on the grounds that this knowledge would enhance their understanding of art and design.[2]

Rays of light reflected from objects are focused by the lenses of the eyes on retinas with rod and cone receptors sensitive to those rays. The retinas convert light rays into electrochemical signals which are then transmitted, via the optic nerves, to the primary visual cortex at the back of the brain. One-third of the brain is devoted to processing these signals. Different pathways in the cortex are concerned with colour, motion, depth and shape or form, but the brain integrates them into a single perception.[3]

Once signals have passed the retinas it no longer makes sense to speak of 'the visual' in isolation. Although people talk about 'the mind's eye', there is not literally a second pair of eyes inside the brain that looks at 'images' coming from the real eyes, otherwise there would be an infinite regress. The fact that we perceive one world rather than five (corresponding to each of the five senses) suggests that inside the brain/mind visual information from the eyes merges with information arriving from the other senses, and with existing memories and knowledge, so that a synthesis occurs. (Psychologists call this process 'apperception'.) And sometimes synaesthesia happens too (this is when colours and shapes come to be strongly associated with sounds, smells and feelings).

Mental images can also occur with the eyes closed: memory enables us to recall familiar people and places, while imagination enables us to conjure up fictional beings, places and events. Dreams and hallucinations also indicate that mental images can occur without conscious control when we are asleep or ill/disturbed/drugged. Scientists have also pointed out that sensations of light can be produced by blows to the head, electrical stimulation of the visual cortex and narcotics.

Furthermore, psychologists have studied phenomena such as afterimages which demonstrate that the eyes are not simply windows on the world. If one looks at a painting consisting of flat fields of two saturated, complementary colours, say cadmium red and viridian green, then the opposite colour afterimages generated within the eyes will mutually intensify the two hues and cause optical flicker at the edge where they meet. The Hard-Edge painting and the Optical art and design of the 1960s made much use of such afterimages and the eyes' dazzled reaction to black-on-white patterns and optical illusions of various kinds (see figure 3).

The value of vision in discovering the truth about external reality is indicated by the folk saying 'seeing is believing'. But there is another saying which contradicts this, namely, 'appearances are deceptive'. In other words, perception and knowledge are frequently at odds with one another. Our knowledge of reality comes from many acts of perception which we compare and subject to logical analysis. This explains how the mind is able to discount misleading visual information: our eyes tell us that a person walking away from us gets smaller and smaller, but our reason tells us people do not shrink, that this phenomenon is an effect of increasing distance.

Vision and the other senses

It is through our senses that we interact with and learn about the world. A number of books discuss the five senses and some contemporary scholars are investigating the ways in which the senses relate to one another, intermingle and are augmented by technological inventions such as the telephone and the cinema.[4]

Hierarchies of the senses have been constructed in which sight has been allocated the top position; it has long been dubbed 'the noblest sense'.[5] However, not everyone has agreed with this ranking order. Martin Jay, in a remarkable intellectual history – Downcast Eyes: The Denigration of Vision in Twentieth-Century French Thought (Berkeley, Los Angeles, London, University of California Press, 1993) – explained that 'ocular-centrism', the traditional privileging or hegemony of the eye in Western thought, gave rise to a counter-current that criticised vision and spoke up on behalf of the other senses. Vision, its critics considered, was complicit in social oppression via surveillance and spectacle.

Feminists also objected to vision's high status on the grounds that it was patriarchal, a sign of male dominance. Consider, for example, two quotations from the writings of Luce Irigaray which Jay reproduced:

> Investment in the look is not as privileged in women as in men. More than any other sense, the eye objectifies and it masters. It sets at a distance, and maintains a distance. In our culture the predominance of the look over smell, taste, touch and hearing has brought about an impoverishment of bodily relations. (p. 493)

> The predominance of the visual . . . is particularly foreign to female eroticism. Woman takes pleasure more from touching than from looking, and her entry into a dominant scopic economy signifies, again, her consignment to passivity: she is to be the beautiful object of contemplation. (p. 535)

Donald Lowe, in *History of Bourgeois Perception* (Chicago, University of Chicago Press/Brighton, Harvester Press, 1982), argued that perception had a history and that social classes had specific ways of perceiving the world.[6] He also claimed that at different times there have been different hierarchies of the senses. He provided a table which divided European history into five periods. In the first period – the Middle Ages – hearing and touching, he claimed, were valued more than seeing. Then, during the second period – the Renaissance – sight gained primacy partly as a result of the emergence of the system of linear perspective. The third phase belongs to estate society, and is to do with representation in space, according to Lowe. Bourgeois society, the fourth phase, was characterised by 'the extension of sight' (by such inventions as photography) and 'development in time'. The fifth period – the twentieth century – Lowe defined as 'corporate capitalism, a bureaucratic society of controlled consumption'. It was 'constituted by the electronic culture; the extrapolation of sight and sound'.

Lowe considered that the change between the bourgeois era and the present age occurred during the period 1905–15 when 'the objective reality of bourgeois society' defined 'from a single perspective' was undermined by 'a perceptual revolution'. The new perceptual field was 'multiperspectival and environmental'. The new field did not totally replace the previous one; instead there was a superimposition or sedimentation. Lowe's new field of 1905–15 corresponds to Cubism and modern abstract art which broke with the conventions of linear perspective. However, the latter has surely continued in mass media representations.

Unlike Lowe, we suspect that the sense of sight is and always has been the most important sense because of the sheer quantity of information about the external world it conveys to the brain (seventy per cent, more than all the other senses combined). In spite of the essential role of language in human relations, vision is arguably more vital: one can see strangers and tell much from their appearance well before one can converse

3 Donald MacKay figure. This figure is designed to excite the eyes. If the viewer focuses upon centre, powerful *moiré* effects will be generated followed by spectral colours. This kind of figure was reproduced in psychology of perception textbooks which were influential in terms of the development of Op art during the 1960s. It also demonstrates the point that the eyes are not simply windows on the world, that they themselves modulate what is seen.

with them. In the past there may have been a dearth of images compared to words, but today we live in a media-saturated environment and therefore the eyes experience a glut of imagery.

Visuality

Viewers are not merely pairs of eyes – they have minds, bodies, genders, personalities and histories. A baby's eyes may be 'innocent' but this phase does not last long. Infants rapidly learn to see and to become social beings: they learn to speak a language (a 'mother tongue', which names and classifies reality in particular ways) and they acquire knowledge of the world and of previous imagery. This knowledge informs and modulates their seeing; it makes recognition and meaning possible. At this point the difference between the terms 'vision' and 'visuality' can be explained. Theorists have argued that the former refers to a physical/physiological process in which light impacts upon eyes, while the latter refers to a social process: visuality is vision socialised. Norman Bryson elaborates:

> When I look, what I see is not simply light but intelligible form: the *rays* of light are caught in . . . a network of meanings . . . For human beings collectively to orchestrate their visual experience together it is required that each submit his or her retinal experience to the socially agreed description(s) of an intelligible world . . . Between the subject and the world is inserted the entire sum of discourses which make up visuality, that cultural construct, and makes visuality different from vision, the notion of unmediated visual experience . . . when I learn to see socially, that is, when I begin to articulate my retinal experience with codes of recognition that come to me from my social milieu(s), I am inserted into systems of visual discourse that saw the world before I did, and will go on seeing after I no longer see . . . It may . . . be that I always feel myself to live at the center of my vision . . . but . . . that vision is decentered by the network of signifiers that come to me from the social milieu.[7]

Furthermore, vision is informed by the various interests and desires of the viewer, and by the social relations that exist between the perceiver and the perceived. As an example, think of the different ways a young, peasant woman minding cows in Brittany during the late nineteenth century would have been perceived by different viewers: tourists, anthropologists, the painter Paul Gauguin, costume historians, her lover, parents, friends, employer and fellow workers.

Mediated vision

Those studying visual culture are not primarily concerned with how people see the world but with how people see still and moving images and other artefacts that have been made, in whole or in part, to be looked at. (Some theorists speak of 'unmediated' vision – seeing the world – and 'mediated vision' – seeing images.) Of course, there is a reciprocal relationship here: we see certain pictures as realistic portrayals of the world, and pictures can in turn influence the way we perceive reality – hence the term 'picturesque' applied to a view of the land.

Visual representations differ from perceptions of nature by being intentional, encoded communications, and by being representations *of* something. Most buildings and designed goods, of course, are not depictions of anything; they are new inventions, additions to nature. Because drawings and paintings are constructed, they need not limit themselves to what already exists, they can present imaginative visions of fictional worlds and creatures – such as fairies and aliens from outer space – which can still have a compelling reality effect.[8] As Paul Klee once remarked: 'Art does not reproduce the visible; rather it makes visible'.[9]

Modern culture, John B. Thompson reminds us, is characterised by mediasation: 'What defines our culture as "modern" is the fact that the production and circulation of symbolic forms have, since the late fifteenth century, become increasingly and irreversibly caught up in the process of commodification and transmission that are now global in character'.[10] As media simulations become ever more pervasive they gradually encroach upon our experience of 'first order' reality. We become more and more dependent upon, say, television news and documentaries for our knowledge about the world.

Art forms that address more than the eyes

The importance of foregrounding the visual characteristics of visual culture in any analysis was stressed in the introduction. The point was also made that the visual arts may involve other senses besides sight. Sculpture, for example, appeals to the sense of touch as well the sense of sight. In museums touch has to be invoked via vision because visitors are normally forbidden to caress sculptures (Bernard Berenson (1865–1959), the connoisseur of Renaissance art, used the term 'tactile values' in this regard.[11]) Periodically exhibitions of sculpture aimed specifically at blind people are mounted by museum curators; consequently, in these instances, a so-called 'visual' art form can be appreciated to some degree by people lacking the sense of sight. (Some blind people have even made sculptures.) Plastic 'thermoforms' showing the content of paintings in relief also enable the blind to appreciate the art of painting. Similarly, the blind can appreciate films and television programmes to a certain extent by listening to their soundtracks.

There is no doubt that architecture is a visual art form. The outward appearances of buildings, their various shapes and styles, are extremely important. Indifference to the visual dimension by some town planners and architects has resulted in many mediocre and ugly urban developments. But we do not just stand and stare at buildings – we enter them and move around their internal spaces. Since we experience buildings as all-encompassing environments, the whole body is involved in their appreciation not merely the eyes. (There is a discipline concerned with spaces called 'Proxemics'.[12]) In the case of certain kinds of designed goods – cars, clothes and furniture, for instance – the relation of the artefacts to the sense of touch and the whole human body is particularly evident.

Furthermore, we live, work and participate in ritual activities inside buildings. In other words, we use them for a variety of private and public purposes. It follows that buildings, and for that matter designed goods, ought not be judged on aesthetic or stylistic grounds alone. Judgement of their performance depends on how well they fulfil the purposes for which they were designed.

Mixed media

Many forms of communication are mixed or hybrid in the sense that two or more media are employed. For example, lots of books are illuminated or illustrated; consequently they cannot be regarded as either purely visual or purely literary. Similarly, paintings are normally accompanied by titles, by catalogue statements written by the artists, plus texts by critics and historians; some paintings even include words, inscriptions and signatures as part of their content. Magazine and billboard advertisements almost invariably involve a combination of images and words. (Peter Wagner employs the term 'iconotexts' and W.J.T. Mitchell the term 'imagetext ' to describe works that are a mixture of images and words.[13])

The performing arts generally use a combination of media that appeals to more than one sense. For instance, musicals on stage and screen involve sounds – speech, songs, music – but also visual elements – dance, acting and gesture, costumes, stage sets and lighting effects. In the case of other multi-media forms – *audio*-visual media – such as rock and pop music concerts, slide-tape presentations, films and television programmes, it would be absurd for scholars to limit discussion to their visual aspects alone.

This means that although visual culture theorists may emphasise the visual, they cannot sensibly exclude the haptic (the sensations of touch, texture and contour) and the kinaesthetic (the sensation of movement or strain in muscles, tendons, joints) altogether. In addition they also need to consider the ways images, designs, textures, words, music and sounds interrelate: they can be complementary or contrapuntal. The sounds in a modern feature film are normally integral to the sequence of shots and the dramatic unfolding of the narrative.[14] (Psychoanalysts refer to the human desire to see as 'the scopic drive'; similarly, they refer to the desire to hear as 'the invocatory drive'.) Paradoxically, there are some fine artists working within the context of the *visual arts* whose primary media are words and sounds: Conceptual and sound artists.

We also need to remember that one visual medium can encompass and relay other forms of visual communication. For instance, non-verbal types of communication such as facial expressions, bodily gestures, adornment, tattoos and dress fashions can be relayed by painting, photography, film and television. One visual medium can also take as its subject matter another visual medium[15] – for example, a television arts documentary about the fashion designs of Vivienne Westwood. In such instances, the visual character of the medium that is the content of the first visual medium is altered to some degree. Today, in fact, visual media of different ages co-exist. These media do not just run in parallel – they overlap and collaborate in ways too numerous and complex to describe here.

Visual representation

There is no reason to think that the physiognomy of the eyes has altered during recorded history, or that the optical apparatus of an American is significantly different from that of an African, but a cursory examination of pictures and artefacts from different periods and cultures reveals that ways of depicting or representing the world have varied immensely. In other words, different 'scopic regimes' or 'ways of seeing' have given rise to different systems of representation. Linear perspective, which had its origins in the paintings of ancient Greece and Rome and was developed further by Italian Renaissance architects and artists, was one such system.

Achieving resemblance was usually the goal of such systems. (Virtual reality is only the latest of a long series of attempts to produce illusionistic simulations.) However, while the majority of the world's cultures have generated representations which depict the visible world, human figures and animals, these representations have usually been subject to *stylisation* which prompts many people to describe them as 'distorted'.

The existence of different representational systems and styles has puzzled theorists. They have wondered: 'How and why did such systems emerge? Are they a particular form of ideology associated with particular cultures or social classes? Why do they vary from time to time and from society to society? What is the relation between visual representations and reality?' (That is, the issue of realism in art.)

In 1960 Ernst Gombrich's influential book *Art and Illusion: A Contribution to the Psychology of Pictorial Representation* (London, Phaidon Press) appeared. As its subtitle indicated, Gombrich thought questions of style and representation could be explained by reference to the findings of the psychology of perception.[16] Texts informed by psychoanalytic theory by Adrian Stokes and Anton Ehrenzweig were also read by art school staff and students during the 1960s.[17] At the time it seemed that 'reading' visual material through the 'lens' of external disciplines such as psychology and psychoanalysis (both Freudian and Jungian) would be useful to practitioners and theorists alike. It was not long however before these sciences were accused of neglecting the social dimension and historical context of visual culture.

Nevertheless, psychoanalysis – in particular that associated with the post-Freudian writings of Jacques Lacan – continues to play a role in helping to illuminate the mechanics of image formation, identification, fetishism, pleasure and meaning. As we shall discover in Chapter 7, spectatorship and the gaze – as manipulated by various media – have been topics of much theoretical reflection.

An insight derived from linguistics is that, while we speak languages, languages also – in a sense – speak us. That is, once a system of representation exists it conditions the way we perceive and think about the world. Nietzsche once called language a 'prison-house'[18] but this formulation is surely too negative because, while languages may impose limits, they also facilitate description and communication. Everyone can make use of such systems of representation and there is scope for creativity too (for instance, new words are constantly being invented). Artists, film-makers and others have a special interest in them because they are professionally concerned with pictorial conventions. They learn about and use inherited conventions but radical artists also seek to develop, subvert or change them, so as to avoid endless repetition, and in order to respond to an ever-changing world.

As Jackson Pollock and other artists recognised in the 1940s, the new atomic age could not be convincingly represented in painting via the pictorial systems of the past. The new age demanded the abandonment of naturalistic scenes, perspectival representations of space; it demanded the invention of new painting techniques. Pollock's Action painting method of pouring liquid paint from cans with the aid of brushes and sticks while moving around canvas laid on the floor is now famous. It is pertinent to this text because, first, it reminds us that visual images are made from specific materials and that these will determine, to varying degrees, the images' final character; and second, it reminds us that not just the painter's eyes are involved in the production of images: arms, hands, or the whole body play a part too. This means that the image may manifest traces of the bodily labour involved. In the case of a Dutch-period landscape by Van Gogh, thick pigment and brushmarks are integral to the work and its meaning but, of course, they were not part of the view he transcribed.

Within film too there are directors like Jean-Luc Godard who experiment with imagery and sounds, and call attention to them, in order to remind the viewer that what is on screen is not simply a transparent window on the world. In short, for modern artists, visual representation is a perpetual site of creative struggle and experimentation.

Retinal and anti-retinal art

As already indicated, much visual culture is the result of *invention* and *construction* rather than recording appearances. However, in the history of painting there have been certain movements that have involved artists painting directly from motifs. Paul Cézanne's long struggle to realise his visual sensations via brushmarks on canvas in front of nature or still life arrangements has become legendary. Impressionism in particular stressed the artist's immediate response to visual sensations experienced in sunny garden or country locations. (Of course, Impressionist paintings were *constructed* from hundreds of brushstrokes.) Claude Monet, Cézanne once remarked, was 'Merely an eye'; however, he then added, 'But what an eye!'. Some years later Marcel Duchamp reacted against Impressionism because he considered it to be 'retinal art'. It pleased the eye but did nothing for the intellect because it lacked narratives, important themes and ideas. Paradoxically, Duchamp's 'readymades' now count as part of the history of the visual arts but when they were first selected and bought from shops it was on the grounds that they had no aesthetic or visual appeal whatsoever. Given Duchamp's anti-retinalism, it is not surprising that he was later hailed as the founding father of Conceptual art.

Like Duchamp, Theodor Adorno, the German critical theorist, reflected on the relation between the visual and the conceptual.[19] Adorno decided that art's visual character was paradoxical because, although the latter marked 'the difference of art from discursive thinking', art could not be purely visual because it was 'pervaded by conceptual elements'. He observed: 'If art were visual through and through, it would become like the empirical life it wants to leave behind'. For Adorno, art – modern art in particular – was a response to reality not a replica of it. Moreover, 'the visual aspect of art differs from empirical perception because it always points beyond empirical perception to spirit. Art is a vision of the non-visual.'

To cite an example of Adorno's apparently contradictory last remark: much of the work of the British artist John Latham (b. 1921) has been concerned with time. But this is a dimension of reality for which we have no dedicated sense and which is not visible to the eyes. Latham's task, then, was to find a visual means of representing a non-visual dimension.[20]

Artefacts and viewers

Having touched upon what might be called 'the producer's share' it is now time to consider what Gombrich called 'the beholder's share'. Mass audiences watching television are often dismissed as 'passive' but some theorists have argued that viewing is an active, mental process. The use of the word 'reading' in relation to images implies that some labour is involved in extracting meaning. Puzzle pictures with 'hidden' figures are designed to make viewers scrutinise images with more than normal intensity. Just as cultural capital varies from person to person, from social group to social group, so do visual skills. As already explained, some art historians have maintained that there are societies at certain times which develop an especially acute sense of the visual.

Clearly, there is no seeing or aesthetic experience without viewers, but theoretical questions arise, namely, 'Are the general laws of psychology or the workings of the minds of millions of viewers the proper subject of Visual Culture Studies? Is not the actual object of study external to the body (artefacts, buildings, etc.) rather than internal?' The multiple meanings of the word 'image' highlight the problem: pictures, photographs and reflections occur outside the body; visual perceptions and memories, hallucinations and dream images occur inside the mind (itself divided into conscious and unconscious). There are also intermediate phenomena like 'found' images (which are actually projected by the viewer) such as those detected in fires or on rockfaces. Gustave Courbet, a self-styled realist, was fond of painting pictures of rock faces in which human faces appeared.

Evidently, there is a need for a theory capable of overcoming the dualism subject/object (or internal/external), a theory capable of accounting for the whole process of interaction that takes place between living subjects and material objects. Understanding will also be facilitated if the production and consumption phases – the making and experiencing of cultural products – are distinguished and considered as a temporal sequence. (See Chapter 5.)

Even if one concluded that the proper object of study is external, this need not prevent critics and historians from citing their personal responses to images, films, etc., and/or the documented responses of others. In fact, a study of the reception and effects of works of art, films, etc., does exist as a branch of Visual Culture Studies: Reception Aesthetics/Theory/ History and/or Impact/Audience studies. However, it is important for critics and theorists to distinguish their own reactions from those of others in order to avoid the danger of universalising their own experiences, and in order to make it clear that responses are often differential, that is, they vary across society now and also historically.

Summary

This chapter has explored both the physical and the mental aspects of experiencing the visual, and has examined the notion of visuality which emerges from debates within psychoanalysis and psychology to differentiate between vision as a biological process and the interpretation of what is seen.

Notes and further reading

1   On the visual, visuality, visual systems of representation, etc., see: Hal Foster (ed.), *Vision and Visuality*, (Seattle, WA, Bay View Press/Dia Art Foundation, 1988); Martin Jay, *Downcast Eyes: The Denigration of Vision in Twentieth Century French Thought*, (Berkeley, Los Angeles, London, University of California Press, 1993); W. J. T. Mitchell's *Picture Theory: Essays on Verbal and Visual Representation*, (Chicago & London, University of Chicago Press, 1994); and Chris Jenks (ed.), *Visual Culture*, (London & New York, Routledge, 1995).

2   Rudolf Arnheim, *Art and Visual Perception: A Psychology of the Creative Eye*, (London, Faber & Faber, 1956); Richard L. Gregory, *Eye and Brain: The Psychology of Seeing*, (London, Weidenfeld & Nicolson, 1966); James J. Gibson, *The Senses Considered as Perceptual Systems*, (Boston, MA, Houghton Mifflin, 1966). Later books on the psychology of perception include: James Hogg (ed.), *Psychology and the Visual Arts: Selected Readings*, (Harmondsworth, Middlesex, Penguin Books, 1969); Richard L. Gregory, *The Intelligent Eye*, (London, Weidenfeld & Nicolson, 1970); M. H. Pirenne, *Optics, Painting & Photography*, (Cambridge, Cambridge University Press, 1970); Nicholas Wade, *Visual Allusions: Pictures of Perception*, (Hove, London & Hillsdale, Lawrence Erlbaum Associates, 1990); Robert L. Solso, *Cognition and the Visual Arts*, (London & Cambridge, MA, MIT Press, 1994); Richard Gregory, John Harris, Priscilla Heard and David Rose, (eds), *The Artful Eye*, (Oxford, Oxford University Press, 1995).

3   See the informative television programme *Mystery of the Senses Part 4: Vision*, (20 August 1995), a Green Umbrella Production/Channel 4 television. The television series was produced by Peter Jones and was based on Diane Ackerman's book cited in note 4.

4   Studies of the senses include: Mick Csáky (ed.), *How Does It Feel? Exploring the World of Your Senses*, (London, Thames & Hudson, 1979); Diane Ackerman, *The Natural History of the Senses*, (New York, Random House/London, Chapmans, 1990); David Howes (ed.), *The Varieties of Sensory Experience: A Sourcebook in the Anthropology of the Senses*, (Toronto, University of Toronto Press, 1991); Constance Classen, *Worlds of Sense: Exploring the Senses in History and Across Cultures*, (London, Routledge, 1993); Michael Taussig, *Mimesis and Alterity: A Particular History of the Senses*, (London, Routledge, 1993).

5   See, for example, Hans Jonas, 'The Nobility of Sight: A Study in the Phenomenology of the Senses', *The Phenomenon of Life: Toward a Philosophical Biology*, (New York, Delta Book/Dell Publishing, 1966), pp. 135–51.

6   D. M. Lowe, *History of Bourgeois Perception*, (Chicago, University of Chicago Press/Brighton, Harvester Press, 1982).

7   N. Bryson, 'The Gaze in the Expanded Field', *Vision and Visuality*, ed. H. Foster, (Seattle, WA, Bay View Press/Dia Art Foundation, 1988), pp. 91–4.

8   At Middlesex University an Art and Design History module was taught (by Dr Peter Webb) for a number of years with the title *Imagination in Nineteenth Century Painting*.

9   P. Klee, 'Creative Credo' (1920), *The Inward Vision: Watercolors, Drawings and Writings by Paul Klee*, (New York, Abrams, 1959), p. 5.

10   J. B. Thompson, *Ideology and Modern Culture: Critical Social Theory in the Era of Mass Communication*, (Cambridge, Polity Press, 1990), p. 124.

11   Berenson asserted: 'to realise form we must give tactile values to retinal sensations . . . the chief business of the figure painter . . . is to stimulate the tactile imagination', *The Italian Painters of the Renaissance*, (London, Phaidon Press, 1952), p. 43. Berenson's ideas derived from Adolf von Hildebrand (1847–1921), who discussed the difference between art perceived close up and at a distance, and also from the

ideas of Alois Riegl (1858–1905), who argued that some styles and periods of art were tactile or haptic, and other kinds were optical. On the work of Riegl see: Margaret Iversen, *Alois Riegl: Art History and Theory*, (London & Cambridge, MA, MIT Press, 1993).

12   The *Encyclopedia Britannica* defines proxemics as 'the study of the communicative values of space, time, body positions, and other non-verbal factors in various cultures'. The term 'silent language' has also been used by the American anthropologist Edward T. Hall. (For more on proxemics see E. T. Hall, *The Hidden Dimension: Man's Use of Space in Public and Private* (London, Bodley Head, 1969); Robert Sommer, *Personal Space: The Behavioral Basis of Design* (Eaglewood Cliffs, NJ, Prentice Hall, 1969); R. G. Haper, A. N. Wiens and J. D. Matarazzo, *Non-Verbal Communication: The State of the Art* (New York, John Wiley, 1978).) Space has also been of interest to architectural historians, witness Siegfried Giedion's *Space, Time and Architecture*, (London, Oxford University Press, 1941, 5th edn 1971), to French philosophers, witness Gaston Bachelard's *The Poetics of Space*, (Boston, MA, Beacon Press, 1969) and to women, witness Shirley Ardener (ed.), *Women and Space*, (London, Croom Helm, 1982) and B. Colomina (ed.), *Sexuality and Space*, (Princeton, NJ, Princeton University Press, 1992).

13   See Peter Wagner, *Reading Iconotexts: From Swift to the French Revolution*, (London, Reaktion Books, 1995) and W. J. T. Mitchell, *Picture Theory*. The relation between words and images has attracted much scholarly attention. There is an International Association of Word and Image (IAWI) which holds conferences and there is a journal entitled *Word & Image* (1985–).

14   The role of sound – dialogue, music, noises – in films has not attracted as much scholarly attention as the role of images. Nevertheless, the French theorist Michel Chion has written three volumes on the subject. See also: Elizabeth Weis and John Belton, *Film Sound: Theory and Practice*, (New York, Columbia University Press, 1985); and Philip Brophy, 'The Architecsonic Object: Stereo Sound, Cinema and Colors', *Culture, Technology and Creativity in the Late Twentieth Century*, ed. P. Hayward, (London, Paris, Rome, John Libbey, 1990), pp. 90–110.

15   For two books exploring mass media which represent the fine arts see: John A. Walker's *Art and Artists on Screen*, (Manchester & New York, Manchester University Press, 1993) and *Arts TV: A History of Arts Television in Britain*, (London, Paris & Rome, Arts Council & John Libbey, 1993).

16   Ernst H. Gombrich, *Art and Illusion: A Contribution to the Psychology of Pictorial Representation*, (London, Phaidon Press, 1960). See also: Gombrich's *The Sense of Order: A Study in the Psychology of Decorative Art*, (Oxford, Phaidon Press, 1979 and *The Image and the Eye: Further Studies in the Psychology of Visual Perception*, (London, Phaidon Press, 1982).

17   Adrian Stokes, *Three Essays on the Painting of Our Time*, (London, Tavistock, 1961). Anton Ehrenzweig, *The Psychoanalysis of Artistic Vision and Hearing*, (New York, George Braziller, 2nd edn 1965) and *The Hidden Order of Art: A Study in the Psychology of Artistic Imagination*, (London, Weidenfeld & Nicolson, 1967).

18   F. Nietzsche, quoted in Fredric Jameson's *The Prison-House of Language: A Critical Account of Structuralism and Russian Formalism*, (Princeton, NJ, Princeton University Press, 1972).

19   T. W. Adorno, *Aesthetic Theory*, (London, Routledge & Kegan Paul, 1984), pp. 139–45.

20   On Latham see: John A. Walker, *John Latham – The Incidental Person – His Art and Ideas*, (London, Middlesex University Press, 1995).

3 Visual culture as a field of study, and the origins of Visual Culture Studies

THIS CHAPTER attempts to identify the contents of the field of study called visual culture and to give a short history of the emergence of the discipline Visual Culture Studies.

The field of visual culture

Figure 4 displays the field of visual culture, defined in terms of its constituent arts, crafts, design and mass media, as it exists at the end of the twentieth century. A diagram showing the state of visual culture in Europe in 1500 would, of course, feature far fewer items. Such diagrams, therefore, are synchronic 'snapshots' showing the state of play of visual culture at particular moments. They are static rather than dynamic. Only by comparing diagrams showing different periods could one detect the changes that have taken place historically.

The word 'field', of course, is a spatial metaphor. Before thinking about the contents of this field further, we need to consider the character of the field as a whole. The writings of Pierre Bourdieu on cultural production are particularly illuminating in this respect.[1] In his opinion, individual artists, art works and art forms cannot be understood in isolation; they have to be regarded as manifestations of the whole field of cultural production. The latter consists of 'structural relations . . . between social positions that are both occupied and manipulated by social agents which may be individuals, groups or institutions'.[2] 'The literary or artistic field', he argues, 'is a *field of forces*, but it is also a *field of struggles* tending to transform or conserve this field of forces.'[3]

The social positions represent varying degrees of power and they are all relative to one another: if one position alters, the position of all the others changes too. (Painters will understand this: every mark added to a semi-completed painting changes the whole ensemble of marks.) To allow for change and development, Bourdieu acknowledges possible or potential positions: new artists, groups and media can enter the field and become powerful within it. For example, the invention and spread of photography during the nineteenth century had an immense impact on the existing art of painting. The new visual medium did not totally destroy or replace the older one but it did influence the look of paintings and reduce painting's social importance. It also provided fine artists with an alternative medium of expression.

Bourdieu maintains that the field of cultural production exists within a larger field of production, the field of general manufacturing, economics and politics which he sometimes calls 'the field of power'. While the field of culture has a relative autonomy, its boundaries are permeable, and it is subject to influences and determinants from the enclosing field. Also, what is at stake in the field of culture is comparable to that of the wider field: the competition for wealth, property, power and social status. But what distinguishes the cultural field from the field of economics is that power is often symbolic: it consists of aesthetic achievements, high status, peer group recognition, and the award of degrees and honours.

Disinterested creation

Bourdieu identifies one peculiar characteristic of the field of culture which apparently inverts ordinary economics, namely, 'disinterested' creation (making works without regard to monetary rewards). This is normally experimental, avant-garde art by artists who strive for complete autonomy. Their work is really aimed at other producers. (Bourdieu thinks art for the sake of art is really art for other artists.) Sometimes such 'idealist' and 'self-sacrificing' artists receive no income from their output during their lifetimes. (Those in charge of a film company or an advertising agency would think it crazy to ignore the profit motive.) But Bourdieu goes on to claim that the artists concerned do have an interest in disinterestedness: if they gain the recognition of fellow artists, they acquire symbolic value which may in the end translate into fame and fortune.

The quantity problem

Given the fact that the content of the field of visual culture is so wide and heterogeneous, a book with the Gombrich-like title *The Story of Visual Culture* is hardly thinkable – except in terms of a multi-volumed/authored encyclopedia. The field encompasses billions of cultural products generated throughout history by the peoples of world. Such a mass of material exists – a mass that continually enlarges as time passes – it is hard to envisage its outer limits. And so many varieties of visual culture exist that there is a danger that any one will be treated in a superficial manner during a three-year degree programme. The advantage of such a large and diverse field is that there is plenty of scope for original research. And even when scholars tackle the same object of study, by applying different disciplinary approaches, they can arrive at different interpretations.

On the one hand, the expanded nature of the field requires scholars to

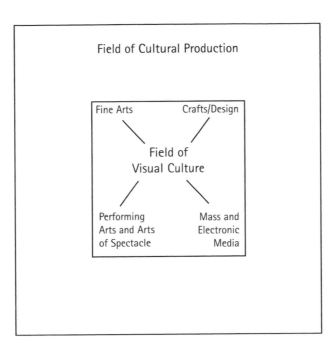

4 The field of visual culture.

Fine arts: painting, sculpture, print-making, drawing, mixed-media forms, installations, photo-text, avant-garde films and videos, happenings and performance art, architecture.

Crafts/design: urban design, retail design, corporate design, logos and symbols, industrial design, engineering design, illustration, graphics, product design, automobile design, design of weapons of war, transportation and space vehicle design, typography, wood carving and furniture design, jewellery, metalwork, shoes, ceramics, set design, computer-aided design, subcultures, costume and fashion, hair styling, body adornment, tattoos, landscape and garden design.

Performing arts & the arts of spectacle: theatre, acting, gesture and body language, playing musical instruments, dance/ballet, beauty pageants, striptease, fashion shows, the circus, carnivals and festivals, street marches and parades, public ceremonies such as coronations, funfairs, theme parks, Disneyworlds, arcades, video games, sound and light shows, fireworks, illuminations and neon signs, pop and rock concerts, panoramas, waxworks, planetariums, mass rallies, sporting events.

Mass and electronic media: photography, cinema/film, animation, television and video, cable and satellite, advertising and propaganda, postcards and reproductions, illustrated books, magazines, cartoons, comics and newspapers, multimedia, Compact-Disc Interactive, Internet, telematics, virtual reality, computer imagery.

learn about more and more subjects, while, on the other hand, to retain their sanity scholars have to be selective, they have to specialise. Students too, when planning research for dissertations, have to set themselves manageable, precisely formulated tasks. Most schools of Visual Culture provide modules with titles like *Historiography* and *Methodology* which are designed to assist students in identifying and solving problems of research, theory and history-writing.

The corpus

Traditionally, individual scholars have narrowed down their subject matter in three main ways: first, by limiting themselves to one particular form or type of visual culture (say, architecture, building type: cinemas); second, by selecting the best, the exceptional examples of any particular art form or medium (the 'masterpieces' of sculpture); and third, by selecting examples deemed to be typical or representative. In cases two and three, the scholar's act of selection implies that he or she is already familiar with a certain corpus of material. Gaining a thorough knowledge of that corpus can take decades of labour. Consider, for example, the survey of the notable buildings of England undertaken by the architectural historian Nikolaus Pevsner from 1949 to 1974. (He and his wife travelled by car to every shire in the land. They were also helped by research assistants.) His findings were published by Penguin Books in a series of volumes, forty-six in all.[4] Clearly, in order to pick out 'notable' buildings from the totality of English buildings, Pevsner must have been armed with some criteria of discrimination. Contemporary architectural theorists are critical of Pevsner's methodology, but there is no gainsaying the fact that his survey was a remarkable feat.

Students will not have as much time as Pevsner to devote to empirical research, but often they can draw upon personal experience – of, say, subcultural artefacts and styles – which enables them to write original essays and dissertations on subjects about which they know more than their tutors. Where the tutor can help is in helping to pose questions to the raw material, in suggesting theoretical approaches that will illuminate the images and objects concerned.

A problem students need to address when writing essays and dissertations is that of deciding upon a certain corpus of material and a set of examples to discuss. (A current exhibition could be regarded as a readymade corpus.) Analyses of specific images, films, designed goods is an opportunity for students to demonstrate how well they have assimilated theoretical concepts; they are also an opportunity for the student to contribute some fresh, personal insights and reactions. But all too often the number of examples is too small and the grounds for their selection are arbitrary. Doubt is then thrown on any generalisations and conclusions based upon them. This problem is especially evident when discussing a subject such as advertising where there are millions of potential examples and so many possible grounds for selection. Obviously, in the space of a short essay, the writer cannot hope to discuss more than a few examples but this makes it all the more vital to select them with care and to devise a rationale – which normally derives from the underlying question motivating the research – for the choices made.

Addressing the vast field of visual culture requires a collective effort. Schools of Visual Culture normally employ teams of full- and part-time staff whose expertise covers a range of subjects and methods. Gaps in knowledge can be filled by commissioning additional lectures from visiting academics. Particularly valuable are contributions by visiting scholars to seminars of the *Ideas in Progress* type because students are exposed to the latest thinking on particular subjects. Whenever possible students should attend the annual conferences of such bodies as the College Art Association (USA), the Association of Art Historians (UK) and the Design History Society (UK), because in this way they will discover who are the leading scholars and what is the latest state of research and scholarship. In addition, of course, there are numerous, one-off thematic conferences organised by universities, museums, arts centres and cultural societies that may be worth attending.

Origins of Visual Culture Studies

Culture has been studied by scholars for centuries and it has been argued that the discipline of Art History can be traced back to 1550, the year in which Giorgio Vasari's *Lives of the Most Excellent Painters, Sculptors and Architects* appeared. However, such an in-depth history is beyond the scope of this chapter. It limits itself to the recent past – 1960s to 1990s – that is, the immediate, preceding context, the period in which Visual Culture Studies emerged.

Radical political and artistic movements during the 1960s prompted a re-evaluation in many intellectual fields and innovations continued for two decades. There is not space here to detail all the influences that anthropology, Frankfurt School philosophy, psychoanalysis, Russian formalism, semiotics and so forth had upon the development of Visual Culture Studies. The core realms Art and Design History and Architectural History will be considered plus those realms where an overlap exists, that is, Communication/Cultural/Film/Media Studies.

Generally speaking, during the 1960s and 1970s, scholars became much more self-conscious than the previous generation in regard to theoretical assumptions, methodological issues and cultural politics. They questioned the very nature and function of their disciplines and professions. They became much more aware of their role as intellectuals and educators in the reproduction of society. Many of them were or became socialists and concluded they could not remain 'neutral/objective/detached' observers, that they had a duty to intervene in ways that contributed to the building of a socialist society.

Predictably, conservative staff and students complained about hidden agendas or outright political propaganda, brainwashing students instead of educating them. Traditionalists objected to what they saw as the politicisation of their disciplines. They failed to see that the disciplines were already ideological and political and what they were really objecting to was the challenge to their complacency, entrenched positions and the switch from Right-wing, liberal and patriarchal positions to socialist and feminist ones. Once the latter had become established, the traditionalists changed their tune and began to complain about 'political correctness'. After the battle within the academy had subsided, attacks on the study of visual culture continued in the press: visual culture, one journalist declared, was 'undermining the literary'; her bleak conclusion: 'the age of the Philistine has arrived.'[5]

Art History and fine art

In Britain a significant expansion in the number of art historians occurred during the 1960s and 1970s as a result of demands for their knowledge in art and design colleges. (Complementary Studies lecturers were also appointed at the same time.) This was because those charged with reforming art education thought some intellectual stiffening was required to make practical, studio-based courses academically respectable, that is, worthy of degree status. Naturally enough painters and sculptors often resented (and still resent) the fact that their practices were not considered intellectual activities in their own right, but at least they were taught the histories of their practices. The art historians taught the history of European fine arts despite the fact that the majority of students were trainee designers rather than budding artists or architects. Consequently, it soon became clear that what design students received from Art History was largely irrelevant to their studio specialisms and vocational needs (see below, Design History).

Art historians who taught fine art students during the 1960s and 1970s also discovered that a knowledge of the history of European art was not sufficient to satisfy the interests and needs of their students. Since the majority of the latter were concerned with living, contemporary art, what they most wanted was information about the latest trends.[6] Furthermore, histories of painting and sculpture proved too narrow because fine art was itself expanding and diversifying in terms of new materials and media, and unusual mixtures of media. Art historians trained at the Courtauld Institute to be experts on the Italian Renaissance were ill equipped for this situation: consequently lecturers had to be recruited from elsewhere. Many of those appointed were fine art graduates with an interest in history and theory.

Today, the fine arts remain part of the field of visual culture but they no longer occupy a position of centrality. (In art colleges fine art used to be regarded as the basis for all design practices because it was concerned with such fundamentals as colour, form, space, objective drawing and so forth.) Painting and sculpture are still discussed in modules but alongside video art, avant-garde film, installation and site-specific art, virtual reality, etc., etc. In some instances the arts of ancient Egypt, Greece, Rome and Renaissance Italy have vanished from the curriculum altogether or they have been reduced to a rump. (Introductory, chronological survey modules tend to concentrate on modern art and to commence in the mid nineteenth century.) Modernism is still considered relevant but, as in Architectural History, the primary focus in recent years has been on its successor: post-modernism.

A combination of the Social History of Art and Business/Professional Studies for fine art students has prompted lectures on social context, and on economic and institutional factors. The art world and its infrastructure, the parts played by galleries and museums, art critics, dealers, patrons and collectors, are subjects far more in evidence than they were three decades ago.

The New Art History

During the 1970s some younger lecturers looked beyond the discipline of Art History for new ideas and methods because it had become an orthodoxy and was too uncritical and connoisseurial. (John Berger's television series and paperback *Ways of Seeing* (London, BBC/Harmondsworth, Middlesex, Penguin Books, 1972) was an inspiration to many because it mounted a crucial challenge to traditional accounts.) In the following decade this gave rise to the phenomenon called 'the New Art History' (a polemical title) which in turn became an orthodoxy in certain institutions.[7] But even the New Art History was, in some instances, too narrow in terms of its subject matter. For example, radical Left-wing scholars such as T. J. Clark made important contributions to the social history of art but they tended to write about the work of the same canonical, male, French artists (Gustave Courbet, Edouard Manet) and the same art forms (painting, sculpture) as the orthodox art historians they had reacted against.

Feminist Art History

The impact of feminism produced a significant transformation of the discipline of Art History by posing a whole new set of questions beginning, in 1971, with 'Why have there been no great women artists?'[8] At first research focused upon excavating the work of neglected women artists, the issues of femininity/sexual difference, and visual representations of women, but later on analysis was extended to masculinity and images of men. (After a while homosexual scholars also began to consider the latter topics, hence the emergence of so-called 'Queer theory'.) Leading scholars included the Americans Carol Duncan, Linda Nochlin, Lucy Lippard, and Whitney Chadwick, and the Britons Tamar Garb, Germaine Greer, Griselda Pollock, Rozsika Parker and Lisa Tickner. Laura Mulvey also contributed an important Freudian critique of Allen Jones's erotic (some would say 'sexist') paintings and sculptures to the magazine *Spare Rib* 8 (February 1973) and wrote feminist accounts of film. The Women's Movement naturally encompassed practitioners as well as historians and theorists, so a close relationship developed between feminist artists and feminist historians, critics and curators. Collaborations based on shared political aims occurred when a series of important feminist art exhibitions were mounted in the United States and Europe.

Post-colonial theory

During the period 1940s–90s, as European states lost or relinquished their colonies around the world, historians and theorists in the West became increasingly conscious of the legacies – both positive and negative – of the ages of slavery, colonialism and imperialism. Edward Said's books *Orientalism* (London, Routledge, 1979) and *Culture and Imperialism* (London, Chatto & Windus, 1993) were highly influential. The relation between 'centre' and 'periphery' and the concept of 'the Other' – anyone distant, different, foreign – began to be scrutinised. Western attitudes to the Other were ambiguous: other races and cultures were perceived as both threatening and attractive. Today, some universities provide modules with titles like *Representing Other Cultures* which attempt to examine critically images of the Other in a variety of media. In Film Studies the Western genre has provided plenty of examples of the generally negative depiction of native American tribes.

Primitivism, that is the cult and appropriation of the arts of 'primitive' or tribal peoples by modern artists such as Gauguin, Brancusi, Picasso and Moore, was documented by Robert Goldwater in 1938 but a large-scale survey exhibition – *'Primitivism' in Twentieth Century Art* – was mounted by the Museum of Modern Art, New York, in 1984.

Aside from its influence on modern artists, tribal material culture itself was generally omitted from Euro-centric histories of art written by white scholars on the dubious grounds that it was non-historical. However, as more and more exhibitions of African and Aboriginal art have been mounted, knowledge has expanded and it has become evident that this kind of art is contemporary as well as historic: there are significant black living artists working in Africa and Australia employing both traditional crafts and modern media. Awareness of the creative achievements of so-called 'Third World' countries gave rise to books and university lecture series on such topics as Third, or Third-World, Cinema.

'Orientalism' is a term that has been used by various scholars to describe the conceptions and images of the Orient, that is, the Arab Near East rather than China, propagated by Western artists and intellectuals. The taste for representing the Orient dates primarily from the nineteenth century when artists such as Gros, Delacroix, Gérôme, Gleyre, Tissot, Ingres, Renoir, Bonington and Lewis delighted in the exotic appeal of scenes set in North Africa, Turkey and the Middle East: paintings of harems, odalisques, despots, the desert, mosques and so on. Several twentieth-century artists too have been intrigued by the same kind of subjects, Matisse and Brangwyn for instance. Some artists visited the Orient in order to make first-hand observations but others simply relied on their imaginations and existing records. Critics of Orientalism have argued that the representations were mythical and an aspect of European colonialism. In the 1980s a number of visual artists explored the theme of Orientalism in an analytical fashion in their work, for example, Olivier Richon and Deanna Petherbridge. During the same decade museum curators also mounted a series of exhibitions on the theme of Orientalism.

One striking legacy of colonialism is the presence in Western cities of ethnic minority communities deriving from the old European colonies in Africa and Asia. Rasheed Araeen (b. 1935), an artist and writer who emigrated from Pakistan to Britain in 1964, established a magazine entitled *Third Text* in 1987 in order to provide 'a critical forum for the discussion and appraisal of the work of artists hitherto marginalised through racial, sexual and cultural differences'. Araeen's own artwork questioned the category of otherness by drawing upon Western avant-garde art tendencies such as Minimalism. Araeen also curated the 1989 Hayward Gallery exhibition *The Other Story* which documented the contribution to British art during the post–1945 era of Afro-Asian artists – Frank Bowling, Sonia Boyce, Avinash Chandra, David Medalla, Francis Souza, etc. – who were either resident or born in Britain.

As a result of the Civil Rights movement in the United States in the 1960s, black consciousness increased and this gave rise to separatist Black art activities, galleries and organisations in North America and in Europe. More recently there has been an integrational tendency known as 'multi-culturalism' or 'new internationalism'. Symptomatic of this new consciousness was the Paris show *Magiciens de la Terre* (Paris, Centre Georges Pompidou, 1989) – judged to be the first global art exhibition – and the foundation by the British Arts Council of INIVA – Institute of New International Visual Arts (1992–) – intended to encourage 'inter-cultural dialogue and exchange'.

The publication during the 1990s of a spate of books and articles discussing post-colonial issues and theory demonstrates that it is now an established sub-category of Literary and Visual Culture Studies.[9] Three noted scholars in this field are Gayatri Spivak, Homi Bhabha and bell hooks.

Design History

To meet the particular needs of design students, a number of art historians re-educated themselves to become design historians. In 1977 they seceded from the Association of Art Historians (1974–) and founded their own professional organisation: the Design History Society. They then held annual conferences, published papers, wrote textbooks and established an academic journal – *The Journal of Design History* (1988-).[10] In the United States a caucus on Design History was held at the 1983 College Art Association annual meeting which resulted in an organisation and newsletter called the Design History Forum. Victor Margolin, of the University of Illinois, began to edit the new theoretical journal *Design Issues* (1984–) which published two important articles about the state of the discipline of Design History by the leading British design historian Clive Dilnot.[11]

As a result of the increase of interest in design, the remit of Visual Culture Studies now includes many design, decorative arts and crafts topics. Some faculties of Art and Design also encompass the performing arts. Design is involved here too in terms of costume and set designs for the theatre, films, television and rock music concerts.

In Britain the period 1980–90 was dubbed 'the design decade' because design and designers achieved such a high profile during that era. This was a time when advertising, markets, business, shops and shopping became very important. Design and style came to be seen as the added values that could make the difference in persuading customers to buy new goods. Supermarkets, shopping malls and retail chains proliferated and so designers of shop interiors and exteriors flourished. Magazine design and typography also became fashionable and innovative – witness *The Face* (1980–), founded and edited by Nick Logan. This youth culture, fashion and pop music magazine became notable for the priority given to striking photographs, bizarre layouts and experimental typography. Its distinctive look was primarily due to the inventiveness of Neville Brody, its designer from 1981 to 1986.

A Design Museum was opened in London in 1989 and this meant that historical and contemporary exhibitions were mounted that treated design as a subject as important as art, and treated individual designers as if they were major artists.

Design historians, critics and journalists undoubtedly benefited from the surge of interest in design. New design magazines were established and publishers commissioned a spate of new books about many aspects of design. At the same time, however, some academics were repelled by the rampant commercialism and shallowness of design in the 1980s, its prioritising of style over substance and function, its indifference to design for social need, public spaces and services.

Some scholars began to raise ecological issues because the Green Movement had highlighted the dangers of pollution, over-production and consumption. Students of design are generally more conscious of commerce and the job market than fine art students, but some still care about the environment. By writing dissertations about recycling, design students were able to tackle ecological issues while simultaneously investigating new business opportunities.

Increasingly, designing occurs on computer screens rather than on paper, especially in the realm of graphics or VCD (Visual Communication Design). Students cannot help, therefore, but be aware of the impact of new technology on the design process. Essays and dissertations written for Design History modules proved useful because they provided opportunities for students to consider technological change historically and to reflect upon their studio experience.

In Britain three-dimensional or product design has experienced something of a crisis in recent decades because a decline in many manufacturing industries has reduced the need and demand for product designers. One response to this has been to shift design in the direction of art, craft, and niche marketing; for example, to make expensive, one-off or limited edition ceramics rather than prototype pots for cheap, mass production. British crafts were encouraged by craft fairs and by organisations like the Crafts Council (see Chapter 6, on institutions). They were also given a new importance and value via the writings of feminist art historians and the work of feminist artists who celebrated the aesthetic achievements of women quilters, embroiderers, potters and so on.

Architectural History

One has only to picture the Egyptian pyramids to be reminded that architecture is an ancient art of immense power and prestige, and, despite all the changes that have taken place in society over the centuries, it is still significant today. (Especially when one considers the enormous aggregations of buildings that constitute modern metropolises.) Architecture was once thought of as 'the mother of the arts'; consequently for generations it featured in most history of art courses. To a limited extent the history of architecture is still taught to studio-based art and design students, and to academic-stream visual culture students, but if a young person wishes to become a full-time professional architect then he or she normally has to attend a specialist university department or a private school like the

Architectural Association in London. Such places are generally staffed by qualified architects who act as studio tutors. Architectural historians employed in these departments do not enjoy quite the same freedom as their colleagues in art and design colleges, and they are often expected to perform extra duties by assisting in the assessment of the students' studio projects.

In Britain the training of architects takes a minimum of seven years and includes periods of placement and practical experience. Furthermore, the education of architects has to meet national standards laid down by external professional bodies such as the Royal Institute of British Architects, consequently the curriculum architectural historians are expected to deliver is narrower – but much deeper – than that found in schools of Visual Culture.[12]

Many academic-stream visual culture students appear to be indifferent to architecture and find it a boring subject to study. This is a pity given that it is such a public art and we all see and experience architecture every day. Clearly, much depends on the skills and enthusiasm of the lecturer. By taking a broad theme like 'The City' a fascinating lecture programme can be delivered which examines the topic from a variety of perspectives without being a dull, chronological slog through the history of urban design.

The key development in architecture in recent decades was the shift from modernism to post-modernism. Since the latter inverted many of the principles and values of the former, students still needed to learn about the International Style. (Modules with titles like *International Modernism* persist.) Histories of architecture by writers like Pevsner, which presented a single-strand development of heroic male geniuses whose logical conclusion was modern architecture, were replaced by histories which acknowledged a plurality of traditions. Charles Jencks is the prolific architectural critic and historian who did most to promote plurality. His ideas, following on from those of the American architect and theorist Robert Venturi, were crucial to modules about post-modernism.

At present female staff and students in architectural schools are still few because architecture is an overwhelming masculine art and profession. During the 1970s and 1980s European and American feminist scholars undertook research and published polemical texts in order to redress this situation. The Open University also produced a video that examined the issue of gender and architecture, the historiography of architecture (Lynne Walker was the consultant art historian), and showed examples of buildings designed by women, and women-only architectural practices, such as Matrix, that design buildings for women clients.[13]

Architecture's close relationship to power – economic, political, institutional – has been an issue of interest to many architectural historians, and the writings of the French philosopher Michel Foucault have been a major source of inspiration for them.[14]

During the 1980s, architecture became a topic of concern outside of architects' offices and university departments as a result of Prince Charles's attacks upon modern buildings via speeches, books and television programmes. The Prince is aware that the majority of people find difficulty in relating to architecture except in a negative way. A magazine inspired by Prince Charles – *Perspectives on Architecture*, 1:1 (April 1994) – was founded with the aim of bridging 'the gap between the public and the building professionals'. He also encouraged the foundation of a new school of architecture to provide an alternative curriculum. Some academics, in their lectures and seminars, have made use of the conflict between Prince Charles and leading contemporary architects in order to encourage students to consider both sides of the argument.

Architects take more of an interest in new theoretical developments than many other groups of practitioners. For example, the French philosophical tendency called 'deconstruction' associated with Jacques Derrida and Jean-François Lyotard had an impact on architecture in the late 1980s. 'Deconstructivist' architecture by Frank Gehry, Bernard Tschumi and others was the result.

Film/Media/Communication Studies

Currently, the field of visual culture includes a variety of still and moving-pictures media but it excludes radio. The nineteenth and twentieth centuries saw the emergence and rise to cultural power of a succession of new media technologies which, as Marshall McLuhan explained in the 1960s, extended and augmented the human senses.[15] In the case of vision, for example, X-ray photography enabled doctors to see inside the human body without cutting it open. Today, visual media supply a cornucopia of imagery both realistic and imaginative that, in most households in developed countries, now absorbs several hours of viewing time every day.

The new media in turn gave rise to a language-based discourse, that is, massive quantities of commentary and analysis both journalistic and scholarly. Most advanced nations now have an organisation like the British Film Institute whose purpose is to foster the production, preservation, appreciation and study of films. Journals such as *Screen* and *Screen Education* issued by the BFI and SEFT (Society for Education in Film and Television) were highly influential during the 1970s in disseminating theory about film and encouraging education about it in secondary schools. The enormous number of books and articles devoted to every aspect of film-making/viewing is a tribute to the cultural importance of the cinema. Theoretical writings on film by Jean-Louis Baudry, Jean-Louis Commolli, Christian Metz, Stephen Heath, Laura Mulvey and others tended to be more sophisticated and innovative than writings on art and design (because they took note of developments in other disciplines);

consequently film theory influenced the thinking of many art and design historians.

In the past three decades Communication, Film, and Media Studies[16] departments have been established in universities around the world. This means that today there are some universities which have schools of Visual Culture and schools of Media Studies (plus schools of Cultural Studies) all considering movies and the other mass media. It may seem, therefore, that needless duplication is occurring. However, there are differences of approach: Media Studies is more concerned with theoretical concepts such as ideology and hegemony, with the ownership of the media, with media institutions, with the press, and statistical methods and Audience Studies, while Visual Culture Studies is more concerned with the aesthetic and design aspects of the media. Visual culture academics also teach the history of the fine arts and design/crafts which Media and Cultural Studies scholars normally do not.

Although it is an over-simplification, compared to the fine arts of the past the mass media are industrial and technological, they deliver popular culture to huge audiences quickly and cheaply. Advertising is generally thought of as one such a mass medium although it is really a mixed form of communication that reaches its target audiences by various means: newspapers, magazines, cinemas, billboards, television and radio, the shirts of sports stars and business sponsorship. As stated earlier, advertisements normally combine images and words, moving pictures and sounds, consequently they cannot be treated as purely visual phenomena.

During the 1960s a key interpreter of the mass media was the Canadian literary theorist McLuhan. In his crucial text *Understanding Media* (New York, McGraw-Hill/London, Routledge & Kegan Paul, 1964), McLuhan argued that education is 'ideally civil defence against media fall-out'.[17] Many academics agree with him – they see their task as one of demystifying and demythologising the media in the belief that such knowledge will arm students against the blandishments and lies of the commercial media and political propaganda. (Of course, the power and resources of the higher education sector are dwarfed by those of the media, and lectures are not normally as entertaining as Hollywood blockbusters. It is also the case that the media contain much material that is critical of society and some material which is self-critical.)

There is a degree of hypocrisy here: like their students, academics are enthralled by mass culture. Also, they use media in their teaching and they are happy to write reviews for newspapers and to appear on radio and television arts programmes. Some academics – Camille Paglia and Christopher Frayling, for instance – even write and present television programmes and series. Media analysis thus percolates back into the media.

One of McLuhan's early books – *The Mechanical Bride* (New York, Vanguard Press, 1951) – was a critique of American advertising. It influenced the ideas of the Independent Group, a cultural think-tank consisting of younger members of the Institute of Contemporary Arts, London, who met during the early 1950s to discuss such subjects as science, philosophy, technology, art, design and popular culture.[18] IG members were the pioneers of a new, quasi-anthropological approach to art, design and popular culture which they characterised as 'non-Aristotelian'. This meant that the traditional, hierarchical conception of culture – high, middle-brow and low – was rejected in favour of 'a long front of culture' in which the various forms of art, design and media were treated as of comparable value and interest. For example, an Action painting and a Hollywood sci-fi movie were both regarded as subcategories of visual communication employing certain kind of signs which required decoding. Mass, industrial, commercial forms of culture were respected and enjoyed and considered as seriously as the modern art of Paul Klee and Marcel Duchamp. The artist Richard Hamilton and the critic Reyner Banham in particular also tried to dismantle the division between the fine and applied arts. The open-mindedness of IG members served as a model for Visual Culture Studies, and their faith in the value of popular culture was confirmed by the vibrant Pop art and design, and mass media of the 1960s.

In Italy and France the mass media attracted the critical attention of such brilliant scholars as Umberto Eco and Roland Barthes. Eco has written demanding theoretical papers and a book about semiotics, but also newspaper columns about popular culture, plus a best-selling novel – *The Name of the Rose* (1983) – that has been turned into a movie starring Sean Connery. Clearly, Eco is a man who spans the divide between the worlds of the academy and the mass media. Barthes's *Mythologies* (France 1957, Britain (London, Jonathan Cape) 1972) was a highly influential text analysing the political and ideological dimensions of the myths in the media and daily life of France. Much of Barthes's later writing was devoted to literature, but he also published notable texts on semiology, fashion, pleasure, advertising and photography.

Judith Williamson, currently a professor at Middlesex University, is the author of a 1978 book about advertising – *Decoding Advertisements* (London, Marion Boyars) – which quickly became a standard textbook. (She has also made a film about the subject: *A Sign is a Fine Investment*.) Williamson treated adverts as signs that required to be analysed in order to reveal their semiotic mechanisms and their disguised ideological and political meanings. Critiques of these kind are essential but they do tend to be ahistorical and they also tend to ignore the role of the designer and the design process. Design historians interested in graphics, posters and typography are much more likely to pay attention to the latter issues, but also to overlook semiotic and political dimensions. Both kinds of theorists often neglect the empirical study of the effects of advertisements on actual audiences.

An important ingredient of advertising is photography. This is another medium that has received much attention and analysis in recent decades. While some conservative thinkers continued to maintain that photography is not an art, this did not prevent magazines, book publishers, galleries and museums from treating certain photographers as if they were great masters. Nor did it prevent many fine artists from using photography as a medium of expression. Roland Barthes, Alan Sekula, Susan Sontag and John Tagg contributed important theoretical analyses, while the British photographers/writers Jo Spence and Victor Burgin made contributions to both theory and practice. In Britain the London organisation Camerawork was influential: it was a centre for community photography; it mounted and circulated exhibitions of photographs; and it published a magazine – *Camerawork* (1976–85) – devoted to a critical and contextual examination of photography. The latter systematically addressed the various genres of photography – advertising, art, commercial, community, documentary, family, fashion, portrait, war – and discussed the ethics and politics of photographic practices.[19]

Exhibitions and books about the work of the German communist monteur John Heartfield encouraged a fresh interest in the technique of photomontage, and Left-wing artists such as Klaus Staeck and Peter Kennard produced critical images and slogans in the service of many political causes. In 1983 Kennard assisted Chris Rodrigues and Rod Stoneman in the production of a videotape entitled *Photomontage Today: Peter Kennard* which is helpful to academic-stream students unfamiliar with montage theory and technique.

Cultural Studies

In Britain Cultural Studies became established at the University of Birmingham when a postgraduate research centre – the Centre for Contemporary Cultural Studies – was opened by Richard Hoggart in 1964. Hoggart came from an adult education/English literary criticism background. He was the author of *The Uses of Literacy* (London, Chatto & Windus, 1957) an important text concerned with the impact of popular culture on the working classes. The Centre took on a more sociological character under the leadership of Professor Stuart Hall (now of the Open University) in the 1970s. Culture was defined in the anthropological sense – described earlier – as all the habits and customs of people. Also, as the name of the Centre indicated, the focus was contemporary culture not the cultures of the more distant past. Culture included the mass media and they were examined in relation to such factors as politics, race, gender and class. Research within Cultural Studies was seen as committed or engaged, that is, capable of being a cultural intervention in its own right.

The researchers at Birmingham absorbed the critical theories emanating from European intellectuals but in addition they undertook empirical studies. Some were fascinated by British working-class and middle-class cultures, in particular the youth and subcultural styles characteristic of the 1950s, 1960s and 1970s. The thesis that such styles were a form of 'resistance through rituals' became highly influential.

Intelligent young scholars such as Dick Hebdige and Angela McRobbie emerged. Hebdige later became noted for his book *Subculture: The Meaning of Style* (London, Methuen, 1979). He succeeded in combining theory derived from Left-wing thinkers and structuralists with empirical and personal knowledge of youth, music and dress styles such as Punk. He went on to teach in polytechnics (he is now a lecturer in the United States) and contributed articles to the Middlesex Polytechnic journal *Block* founded in 1979 by a group of art and design historians mostly from Left-wing and feminist standpoints. This periodical published important articles by Hebdige (most notably on the Italian motor scooter and the British Mod subculture) and also by Tim Putnam, Fran Hannah, Jon Bird, Barry Curtis, Jo Spence, Lisa Tickner, John Tagg and others.[20] *Block* also sought to overcome the theory/practice divide by inviting artists to contribute articles and visual layouts.

There is not space to provide a history of Cultural Studies in the United States but, given the immense power of the American media, it is no surprise that they flourish there. To cite just one stimulating collection of essays about a pop music star: *The Madonna Connection: Representational Politics, Subcultural Identities and Cultural Theory*, (1993), edited by Cathy Schwichtenberg of the University of Georgia.

The field of Cultural Studies is broader than that of Visual Culture Studies because it includes more kinds of culture – literature, music and radio, for example. Some other points of difference: Cultural Studies does not foreground 'the visual' to the same extent as Visual Culture Studies. Cultural Studies academics often come from a sociological rather than an arts/humanities background. However, the differences should not be exaggerated: there is clearly an overlap between the two, and some art and design historians have taught in both realms.

Despite the undoubted achievements of Cultural Studies, they have recently been subjected to criticism.[21] For instance, Colin MacCabe complained they lacked historical perspective: the preference for the contemporary period meant that the cultures of the past – which art historians have traditionally addressed – were neglected; and they also avoided judgements of quality and comparative value.[22] During the late 1980s Michèle Barrett argued that Cultural Studies was preoccupied with 'a conception of meaning stripped of traditional aesthetic questions, one that does not engage with the issue of the senses'.[23] Lawrence Grossberg, an American academic, also found Cultural Studies guilty of political impotence and a failure to analyse the links between popular culture and the success of the New Right during the 1980s.[24]

Summary

This chapter has shown that the origins of Visual Culture Studies can be traced back to several, different historiographic traditions and that these Studies were subsequently shaped, first, by the changing demands of art and design education; and second, by theoretical developments in Art, Architectural and Design History, and in Cultural, Film and Media Studies.

Notes and further reading

1 See: P. Bourdieu, *The Field of Cultural Production: Essays on Art and Literature*, (Cambridge, Polity Press, 1993).

2 *Ibid.*, p. 29.

3 *Ibid.*, p. 30.

4 N. Pevsner, *Buildings of England*, 46 vols, (Harmondsworth, Middlesex, Penguin Books, 1949–74).

5 See Melanie Phillips, 'The Videotic Age of the Philistine', *The Observer*, (13 August 1995), 25.

6 An anthology edited by David Thistlewood that reviews the problems of teaching the history of art and critical studies to students on practical courses is *Critical Studies in Art and Design Education*, (London, Longman/NSEAD, 1989).

7 On the New Art History see: A. L. Rees and F. Borzello (eds), *The New Art History*, (London, Camden Press, 1986); N. Bryson (ed.), *Calligram: Essays in New Art History from France*, (Cambridge, Cambridge University Press, 1988); S. Bann (ed.), 'The New Art History', *History of the Human Sciences*, 2:1 (February 1989); D. Preziosi, *Rethinking Art History: Meditations on a Coy Science*, (New Haven, CT, & London, Yale University Press, 1989).

8 The literature on feminism and Art History is so extensive we will cite only one substantial article that gives an overview: Lisa Tickner, 'Feminism, Art History and Sexual Difference', *Genders*, 3 (Fall 1988), pp. 92–128.

9 See: Iain Chambers and Lidia Curti (eds), *The Post-Colonial Question: Common Skies, Divided Horizons*, (London & New York, Routledge, 1991); Francis Barker and others (eds), *Colonial Discourse/Postcolonial Discourse*, (Manchester & New York, Manchester University Press, 1994); Ella Shohat and Robert Stam, *Unthinking Eurocentrism: Multiculturalism and the Media*, (London & New York, Routledge, 1994).

10 For more on the emergence of Design History see: John A. Walker, *Design History and the History of Design*, (London, Pluto Press, 1989) and Hazel Conway (ed.), *Design History: A Student's Handbook*, (London, Allen & Unwin, 1987); Victor Margolin, 'A Decade of Design History in the United States 1977–87', *Journal of Design History*, 1:1 (1988), 51–72.

11 C. Dilnot, 'The State of Design History: Part One, Mapping the Field', *Design Issues*, 1:1 (Spring 1984), 4–23; 'Part Two', *Design Issues*, 1:2 (Fall 1984), 3–20.

12 For a critique of architectural education see: Necdet Teymur, *Architectural Education: Issues in Educational Practice and Policy*, (London, ?uestion Press, 1992). See also: Mark Crinson and Jules Lubbock, *Architecture – Art or Profession? Three Hundred Years of Architectural Education in Britain*, (Manchester & New

York, Manchester University Press, 1994) and Hazel Conway and Rowan Roenisch, *Understanding Architecture: An Introduction to Architecture and Architectural History*, (London & New York, Routledge, 1994).

13 Several versions of the video have been transmitted. See: *Personal Details: Women, Architecture and Identity*, (BBC–2, 1992), made originally for the Open University's 'Issues in Women's Studies' course. For an overview article see: L. Walker, 'Women and Architecture', *A View from the Interior: Feminism, Women and Design*, eds J. Attfield and P. Kirkham, (London, The Woman's Press, 1989), pp. 90–105.

14 See: Paul Hirst, 'Foucault and Architecture', *AA Files*, 26 (December 1993), 52–60; Thomas A. Markus, *Buildings and Power: Freedom and Control in the origin of Modern Building Types*, (London & New York, Routledge, 1993).

15 M. McLuhan, *Understanding Media: The Extensions of Man*, (New York, McGraw-Hill/London, Routledge & Kegan Paul, 1964).

16 There are several books concerning Media and Communication Studies: J. Hartley, H. Gouldon and T. O'Sullivan, *Making Sense of the Media*, (London, Comedia, 1985); L. Masterman, *Teaching the Media*, (London, Comedia, 1985); B. Dutton, *Media Studies: An Introduction*, (London, Longman, 1989); G. Burton, *More than Meets the Eye: An Introduction to Media Studies*, (London, Edward Arnold, 1990); D. Lusted (ed.), *The Media Studies Book: A Guide for Teachers*, (London, Routledge, 1991); A. Hart, *Understanding the Media: A Practical Guide*, (London & New York, Routledge, 1991); J. Corner and J. Hawthorn (eds), *Communications Studies: An Introductory Reader*, (London, Edward Arnold, 4th edn 1993); J. Watson and A. Hill, *A Dictionary of Communication and Media Studies*, (London, Edward Arnold, 3rd edn 1993); S. Price, *Media Studies*, (London, Pitman, 1994); T. O'Sullivan, B. Dutton and P. Rayner, *Studying the Media: An Introduction*, (London, Edward Arnold, 1994).

17 McLuhan, *Understanding Media*, p. 208.

18 For a recent history of the IG see: Anne Massey, *The Independent Group: Modernism and Mass Culture in Britain, 1945–59*, (Manchester & New York, Manchester University Press, 1995).

19 See also: Jessica Evans and Barbara Hunt (eds), *The Camerawork Essays: History and Context*, (London, Rivers Oram Press, 1996).

20 *Block* ceased publication in 1989 having accomplished its initial objectives. However, a series of annual conferences were then organised by the journal's editors at the Tate Gallery, with financial help from the Arts Council, and the proceedings of these conferences were published in book form by Routledge. See, for example, *Mapping the Futures: Local Cultures, Global Change*, eds Jon Bird and others, (London & New York, Routledge, 1993). A selection of articles from *Block* was published by Routledge in 1996.

21 There are several surveys of Cultural Studies: D. Punter, *Introduction to Contemporary Cultural Studies*, (London, Longman, 1986); Stuart Hall and others, *Cultural Studies: An Introduction*, (London, Macmillan, 1988); Graeme Turner, *British Cultural Studies: An Introduction*, (London, Unwin Hyman, 1990); Antony Easthope, *Literary into Cultural Studies*, (London, Routledge, 1991); Ben Agger, *Cultural Studies as Critical Theory*, (Brighton, Falmer Press, 1992); Lawrence Grossberg and others (eds), *Cultural Studies*, (London & New York, Routledge, 1992); David Buckingham and Julian Sefton-Green, *Cultural Studies Goes to School: Reading and Teaching Popular Media*, (Basingstoke, Taylor & Francis, 1995); Ioan Davies, *Cultural Studies and Beyond: Fragments of Empire*, (London & New York, Routledge, 1995).

22 John Davies, 'Perspective', *Times Higher Education Supplement*, (10 March 1995), 15.

23 M. Barrett, 'The Place of Aesthetics in Marxist Criticism', *Marxism and the Interpretation of Culture*, eds C. Nelson and L. Grossberg (Basingstoke, Macmillan Education, 1988), pp. 697–713.

24 L. Grossberg and others, *It's a Sin: Essays on Postmodernism, Politics & Culture*, (Sydney, Power Publications, 1988).

4   Coping with theory

We are in the age of the Theory student, the Theory course, the Theory degree, and so the Theory handbook for the Theory student on that Theory course. (Valentine Cunningham)[1]

Theory is more sadistic than politics. It beats you every time. The enforced discipline of theory expels the lazy reader. I read each sentence again and again. Slight distractions flaw me. Trying to get my head round this is like a snake swallowing a pig. The incessant return demanded by the authoritarian tone of rigorous theory affords little respite. (John Cussans)[2]

Hostility to theory usually means an opposition to other people's theories and an oblivion of one's own. (Terry Eagleton)[3]

A DICTIONARY DEFINES theory as: 'a coherent group of general propositions used as principles of explanation for a class of phenomenon'. Some theories have been thoroughly tested and are therefore widely accepted but, as another definition reminds us, 'theory' can also mean: 'a proposed explanation whose status is still conjectural'. In the humanities theories are not so easily tested as in the sciences; consequently students will find that many of the theories they encounter are of the conjectural variety. (The work of the philosopher Karl Popper and the historian of scientific revolutions Thomas Kuhn has shown that all theories are hypotheses/paradigms which are provisional and may be overthrown by the discovery of new information.) The word 'theory' is often linked with 'practice', therefore it also refers to the principles and methods that underpin a particular activity.

Most students decide to study visual culture at university because they enjoy looking at art and watching films, television, etc. They may be surprised and dismayed to discover that they are expected to read and master a range of theories about their favourite subjects, and that many of these theories prove extremely difficult to assimilate because they seem so far removed from common sense, and are, so often, couched in esoteric, dense and convoluted language.

To new students a three-year degree programme may seem a long time but in fact it is a short time in which to learn the mass of theory that currently exists (and which is being added to all the time). What students should try to bear in mind is that learning continues after graduation, that it is a life-long enterprise. Even so, a lifetime of study will not result in complete knowledge (in part because one has no knowledge of the future after one's death). Therefore, one has to tolerate uncertainty, to accept that one's understanding of reality will always be limited and subject to revision.

Some students will become intoxicated by the new world of ideas and try to swallow too many too quickly. Others will feel intimidated. This chapter has been included in order to reduce anxiety and to suggest coping strategies. Students who feel apprehensive about theory could start by reading books designed for beginners. Despite their emphasis on literature, Terry Eagleton's *Literary Theory: An Introduction* (Oxford, Blackwell, 1983) and Peter Barry's *Beginning Theory: An Introduction to Literary and Cultural Theory* (Manchester & New York, Manchester University Press, 1995), for instance, are helpful, accessible texts. There are also guides to the thought of individual theorists such as *Baudrillard for Beginners* (1996). The latter is one of a series published by Icon Books of Cambridge which are illustrated in a comic-book style.

Huge increases in student numbers in recent years without matching increases in staff and resources mean that mass lectures and large seminar-groups are now the norm. Students experiencing difficulty with theory may not receive the individual help they need because academics no longer have the time to give every student a tutorial. This means that students have to become more self-reliant. One solution is for students to form reading groups so that they can share texts and have an additional discussion forum.

Large student numbers also puts pressure on university libraries. They cannot usually afford to buy multiple copies of recommended textbooks, so students may find they cannot obtain the required reading. However, libraries usually maintain photocopy collections of periodical articles which students can copy for private study purposes. Some module tutors also offer 'readers' – anthologies of selected articles – for sale at cost price. For some time copyright problems have hindered the production of such readers. Today, in some innovative universities, custom-made, print-on-demand readers and teaching packs are now being generated in days from electronic databases containing material whose copyright has been cleared.

Film Studies, an increasingly popular subject in universities, presents particular problems of delivery: first, the theory associated with film is quite daunting; second, the need to screen whole films (often in the inadequate form of video-projections) can eat into teaching time with the result that discussion of theoretical texts is curtailed. Time-based media such as film and television take time to consume and if the university is without a properly equipped cinema or videotheque – as many are – in which programmes of screening can be arranged separately from lectures and seminars, the difficulties cited above will persist. However, many university libraries have collections of films on videotape that can be viewed by students in their own time. Video-recorders with variable speed controls enable students to undertake frame-by-frame analyses of movie-segments.

Language and visual culture

The main medium used to discuss visual culture is language, both verbal and written. There is, of course, an intrinsic limitation in commenting on visual/tactile material via a non-iconic medium of expression. The problem has been subject to theoretical reflection by various art historians and by the film theorist Raymond Bellour.[4] He pointed out that film critics cannot quote from their object of study in the same way that literary critics can. (Dialogue can be quoted but with a loss of sound, tone, etc.) The title of Bellour's article – 'The Unattainable Text' – is rather despairing. However, if we accept that translation between different languages is possible (even though translation is never a hundred per cent), that one can describe in words a visual object with some degree of veracity, then the use of the commonest means of human communication is surely reasonable.

During classical antiquity there was a literary vogue, called *ekphrasis*, for detailed descriptions of works of art. Students should practise writing descriptions of artefacts (paying heed to both form and content) for an imagined reader who has not seen the work in question. Accuracy should be striven for because it is crucial to criticism and interpretation.

No verbal or written description can totally replace the visual experience of seeing a dress, a movie, etc., but this is not usually the aim of such utterances in any case. Scholars consider such issues as influence, artistic intention, patronage, iconography, gender, genre, style and reception. They also provide socio-historical, contextual information. They do analyse and evaluate individual examples, but they also compare and contrast them; indeed, they consider whole categories, types and series of products from different cultures and across different historical periods. In short, their commentaries encompass far more than descriptions of the appearance of single artefacts.

Those who point to the inadequacies of language in regard to visual experience should remember that most visual culture lecturers use illustrations to supplement their words: they project slides and screen clips from films and television arts programmes, and use reproductions in their publications. It should be noted however that illustrations are themselves 'translations' and their accuracy of reproduction is always in question. Anyone who has compared a postcard of a painting to the original will know that the former rarely does justice to the latter. And regular users of slide libraries will know that two slides of the same painting can vary enormously in terms of their colour values. Furthermore, slides and reproductions in books vary in size from the originals and they may have been cropped too. Photographs of sculptures and buildings provide only partial information about the originals. Additional problems face those studying film: still pictures may be publicity shots rather than photos taken from the film itself; obtaining a complete, undamaged print of a film to screen is often impossible. These and other difficulties posed to Film Studies by misrepresentation in image reproduction have been reviewed by Mike Catto.[5]

In the light of the above, students are advised to gain as much direct visual experience of originals as possible, by visiting exhibitions, museums and buildings at home and abroad, by watching films in cinemas with large screens and good sound systems, etc.

Criticism

Criticism can be defined as a genre of writing that describes and evaluates particular examples of visual culture for the benefit of non-specialist readers. Criticism or reviewing – particularly that found in newspapers and magazines – can be distinguished from theory even though the first is often informed by the second. (Criticism is also, normally, a constituent of art-historical writing.) Clement Greenberg, a notable American art critic, can be cited as an example of a writer who produced both criticism and theory: he reviewed current exhibitions but he also wrote more general, theoretical articles on such topics as 'Avant-Garde and Kitsch' and 'Modernist Painting'. Some university modules focus on the work of leading critics while others encourage the practice of art and film criticism with vocational ends in mind.

In reading theory and criticism students will, of course, encounter many different writing styles, some journalistic, some academic, some clear, some obscure. (Roland Barthes distinguished between 'readerly' and 'writerly' styles.) Students should make a point of reading good-quality daily and Sunday newspapers and visual culture magazines in order to discover who are the leading reviewers and critics, and to study their writing styles. According to Oscar Wilde, criticism is a minor branch of literature and therefore it should manifest literary qualities. Unfortunately, many student essays disregard this advice. Writing is a creative activity and students should strive to produce essays exhibiting energy and verve.

Intrinsic difficulties

What may disappoint students is that objects of study – films, works of art, etc. – are at times displaced/eclipsed altogether by theory and contextual information. Some lectures are delivered in which references to examples of visual culture occur little or not at all. Modules which are ostensibly about visual culture turn out to be about theories and criticism of visual culture: that is, in a module outline, names of artists and artworks have been replaced by names of theorists and titles of texts. If truth be told, some academics are more excited by the ideas of the French cultural theorist Jean Baudrillard than by the sculptures of Constantin Brancusi.

In recent years certain theorists have become media stars as famous as leading artists and film directors – Baudrillard for instance. He was easily the theorist who had most impact on the contemporary visual arts during the 1980s. So much so that an American artists' collective called Group Material eventually mounted an exhibit in New York in 1987 with the title *Resistance (Anti-Baudrillard)*.[6]

Of course, if a module has been designed specifically to examine the work of leading art critics and theorists then there can be no grounds for complaint, but in those cases where theory and criticism have displaced artists and artworks then it seems students would be justified in feeling aggrieved. As a general rule, students have a right to expect that lectures should be illustrated, that abstractions and generalisations should be explained by reference to specific instances. Even so, it should be borne in mind that many examples of visual culture are themselves complex and difficult – especially works by avant-garde artists. (Witness Duchamp's large glass *The Bride Stripped Bare by her Bachelors, Even* (1913–23).) The fact that one can *see* them is no guarantee that one can comprehend them.

Lecturers vary, of course, in their ability to expound and popularise the theories of major thinkers. Students at one British university once complained about a lecturer teaching a module on post-modernism on the grounds that his lectures were 'very hard to follow', and that when he was asked to clarify he refused on the grounds that the ideas were intrinsically difficult and could not be simplified any further. To the students this appeared to be a failure on the part of the lecturer but it should be acknowledged that such intrinsic difficulties do exist. A module about realism in art, for example, will ask: 'What is meant by the concept realism? Why have so many different kinds of art claimed to be realist?' Eventually, such enquiries encounter fundamental philosophical problems – such as the nature of reality and its representation – that have troubled Western thinkers for thousands of years. Consequently, students cannot expect prepackaged answers, neat and easy solutions to every theoretical question. A proportion of students unreasonably expect all theory to be simplified to the extent that anyone can understand it. Janet Wolff has argued against the 'false populism which maintains that nobody should say anything unless everyone can understand it'.[7]

Academics too find much recent theory hard to follow and accept; consequently there are times when even they abandon the struggle to understand a text. Sometimes the failure is due to the academic's intellectual limitations but sometimes it is due to the theorist's own muddled thinking and impenetrable prose. Baudrillard has been dubbed 'an intellectual terrorist', so it is not surprising that he has succeeded in intimidating many of his readers.

Students should realise that certain philosophers and theorists make their writings difficult because they want a reputation for profundity. They want readers to struggle with their texts time and time again – if the readers do, in the end, understand what is being argued they will have a greater sense of achievement, a sense of belonging to a select few. Some theorists even generate wild, preposterous ideas precisely in order to cause mental agitation and to prompt speculation. Like avant-garde artists, radical theorists like to shock and astonish. Such behaviour stimulates debate, press profiles and interviews, television appearances, lecture tours and book commissions/sales.

Students are advised to read a set text several times – with intervals between – before they condemn it as 'impossible to understand'. They should also attempt to check the ideas and propositions it contains against specific examples and their own lived experience. When exhausted by texts, students should try sitting quietly and thinking for themselves. They may be agreeably surprised by what this can achieve.

Context and history

Undergraduates often expect Visual Culture Studies to continue the unthinking appreciation of works of art and media they have been used to. Many find that a surfeit of theory interferes with and even ruins the pleasure they take in visual culture. (A minority discover that theory has its own fascination.) They find it unsettling when they discover that aesthetic pleasure is itself scrutinised and problematised and, in the case of some radical feminist theorists, it is actively challenged. Laura Mulvey, for example, wrote a now famous essay – 'Visual Pleasure and Narrative Cinema' (1975) – whose declared aim was to destroy pleasure and beauty by analysing them. Further discussion of this issue will be undertaken in Chapter 10.

Academics are concerned with far more than aesthetic appreciation: they are interested in the history and socio-political functions of visual culture. This means that extensive *contextualisation* is necessary. However, there is again a danger that artefacts will receive short shrift while their social and historical contexts are sketched in. In fact, the relationship between visual culture and society/history – a 'foreground/background' problem – is a complex one which itself poses theoretical problems of historical method. T. J. Clark is one noted art historian whose writings include intelligent reflections on this issue.[8] Arguably, visual representations are not just reflections or refractions of a historical reality, they are historical documents/evidence in their own right. Furthermore, some images – for example documentary photographs – have caused such a public outcry that social change has ensued.

If academics could assume a reasonable level of historical knowledge on the part of students then contextualisation would not be so time-consuming, but unfortunately they cannot. (One fine art student interested in the work of Georg Grosz told her tutor she was having difficulty distinguishing between the First and Second World Wars!) Of course, students vary immensely in the knowledge they bring to university. Mature students in particular are often well informed about certain subjects – this makes it difficult for academics to know at what level to pitch their lectures. What is generally lacking, amongst other things, is a basic understanding of how the present economic system works and the objections to it that have been made its critics. Many academics believe that such an understanding should have been imparted at the secondary level of education. Its absence one can only attribute to a systematic refusal by the state to educate students about the nature of the society of which they are citizens.

Clearly, there is not time to teach and learn about economics and politics in addition to visual culture, but there are ways of illustrating connections. For instance, the relation between images/designs and private property (so crucial to the capitalist system) can be made clear by considering the issue of the copyright and the work of 'appropriation' artists such as Jeff Koons who have ended up in court because they ignored copyright laws. (For more on visual culture and commerce, see Chapter 12.)

All students will find it essential to do some reading about history in order to discover what was happening at the time the artefact they are interested in was produced. To establish exactly what happened when, students will find it helps to construct a chronology of key dates and events. In some instances, the work in question will be about a historical event – Edouard Manet's painting *The Execution of the Emperor Maximilian (III)* (1868–9) for example – in which case the work itself will supply some historical information (its accuracy is another matter). To overcome her ignorance, the fine art student cited above would clearly have to do much more background reading than normal. Students starting from scratch, should feel no qualms about consulting basic reference tools such as the *Encyclopedia Britannica*. Once basic facts and dates have been learnt, they can move on to more detailed and sophisticated histories.

There is a danger that the sheer volume of theory that is ahistorical in character will cause the historical dimension of visual culture to be neglected. (The titles 'Visual Culture Studies' and 'Film Studies', for instance, rather ominously omit the word 'history'.) But there are also theoretical and methodological problems associated with history-writing itself. Many leading historians have published at least one text reflecting on such problems.

The necessity for theory

What is the justification for theory? Is it really necessary? In the first place, theory is crucial and inescapable because without theories and hypotheses we would be overwhelmed by a mass of impressions, by immense quantities of empirical data.[9] Scientific theories underpin all modern machines, instruments, weapons and technologies; political and economic theories underpin the ways nations are governed and organised. Everyone's ideas are based on theories – however crude or mistaken – about the world. In higher education the aim is to make such theoretical assumptions explicit, to consider the more sophisticated theories developed by major thinkers and then to compare and evaluate them.

In the second place, the verbal and written discourse about visual culture contains many concepts and specialist/technical terms which pose problems of definition, have several meanings and have histories of use (a clear demonstration of this is supplied by Raymond Williams's essential paperback *Keywords* (New York, Oxford University Press, rev. edn 1983)).

Every science and academic discipline has a vocabulary special to it which beginners simply have to learn. And theorists constantly coin new terms. Definitions are given in specialist dictionaries and encyclopedias – every discipline has them – which are normally stocked in the reference sections of university libraries. See, for example, John A. Walker's *Glossary of Art, Architecture and Design Since 1945* (London, Library Association/ Boston, MA, G. K. Hall, 3rd edn 1992), Robert Stam and others' *New Vocabularies in Film Semiotics* (London and New York, Routledge, 1992), and Susan Hayward's *Key Concepts in Cinema Studies*, (London and New York, Routledge, 1996), but students need also to note the particular senses in which the terms are used by leading theorists in their own writings.

In the third place, understanding how visual signs generate meanings requires knowledge of theories of communication, iconography and semiotics. If one wishes to understand the mental processes involved in the experience of visual culture, then theories derived from external disciplines such as psychology and psychoanalysis may prove useful. In the case of a module entitled *Psychoanalysis and the Cinema* the challenge facing students is to acquire sufficient grounding in psychoanalytic theory to be able to apply it to films (it has also been used to explain the whole cinematic apparatus). Students who failed to acquire this knowledge in time would probably receive lower than usual essay marks. Students may expect all the modules they take to be comparable in terms of difficulty, but certain modules and certain lecturers, it should be acknowledged, are more demanding than others.

A key difference between the kind of learning undertaken at secondary school level and university level is that the latter is much more self-conscious and critical in relation to its own conceptual assumptions, methods and practices. Most first and second year students write essays without considering the methodological and historiographic problems involved in history-writing. But some awareness of such issues is usually expected when third year dissertations come to be written.

Much of the difficulty of theory at university stems from the fact that students are expected to learn theories and at the same time, or later on, question and criticise them. One cannot place all the concepts one is using into question at once – they should be considered one at a time and taken in rotation. Since theory has to be tackled in manageable chunks, students should plan a programme of reading and stick to it.

French theory

Just as there are dress fashions, there are intellectual fashions. Paris since 1945 has been a prime source of both. The roll-call of French theorists includes Louis Althusser, Roland Barthes, Georges Bataille, Jean Baudrillard, Pierre Bourdieu, Fernand Braudel, Guy Debord, Gilles Deleuze, Jacques Derrida, Michel Foucault, Félix Guattari, Luce Irigaray, Jacques Lacan, Jean-François Lyotard, Claude Lévi-Strauss, Christian Metz and Jean-Paul Sartre. The productivity and creativity of French intellectuals cannot be denied, nor can their influence upon British and American academics, and a number of artists and photographers, be over-estimated.

While there is no substitute for reading the writings of the theorists themselves, there are a number of 'orientation' books worth consulting that provide biographical and intellectual summaries; for example: *The Fontana Dictionary of Modern Thought*, (London, Fontana, rev. edn 1988) edited by Alan Bullock and Oliver Stallybrass, and John Lechte's *Fifty Key Contemporary Thinkers* (London and New York, Routledge, 1994).

The arrival of new theories from France every few years has posed problems of assimilation. Investing time and effort learning a new theory may seem to be a waste of time if it is shortly to become outmoded. (But just because a theory is new does not mean that it is automatically better than an old one.) Students will find that not all academics are enthusiastic about new theories. Some resist them because they dislike being pressurised by media hype and are suspicious of herd-like behaviour. They do not wish to become mere relays for French theories especially since the latter's complexities and contradictions often produce mental confusion rather than illumination. British academics who disagree with what the French theorists say are clearly going to be reluctant to present such ideas to their students.[10] Yet such is the prestige of these theorists that they are often compelled to do so. Traffic is virtually one-way: French theorists pay almost no heed to British and American ones. The strength of many British scholars lies in empirical and historical research rather than grand theory. Unfortunately, the latter seems to be more glamorous than the former.

Other academics ignore theory because they are content with traditional concepts and empirical, ad hoc approaches to the study of visual culture. After a time, students may conclude that the latter yields shallow results.

It is not only academics who are conscious of intellectual trends. Some students are also fashion-conscious: they demand an account of the latest theory and refuse to learn something as fundamental as the Marxist critique of capitalism on the mistaken grounds that it is 'old-fashioned, out of date'.

The various theories students will encounter have different vocabularies, origins and objects of study. Sometimes a concept such as 'fetishism' will recur but often the theories will be incommensurable with one another. To compare and evaluate a range of theories is a demanding philosophical task. It may be too much to ask of undergraduates.

The utility of theory

To sum up: the choice is not between theory and no theory but which theory? Discrimination is needed because not any old theory will do. Some are better or more plausible than others. The multi-disciplinarity typical of Visual Culture Studies means that many scholars adopt an eclectic and pragmatic attitude towards theories – they borrow concepts and methods from a spectrum of disciplines. What matters to them is a theory's utility: will it enhance our understanding of examples of visual culture?[11] Terry Eagleton, the Left-wing Professor of English, calls the view that 'theory is all right as long as it can directly illuminate texts . . . that theory is some humble handmaiden to the still all-centred and all-privileged literary work' the 'standard liberal humanist line'.[12] But is theory, we wonder, an end in itself or does it have a wider objective? Raymond Tallis, a sceptical British commentator, discerns a political aim behind theory: 'a dream of unmasking literature and society at large and in this way contributing to the revolution that will lead to a better future'. Dryly he adds: 'Exactly how this is going to come about is a little unclear'.[13] Eagleton himself admits there are times when 'theory overshoots practice', and that this 'signals a problem in practical social reality'. In such situations, theory may be driven back upon itself and become 'autonomous, self-generating'.

Theory and politics

The terrain of theory is in fact a battlefield on which contending factions fight to win the minds of readers. (Naive students expect all the staff employed by the same school to agree with one another. They find it hard to understand that bitter ideological/political struggles between conservatives and radicals may have been raging for decades.) Therefore, students will encounter many texts that are primarily critiques of other thinkers. For instance, the feminist movement of recent decades has been accompanied by a tremendous volume of writing much of which has set out to *destablise* theories produced by men. As Michèle Barrett and Anne Phillips explain:

> Feminists have long criticised the pretensions of 'grand', 'high' and 'general' theory and have demonstrated the difficulties that attend any such enterprise. Universal claims have all too frequently turned out to be very particular, supposed commonalities false, abstractions deceptive. Feminists have become deeply suspicious of theoretical discourses that claim neutrality while speaking from a masculinist perspective, and have at times despaired of the possibility of 'gender-neutral thought' . . . many feminists have opted for an analysis of the local, specific and particular. Much of this work is 'deconstructive' in character, seeking to destablise – challenge, subvert, reverse, overturn – some of the hierarchical binary oppositions . . . of Western culture.[14]

The issue of gender is now foregrounded by many modules taught in European and American universities. While most such modules in British institutions are concerned with the female gender, there are some that focus on the male gender.

For people who are politically conscious and committed, theory – in the famous words of Marx – is not only a means of *interpreting* the world, it is also a means of *changing* it.[15] To achieve the latter, theory has to inform practice, has to contribute to cultural, ideological and political struggles. Most socialist cultural producers, therefore, are familiar with the Marxist critique of capitalism (which has been extended in the twentieth century by such thinkers as Althusser, Antonio Gramsci, Ernesto Laclau and Ernest Mandel), aware of the need for further theoretical work (to keep abreast of an ever-changing social reality) and the necessity to test theory in practice. For some this means joining Left-wing political parties and using their creative imaginations and skills to further the goals of those organisations. (John Heartfield, the photomonteur and graphic designer who was a member of the German Communist Party, is a well-known historical example.) However, knowledge of capitalist economics and the business side of the culture industries can also benefit budding entrepreneurs.

Theory and practice

Given the fact that academics differ in their theoretical allegiances and political convictions, the questions 'Which theory? Theory for what ends?' haunt any consideration of the application of theory to practice. In art and design colleges and faculties the most immediate sites for the application of theory to practice are the arts, design and media studios. As explained earlier, the existence of separate schools of Art History/Visual Culture means that, although academics attached to those schools 'service' the practical areas by providing inputs of theory and history, a certain distance has been established and formalised. Theory and practice are thus not as fully integrated as they could be. Of course, it is always possible for studio tutors to provide theory and for studio-based students to learn about it via independent study.

Summary

This chapter has been about theory in a meta-discursive sense, that is, theory that has been developed by critics and philosophers (who are usually non-practitioners) as a means of explaining visual culture.[16] But students should be aware that not all the theory they will encounter is of a second-order character. Artistic practice is informed by theory and many modern artists, film-makers, etc., have themselves reflected on their practice and published theoretical statements and manifestos.[17] Examples include: Piet Mondrian's theory of neo-plasticism; Sergei Eisenstein's writings on montage; Bertolt Brecht's statements about the political function of the theatre; Robert Venturi's writings about popular architecture; Victor Burgin's lectures and writings on photography.

Furthermore, in many instances, theory and practice have developed in tandem: for example, John Latham's cosmological, time-based theory was embodied in both visual artefacts and writings.[18] In the case of the Conceptual art group Art & Language, writing essays and publishing a journal were central to their artistic practice during the late 1960s and early 1970s. The so-called 'scripto-visual' work of many radical feminist artists has been described as 'theory-informed', that is, these artists use, say, psychoanalytic theory as one of the sources for their artworks. For instance, Mary Kelly's *Post-Partum Document* (1973–79) traced the early development of her son through the prism of Jacques Lacan's post-Freudian theories of language and the subject.

It follows from the above that students will be expected to read theories generated by practitioners as well as by non-practitioners. In sum: there are not only theories *of* art, but also theories *for* art; theory-informed art, and even theories *as* art.

Notes and further reading

1 Valentine Cunningham, 'Perspective: The Theorists', *Times Higher Education Supplement*, (25 February 1994), 17–18.
2 John Cussans, 'Incessant Text to Corporal Disintegration', *Reading Things*, ed. N. Cummings (London, Chance Books, 1993), p. 132.
3 Terry Eagleton, *Literary Theory: An Introduction*, (Oxford, Blackwell, 1983), p. viii.
4 R. Bellour, 'The Unattainable Text', *Screen*, 16:3 (1975), 19–27.

5 Sir Joshua Reynolds (1723–92), *Theory* (c. 1779). Oil on canvas, 172.7 × 172.7 cm. London, Royal Academy of Arts.

This painting was originally part of the ceiling decoration of the library of Somerset House. The latter was the home of the Royal Academy during the late eighteenth century. The painting was detached in 1837 and eventually moved to Burlington House in 1869. Reynolds's self-imposed task was to find a visual representation of a highly abstract concept. In accordance with the European classical tradition, he personified the 'Theory' (of the Arts or of Painting) somewhat absurdly in terms of a plump, draped woman resting on clouds contemplating the heavens. She holds a scroll which states: 'THEORY is the knowledge of what is truly NATURE'. (Today this seems more like a definition of the sciences rather than the arts.)

Reynolds admired classical sculpture and the painting of High Renaissance Italy and thought artists should be learned individuals. Establishing an academy was a means of raising the social status of English artists and a way of communicating neo-classical aesthetic principles to succeeding generations. Reynolds, the first President of the Royal Academy, himself wrote theoretical texts, namely his fifteen *Discourses*, first delivered as lectures to students between 1769 and 1790. In them he advocated the academic doctrine of the Grand Manner and the rational ideal: consequently his view that the aim of art was the imitation of nature was a universalising, ideal-type tendency opposed to the particularity and detailed naturalism characteristic of Dutch painting. Nature, in other words, was considered to be imperfect; consequently, it had to be corrected by generalising and by reference to the rules of art established by the great masters. 'Theory' could not, therefore, be depicted wearing the purely temporary dress fashions of the eighteenth century. Her 'up in the air' location and upward gaze signifies Reynolds's constant striving for elevation and the perfect beauty that existed as an ideal in the mind of the artist rather than in the world outside.

5   M. Catto, 'Simulacra Et Anobile – Misrepresentation in Image Reproduction', *Screen Education*, 23 (Summer 1977), 39–49.

6   See John Miller, 'Baudrillard and His Discontents', *Artscribe International*, 63 (May 1987), 48–51.

7   J. Wolff, 'The Artist, the Critic and the Academic: Feminism's Problematic Relationship with "Theory"', *New Feminist Art Criticism: Critical Strategies*, ed. K. Deepwell, (Manchester & New York, Manchester University Press, 1995), p. 22.

8   T. J. Clark, 'On the Social History of Art', *Image of the People: Gustave Courbet and the 1848 Revolution*, (London, Thames & Hudson, 1973), pp. 9–20. See also: Norman Bryson, 'Art in Context', *The Point of Theory: Practices of Cultural Analysis*, eds M. Bal and I. E. Boer (Amsterdam, Amsterdam University Press, 1994), pp. 66–78; John A. Walker, 'Context as a Determinant of Photographic Meaning', *Camerawork*, 19 (August 1980), 5–6.

9   Janet Wolff, writing from a feminist perspective, remarks: 'I want to argue. . . for the importance of theory . . . of theory in the most general sense, as *knowledge* – as giving an account of the social world and specifically its structuring around gender. The importance, too, of theory as *critique* – that is, as a more systematic analysis of how gender divisions have been constructed and maintained historically and in the present. And the importance of theory . . . when "Theory" has a capital T . . . signifying post-structural theories which investigate the cultural construction of gendered identity in language, representation . . . and psychic processes.' *New Feminist Art Criticism*, p. 17.

10 One of the few British intellectuals who resisted the importation of French theory was the Marxist historian Edward P. Thompson. In 1978 he wrote a critique of the work of Louis Althusser in which he accused the French philosopher of 'ahistorical theoreticism'. See his essay: 'The Poverty of Theory: or An Orrery of Errors', *The Poverty of Theory and Other Essays*, (London, Merlin Press, 1978), pp. 193–406.

11 For a thoughtful assessment of the use-value of various theories of art, popular culture, mass media and society when applied to the many different kinds of visual images and artefacts produced by the nationalist and loyalist communities of Northern Ireland see: Belinda Loftus, 'In Search of a Useful Theory', *Circa*, 40 (June–July 1988), 17–23.

12 T. Eagleton, *The Significance of Theory*, (Oxford, Blackwell, 1990), p. 77.

13 Raymond Tallis, *In Defence of Realism*, (London, Edward Arnold, 1988), p. 166.

14 M. Barrett and A. Phillips (eds), *Destabilising Theory: Contemporary Feminist Debates*, (Cambridge, Polity Press, 1992), p. 1.

15 Praxis – the unity of theory and practice – is the goal of Marxists. Gen Doy, a British Marxist art historian who is also a political activist, poses this question to her fellow Left-wing lecturers: 'Is it really possible to be a Marxist art or cultural historian while engaging in purely theoretical practice as an academic?' *Seeing and Consciousness: Women, Class and Representation*, (Oxford & Washington, DC, Berg Publishers, 1995), p. 196.

16 There are some leading French philosophers who have produced examples of visual culture as well as theory. Barthes, for instance, dabbled in painting and Derrida organised an exhibition at the Louvre in Paris.

17 See: Herschel B. Chipp (ed.), *Theories of Modern Art: A Source Book by Artists and Critics*, (Berkeley, CA, University of California Press, 1968) and Charles Harrison and Paul Wood (eds), *Art in Theory 1900–1990: An Anthology of Changing Ideas*, (Oxford & Cambridge, MA, Blackwell, 1992).

18 For a detailed account of the British artist's *oeuvre* see John A. Walker's monograph *John Latham – The Incidental Person – his Art and Ideas*, (London, Middlesex University Press, 1995).

5 Production, distribution and consumption model

Art is a mode of production. We sell our labour. It would be very strange to think that artists had perversely different intentions, ambitions and desires from any others in society. (Dinos and Jake Chapman)[1]

THIS CHAPTER is intended as a fleshing out of the content of figure 6, which is itself a schematic representation of one cycle of production, distribution and consumption of cultural goods. Much of it will already be familiar to students but the advantage of such a model is that it is systematic: it attempts to be exhaustive, to plot the relations between the various parts and to show feedback loops. Existing publications, which deal with only one aspect of the cycle, could be mapped by students on to the diagram. It would then become clear where well-trodden and neglected areas of study are located.

Time, for the purposes of this chapter, is assumed to be unidirectional. This means that there is an irreversible temporal sequence associated with visual culture's existence, which can be divided into three phases: production, distribution and consumption. Although phases one and three are distinct, they are also interdependent because, as Marx pointed out, their relationship is reciprocal:

Without production, no consumption; but also, without consumption, no production; since production would then be purposeless . . . Production mediates consumption; it creates the latter's material; without it, consumption would lack an object. But consumption also mediates production, in that it alone creates for products the subjects for whom they are products. The product only obtains its 'last finish' in consumption.[2]

Production

As explained earlier, the present field of visual culture is part of a broader field of cultural production which in turn is part of a field of general manufacture associated with a particular, historical mode of production, that is, the capitalist mode of production. In a diagram the boundary of the field of visual culture should be indicated by a dotted line to show that it is permeable – subject to influences from the economy and politics of society as a whole. Like language, visual culture is assumed to be essentially social,

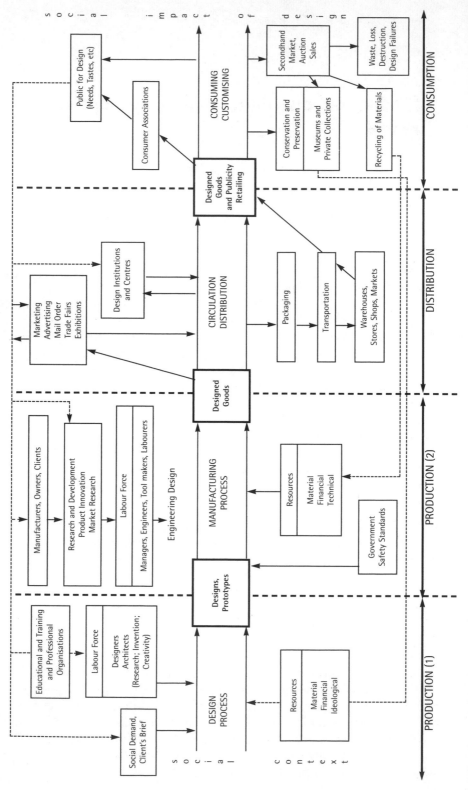

6 Production, distribution & consumption model for the field of design

even when made by solitary producers.³ All humans are assumed to be social as well as biological beings, even those whose behaviour is judged by their fellows to be anti-social. (There are categories of design and visual culture that some would regard as anti-social/human; for example, the design of instruments of torture and weapons of war; badly made goods that are dangerous to users; fascist art; extreme pornography.)

Needs, desires

Since the production of visual culture occurs *within* society, expressions such as 'art *and* society', 'design *and* society', are unhelpful. Visual culture would not exist at all unless it served certain human needs and desires, consequently they are the logical starting point for any analysis. An obvious example of social demand is the need of homeless people for housing. Such a need may prompt a local government authority to commission a new housing estate from an architect's office. Huge projects such as the building of pyramids and cathedrals, and the exploration of space, presuppose a need, a willingness on the part of whole societies – or at least their ruling and managerial classes – to commit enormous public resources to ensure their achievement. Sexual curiosity/lust is a clear-cut example of voyeuristic desire that is catered for by erotic material of various kinds.

People, their needs and desires, are thus crucial to production, but they mainly figure in the consumption phase as the recipients and users of visual culture. Two qualifications: first, it may be argued that someone who keeps a diary and never shows it to anyone is satisfying a personal desire rather than a social need. However, keeping diaries is a common habit; furthermore, diaries can be read by others and published after the author's death. Second, it may be argued that some needs are artificially created by big business in pursuit of profits. Big business certainly does create artificial needs but unless the products designed to satisfy those needs cater for, or build upon, genuine human needs then they will not survive for long. (Once a society develops beyond subsistence level, it becomes hard to distinguish 'artificial' from 'real' or 'basic' needs. Do we 'need' television?) Both small and large-scale producers generate new products 'on spec' in the hope that they will find buyers but the harsh reality is that majority of new products (which are often variations of old products) placed on the market fail either because of their poor quality, inadequate design, expense, lack of appeal to customers, or simply because the marketplace is already saturated with similar goods.

Both producers and consumers have desires of various kinds but if one examines the relations between modern artists and patrons/collectors/the public, then it is clear that often they do not match.⁴ Independent artists seek to fulfil their own artistic ideas and visions, despite pressures to conform to the tastes and demands of potential patrons. What interests many commentators are the struggles of producers to fulfil their personal agendas, to retain their artistic integrity in the face of commercial pressures, and to reconcile their needs with those of their employers or audiences, in circumstances not of their own choosing.

Nevertheless, in the majority of cases, cultural producers are perfectly willing to compromise in order to please their clients or audiences. (Often, no compromise is needed because artists and patrons share the same beliefs, values and goals.) Architects and designers who disregarded the views of their clients and the needs of users would quickly lose public respect and soon be out of business. Problems can arise from the fact that architects and designers often have to please two constituencies – clients and users. For example, a firm of architects may satisfy a local government client by providing system-built tower blocks at a low cost, but the actual inhabitants of such blocks may well be unhappy with this type of accommodation. Some architects and planners defend and represent the interests of the community or users in any struggle or dispute with clients, or work on their behalf – hence the expressions 'advocacy planning', 'community architecture' and 'planning for real'.

Cultural producers

The production of visual culture depends upon human labour both phys-ical and mental – which includes imaginative thinking, construction, invention and play as well as routine tasks – consequently a workforce is required. That workforce is normally sub divided according to the various professional groups – architects, graphic designers, television producers, etc. – associated with each subcategory of culture. Each group is regarded as being engaged in a *signifying practice* whose goal is the production of meaning as well as material artefacts.

Specialist knowledge and skills are normally essential to cultural production, consequently any model must include educational institutions such as art and film schools, plus professional associations and trade unions. (Institutions will be considered in more detail in Chapter 6.) Of course, there are a few artists who become successful – Francis Bacon is an example – who never went to art school.

In the case of the contemporary fine arts, individual production is generally the norm but as soon as one considers major building projects such as skyscrapers or industrialised forms of entertainment like pop music, then large teams, with specialisation and a high division of labour, are involved. Numerous volumes have been devoted to the achievements and lives of individual artists, film directors/stars, etc. Materialists (i.e. those who, in philosophical terms, are the opposite of idealists) regard notions such as 'natural talent', 'creativity', 'genius' and 'expression', typical of traditional accounts of such individuals, as problematic because they mystify rather than clarify. It is certainly the case that individuals are social agents, that they do make unique contributions to culture, but what may be called 'the ideology of absolute artistic individualism', which is so pervasive in Western societies, tends to obscure the social and collective aspects of cultural production.[5]

Authorship

In recent decades much theoretical effort has been expended trying to clarify the relationship between producers and their works, producers and intended meanings, the role of the producers' subjectivities, personalities and private lives (some artworks are more autobiographical than others), and the situation of producers within the economic relations of production. The writing in question is called 'auteur' or 'authorship' theory and was developed within French film criticism during the 1950s.[6] (Today, Film Studies sets taught in certain universities include entire modules devoted to the theme 'authorship and the cinema'.) The French theorists argued that certain directors could be regarded as authors or artists because they stamped their personalities and styles on a series of films despite the fact that actors, cinematographers, etc. were also involved. Later, in 1968, Roland Barthes reversed direction by announcing 'the death of the author' while simultaneously hailing 'the birth of the reader'. In other words, theoretical emphasis had shifted from production to reception.

Resources

Before any cultural production can take place, resources of various kinds – capital, materials (both physical and ideological/aesthetic), tools and technologies – have to be available. As already explained, Marxists have theorised society in terms of a base/superstructure model and placed culture in the upper structure erected upon an economic foundation. The latter is deemed to be 'determinant in the last instance' but, arguably, it is a factor that is omnipresent. While culture depends upon the creation of surplus value and is subject to the behaviour of the economy in general, it too has an economy. It requires capital investment and, via the sales of cultural commodities, it generates income and profits. (The commerce/culture relation will be explored further in Chapter 12.)

Financial investment in culture can vary in size from the small monthly payments the art dealer Theo van Gogh made to his painter-brother Vincent in the 1880s to the $200 million spent by Universal Studios on the Hollywood epic *Waterworld* in the 1990s. (Artists who hope to be completely independent of patrons, investors and buyers require independent incomes.) The Marxist critique of capitalism, which argues that workers (wage-slaves) are exploited because they do not receive the full financial rewards of their labour, applies to the field of culture despite the fact that top earners – Picasso, Madonna, Kevin Kostner, etc. – do become extremely rich. Also, many cultural producers are self-employed people who own and run small businesses; consequently their economic position is different from that of employees working for bosses with the power to hire and fire.

Materials and tools

The materials that cultural producers use are too many and multifarious to be listed here. If the installations so popular with contemporary artists are taken as a guide, then there is no material known to humankind that cannot be deployed. A quantity of sump oil was used by Richard Wilson, a British artist, for a 1978 installation entitled *20:50* (the work is now in the Saatchi collection). In 1961 the Italian artist Piero Manzoni had ninety cans made each of which contained thirty grams of his own excrement. As far as performers and so-called 'body' artists are concerned, their own bodies are their raw material. (Examples include the Americans Vito Acconci, Ron Athey and Chris Burden, the Britons Stuart Brisley and Bruce McLean and the French Orlan.) The use of a non-traditional material by an avant-garde artist is frequently the reason why contemporary art is vilified by the tabloid press and the general public.

New materials are constantly being invented thereby supplying new opportunities for artists and designers.[7] For example, a building material with the absurd name 'Buckminsterfullerene' has become available to architects; new fabrics made from plastics enable fashion designers to experiment. After materials have been selected, they are either presented in a raw state or transformed in different ways by the action of human labour. Artists may do the work themselves or they may subcontract some or all of it to others – hence the phenomenon of 'art by telephone'.

To alter the shape a block of wood or stone, sculptors use simple tools such as saws, hammers and chisels. Besides easel and brushes, the Dutch painter Jan Vermeer is thought to have used a camera obscura as an optical aid. Today, many producers employ the most advanced, most recent technologies. (For further discussion of this topic see Chapter 13.) Clearly, the materials and tools used help to determine the character of the end result. It should be borne in mind, however, that artists can work *with* or *against* their materials and tools; for example, painters can choose to emphasise or to play down pigments and brushstrokes.

Ideological and aesthetic resources

'Ideology' is a word/concept that has provoked numerous analyses that are too lengthy and complex to repeat here.[8] While some theorists contend that art transcends ideology, others argue that it is a subset of ideology – a visual manifestation of ideology. The word 'ideology' has been defined as 'false consciousness' (a mental misrepresentation of the way things really are) or simply 'a particular system of ideas'. In this instance, by 'ideological resources' we mean, first, belief systems such as Christianity or socialism which are external to art but which artists may serve; second, belief systems such as functionalism and neo-plasticism which are internal to artistic practice; and third, particular systems of representation such as linear perspective which can be thought of as ideological in certain respects.

Marxists contend that the dominant ideas of any age are those of the dominant classes.[9] Just like ordinary citizens, cultural producers are victims of dominant ideologies, but if Marxists can escape their grip and arrive at the truth then, presumably, so can others. In many instances, artists affirm and reinforce dominant ideologies (we cannot imagine Michelangelo questioning Christianity), in other cases they criticise and subvert them. Arguably, what critical artists do is to perform work upon ideologies and this generates insights of benefit to society as a whole. Often, the most compelling and valuable forms of culture are those that address social, ethical, moral issues and contradictions, make them explicit and work through them. Even successful, commercial Hollywood movies are capable of doing this.

'Aesthetic resources' encompass the enormous bank of object types, images, symbols, techniques and styles that have accumulated over the centuries. Virtually all examples of new culture are indebted – to a greater or lesser extent – to the past. While some theorists have regarded historic styles as organic manifestations of a society and an epoch, the situation of stylistic pluralism that now prevails makes for a much more self-conscious, appropriational attitude to style. Indeed, the high incidence of borrowing typical of post-modern culture has led to accusations of 'cannibalism'.[10] There is often a sharp difference in the way art historians and artists treat past culture. The former generally try to understand a work of art in its original socio-historical context, whereas the latter are more interested in its contemporary relevance, and in what use can be made of it.

Artefacts/products

In the majority of cases the result of the work performed upon materials is a physical artefact or product of some kind. (But it can also be a live, real-time performance or event.) Many scholars regard such artefacts as the primary object of study. Immanent 'textual analysis', as it were, interests them more than, say, the study of artists, patrons or audiences.

In the case of the fine arts, products are either unique or take the form of limited editions. Most artists and craftspersons make their own works by hand in studios and workshops; consequently a second production phase is unnecessary. In the spheres of design and mass media, however, a second phase is essential because designs, artwork, photos, prototypes and master film/video-recordings, etc. are passed to manufacturers and printers for small batch or large-scale production via machines and assembly lines. In addition it is now commonplace for primary cultural products and events to be accompanied by all kinds of secondary merchandise.

Major businesses will have Research and Development units, Marketing, Publicity and Sales departments. In addition to in-house designers they will employ managers, engineers, tool makers, sales staff and labourers, they will draw upon further financial, material and technical resources, and they will be influenced by economic and market trends, plus external factors such as government laws and regulations relating to standards and copyright.

Distribution, circulation and exchange

Once products have been manufactured they are packaged and then transported/dispersed around the globe. Packaging and transportation clearly involve their own design and manufacturing processes. Many books and articles are devoted to the graphics involved in packaging and to the design of transportation infrastructures (roads, railways, airports, bridges, etc.) and carriers (container ships, aircraft, trucks, vans, trains, etc.). Travel is virtually compulsory in modern societies, consequently millions fly in aircraft in order to holiday in distant places and millions also own motor cars. Automobile design, styling and performance are thus topics that fascinate drivers as well as design historians.

Goods circulate through space and over time. (Information now circulates globally at high speed via the Internet.) The concept of circulation is best illustrated by the example of a war photograph that appears in the mass media around the world until its 'currency' or topicality has been exhausted. Later on, that same photo could achieve a second life by being included in a photo-library or an artist's photomontage, by being reproduced in history books or displayed in exhibitions devoted to the photographer's oeuvre. Objects too can circulate: think of a sixteenth-century clock that is passed from parents to children until it eventually becomes an heirloom/antique, is then exported to a foreign country and sold to a dealer who then sells it on to a collector, etc., etc., down the ages. Anthropologists have argued that the movement of goods tends to follow certain pathways but also that diversions can occur; for example, goods are diverted from their usual routes and destinations by theft, and by plunder in times of war.

In many cases the first destinations of new products are trade events – motor shows, film festivals, art, fashion and furniture fairs that are held annually or biannually in certain major cities – that inform corporate buyers, retailers and the press about the products' existence. (Incidentally, fashion catwalk shows are now significant and popular cultural events in their own right.) Then the bulk of products are dispersed to warehouses, shops, street markets, cinemas, art galleries or, in the case of electronic media, they are transmitted via mass communication systems, in order to reach potential buyers or consumers. Simultaneously, they are marketed, advertised or promoted and then displayed and sold.

Much publicity is originated and paid for by the manufacturers of cultural goods but in addition there is a huge media industry feeding off advertising and providing more independent news and evaluations via the critics who generate reviews and appraisals. By these means consumers learn about the advent of exciting new products and are groomed for the acts of purchase and consumption. Press reports that a new film such as *Independence Day* (1996) has broken all box office records in the United States are often sufficient to arouse curiosity and create a desire on the part of Europeans to see the movie on the dubious assumption that 'it must be excellent to have been so successful in the world's largest market'. Some British films are even released first in the United States in the hope that they will prove successful; if this happens the films will arrive in Britain trailing clouds of glory. This did occur in the case of *Four Weddings and a Funeral* (1994).

Artefacts are exchanged in three mains ways: first, bartered for goods or services of equal value; second, presented as gifts; and third, bought and sold for money. The latter is the most common because money is so flexible: all values are translated into a single medium of exchange. (For further discussion of this topic, see Chapter 12.)

Shops, supermarkets and shopping malls are environments that most people in the developed nations experience every week consequently their signage, exteriors, interiors and layouts are carefully designed by architects, designers and shop display experts in order to draw customers in and to encourage them to buy. In the advanced nations of the world shopping has become a major ritual and leisure activity. Huge shopping malls are public spaces owned by the private sector. They are commercial mini-utopias – enclaves that protect visitors from the weather and provide safe, guarded spaces. Increasingly such malls supply entertainment along with shopping opportunities. Shoppers are controlled and manipulated to some extent but they also exercise a measure of power through their purchasing ability (so-called 'consumer sovereignty'). They also exercise discrimination, taste and creativity in the selection process. For example, someone who constructs a personal 'look' by combining several items of clothing bought from different shops may be deemed a 'bricoleur'. See also, below, the discussion of 'customising'.

Sociologists take a professional interest in such social habits as shopping, and in related activities such as gallery/museum/cinema-going, travel and tourism.[11] In the case of the cinema, huge, lavishly appointed, ornate buildings in fantastic styles were constructed during the 1920s and 1930s in order to provide attractive environments for watching films. Cinema-going was thus a visual experience in a double sense. Today, the trend in new cinema building is for multiplexes which offer viewers a wider choice of movies plus a range of additional facilities such as shops, cafés and bars.

Supermarkets and major fast-food high-street chains with strong corporate identities remind us that food too is now designed for particular groups of consumers. The widespread influence exerted by such chains is indicated by the title of a recent American book by George Ritzer: *The McDonaldization of Society* (London, Sage, rev. edn 1995).

Consumption, reception and use

In today's society manufacturing still continues but recent decades have witnessed the growth of new service and consumer industries. The advent of expressions such as 'post-industrial society' and 'consumer society' indicate that a shift of emphasis has occurred from production to consumption. This in turn has led to an expansion in the literature on consumption as compared to the literature on production.[12] In the past the term 'art appreciation' would probably have been used rather than 'consumption'. The latter term is wider in scope in that it encompasses both appreciation and use. Some artists object to the term 'consumption' because it equates the experience of art with such mundane habits as eating and drinking. Certainly, it should be acknowledged that the two experiences are somewhat different. During eating, food is used up, whereas a mural can be 'consumed' over and over again by the same person; it can also be 'consumed' simultaneously by many viewers.

As indicated earlier, the first consumers of new visual culture are the critics employed by the mass media. They are then followed by the rest of society. Contemporary industries now supply an immense variety of products and variants of one product type. These products are often too numerous and technically sophisticated for ordinary buyers to test and evaluate before purchase, hence the emergence of consumer protection organisations like the Consumer's Association (1951–) in Britain. The latter employs experts to test a range of goods and publishes the results in *Which?* magazine.

Products designed and made to perform some practical function may be bought because of their attractive appearance, but a final judgement of their merits is normally deferred until they have been used for some time to see if they work as well as advertised. (The phenomenon of branding is important here: a well-known brand is some guarantee of quality and reliability.) A client's satisfaction with a new, high-tech building made from metal may wane if, after a few years' occupation, it proves to be full of rust and thus in need of repair and costly maintenance.

Reception Aesthetics (also called 'Reader-Response, Impact/Audience /Spectatorship Studies') is a branch of criticism and history-writing concerned with the impression art, design and media make upon viewers, the way texts, images and objects are 'read', interpreted, evaluated, used and 'consumed' differentially by various individuals and social groups.[13] Since people vary according to their gender, race, religion, age, class, nationality, politics, tastes, etc., the same movie will often provoke different reactions. While the persuasive rhetoric of most mainstream films is designed to elicit a common response or 'preferred reading' from viewers no matter what their politics, politically-conscious viewers are capable of so-called 'oppositional', or 'aberrant, decodings'.

Audiences themselves can contribute to the experience of culture. This is especially obvious in theatres and other live events when audiences respond to, interact with, stage performers. In the case of all-night rave parties held in huge tents in the countryside, the dancers' energy and participation is as crucial as the DJs, the light-show artists and the event's organisers. Many contemporary artists are now striving to design electronic, time-based works with alternative pathways that are more interactive than those of the past.

Reception *Theory* is concerned with developing a theoretical model of the mental process of reception and with the ideal readers or observers implied or constructed by texts, while Reception *History* is concerned with actual readers. Scholars have produced a range of studies: examinations of the critical responses to the paintings of Van Gogh in different countries in the decades after his suicide; sociological studies of the popular cult of Van Gogh;[14] the experience of tenants of the design of new houses; female spectatorship in the cinema; empirical studies of visitors' reactions to exhibitions and the impact on children of watching television.

Violence and pornography in the media and society are matters of continuing concern; consequently there is a growing body of literature about the influence of 'violent' and 'pornographic' imagery upon the behaviour of viewers. David Freedberg is the author of a substantial historical account of the power of images to affect human thoughts, emotions and behaviour.[15] The existence of censorship and censorship bodies testifies to the threat posed to social order by many examples of visual culture. Some artists and performers have been arrested, charged with various offences and then fined or even imprisoned because of what they have produced.

The habit of customising, that is, the alterations and additions many people make to newly acquired clothes, cars, scooters and houses (usually by means of Do-It-Yourself) reveals that not all consumers accept without question what manufacturers and builders supply.[16] Phillipe Boudon undertook a survey of the history of a housing settlement at Pessac, France, designed by Le Corbusier in the 1920s. He interviewed residents as to their experiences of the buildings and recorded the alterations they had made to the architect's design.[17] Customising enables the customer to be creative too, even if this means the designer's immaculate conception is ruined. Some specialist companies offer customising services and today many manufacturers offer products that can be tailored in various ways to meet the customer's personal preferences: thus customising has been anticipated and appropriated by certain manufacturers.

Taste

One of the key variables in reception is taste. This is another subject which has generated a range of studies – philosophical, psychological, historical, nationalistic and empirical.[18] Art and design historians are particularly interested in taste because it is crucial to the histories of patronage and collecting, fads and fashions. Because taste is commonly regarded as the quintessence of subjectivity and individuality, many people regard it as beyond rational explanation – 'There's no accounting for taste'. This is not the view of Bourdieu whose sociological opus *La Distinction* (1979; English translation *Distinction*, London & New York, Routledge & Kegan Paul, 1988) – a study of the taste patterns of the whole of French society – is by far the most ambitious and illuminating contribution to the literature on taste to date.[19]

Preservation and conservation

Every product, by the nature of the materials used and its structural strength, is designed to exist for a certain length of time. Of course, its lifespan will vary according to how carefully or intensively it is used. After a period of use – which can include phases of recycling – the majority of goods are destroyed or end up on the scrap heap. (The vast quantity of used goods and packaging is now causing severe environmental problems. These pose new challenges and opportunities for 'green' or 'eco' designers.) In order to survive in a highly competitive market, modern industry requires a rapid turnover of goods consequently short-life or 'throwaway' products and planned obsolescence are the norm. (The fashion industry encourages stylistic change twice a year.) However, a few products are treasured and become 'classics' or antiques. A minority of works of art enter private and public collections where they are protected and conserved and so they may survive for centuries. Ancient artefacts in museums are thus 'consumed' by people for whom they were not made, who live in societies markedly different from those in which the artefacts originated.

Specialists exist whose vocation is to conserve, clean and repair works of art and craft. When famous works such as Michelangelo's Sistine Chapel ceiling frescos are cleaned, many difficult aesthetic decisions have to be taken and bitter controversies often ensue between those who favour cleaning and those who don't (the latter usually claim that the cleaning will ruin the original). The fact is that so-called timeless works of art are not timeless. Even if they remain untreated, they are subject to the change and decay that the passage of time inevitably brings. High levels of air pollution typical of modern cities accelerates the rate of decay of ancient buildings. The notorious *nefos* (smog) of Athens has damaged the Parthenon.

Social effects

We began by considering social needs and desires, therefore it is logical to conclude by considering the social effects of wave upon wave of new visual/material culture. Estimating the impact of visual culture on society as a whole is perhaps more difficult than judging its impact on individuals because they usually have some insight, and can tell us how, say, a film or an advertisement has altered their attitudes or behaviour. But one has only to think of the consequences – planned and unplanned – of such inventions as the motor car, television and computer to people's lifestyles and the environment, to realise how significant visual/material culture can be.

To cite just one example of a memorable cultural event of recent times that had a measurable social impact: Bob Geldof's humanitarian response to images and news of famine in Ethiopia and impatience with professional politicians prompted him to use his influence as a rock celebrity to assemble a roster of top acts for a concert called *Live Aid* that was broadcast around the globe in July 1985. Although *Live Aid* received much adverse criticism, it was enjoyed by millions of viewers and it raised £40,000,000, which saved and improved the lives of many Africans.[20]

Cycles and social change

The production, distribution and consumption model outlined in this chapter describes, of course, one cycle. In reality millions of such cycles take place simultaneously and successively. However, the word 'cycle' is somewhat misleading because it implies exact repetition, which in fact never occurs. Every new cycle is slightly or even dramatically different than the one before. This is because the socio-economic environment is constantly changing. (Extreme disruptions to the smooth running of the system are caused by such events as earthquakes, recessions, revolutions and wars.) Technological innovations, the introduction of new media and culture, also alter the existing environment. The expansion and popularity of television in the 1950s, for instance, had negative consequences for the cinema which in turn prompted changes in film-making techniques.

Furthermore, self-induced change and constant product improvement are crucial and integral to the capitalist system and its commercial culture – think of the new models car manufacturers regularly introduce. But does such 'neophilia' produce fundamental social change? Gianni Vattimo thinks not. He writes: 'In a consumer society continual renewal (of clothes, tools, buildings) is already required physiologically for the system simply to survive. What is "new" is not in the least "revolutionary" or subversive; it is what allows things to stay the same'.[21]

Summary

This chapter presents a particular model which we think aids an understanding of an entire set of processes, plotting the relations between the production, distribution and consumption of visual culture, showing where there are moments of feedback, and attributing a cyclical quality to the whole network of interrelations.

To understand production, it is important to be able to identify cultural producers, to recognise their role as authors, and to understand the wide range of resources that are deployed, not just physical and financial but aesthetic and ideological, in the creation of an artefact or product.

To understand consumption, the impact of the many needs and desires of the consumer has to be considered, and the way in which these desires are in turn stimulated and manipulated by the media and advertising to motivate a purchase. Theories of reception have been developed to try to take account of the behaviour and response of consumers to visual culture, through examining not only received meanings but also patterns and habits of use which reveal other aspects of our relationship to objects. Activities such as preservation and conservation form a special category of re-use and have a transformative effect on patterns of consumption, which are in themselves informed by attitudes of the day towards the past and the present, old and new.

The role of time in the consideration of the production, distribution and consumption of visual culture is therefore of particular interest to students of visual culture.

Notes and further reading

1   Dinos and Jake Chapman, quoted in, 'Brilliant Bad Boys of the Galleries', by Megan Tresidder, *The Guardian*, (7 October 1995), 29.

2   Karl Marx, *Grundrisse: Foundations of the Critique of Political Economy*, (Harmondsworth, Middlesex, Penguin Books, 1973), pp. 90–4.

3   On the social production of art see: Janet Wolff's *The Social Production of Art*, (London & Basingstoke, Macmillan, 1981, 2nd rev. edn 1993). Further discussions of cultural production are to be found in Terry Eagleton's *Criticism and Ideology: A Study in Marxist Literary Theory*, (London, New Left Books, 1976); Pierre

Machery's *A Theory of Literary Production*, (London, Henley & Boston, MA, Routledge & Kegan Paul, 1978); Raymond Williams's *Marxism and Literature*, (Oxford, Oxford University Press, 1977); and Walter Benjamin's essay 'The Author as Producer' (1934), *Understanding Brecht*, (London, New Left Books, 1977), pp. 85–103. For an account of production within one major entertainment industry see: Keith Negus, *Producing Pop: Culture and Conflict in the Popular Music Industry*, (London, Edward Arnold, 1992).

4   In the early 1980s 'desire' became a buzz word. Witness: Rosetta Brooks (ed.), 'Desire Issue', *ZG*, 7 (1982); Lisa Appignanesi (ed.), *Desire*, (London, Institute of Contemporary Arts, 1984) (ICA Documents – conference papers).

5   This ideology is most vividly embodied in Ayn Rand's 1943 novel *The Fountainhead*, the story of an ultra-modern architect, and in the American movie *The Fountainhead* (1948) based on Rand's book. For an analysis see: John A. Walker's *Art and Artists on Screen*, (Manchester & New York, Manchester University Press, 1993), pp. 95–105.

6   Auteur theory is too extensive and complex to summarise further here. Those interested can refer to: Roland Barthes, 'The Death of the Author' (1968), *Image – Music – Text*, (London, Fontana/Collins, 1977), pp. 142–8; Michel Foucault, 'What is an Author?', *Screen*, 20:1 (Spring 1979), 13–33; J. Caughie (ed.), *Theories of Authorship*, (London, Routledge & Kegan Paul/BFI, 1981); Jack Stillinger, *Multiple Authorship and the Myth of the Solitary Genius*, (Oxford, Oxford University Press, 1992); Sean Burke, *The Death and Return of the Author: Criticism and Subjectivity in Barthes, Foucault and Derrida*, (Edinburgh, Edinburgh University Press, 1992); M. Biriotti and N. Miller (eds), *What is an Author?*, (Manchester & New York, Manchester University Press, 1993); Adam Richardson, 'The Death of the Designer', *Design Issues*, 9:2 (Fall 1993), 34–43.

7   On materials in design see: E. Manzini and others, *The Material of Design: Materials and Design*, (Cambridge, MA, MIT Press/London, Design Council, 1989), and P. Antonelli (curator), *Mutant Materials in Contemporary Design*, (New York, Museum of Modern Art, 1995).

8   On ideology see: Kenneth Thompson, *Beliefs and Ideology*, (Chichester, Ellis Horwood, 1986/London & New York, Routledge, 1993); John B. Thompson, *Ideology and Modern Culture: Critical Social Theory in the Era of Mass Communication*, (Cambridge, Polity Press, 1990); Terry Eagleton, *Ideology: An Introduction*, (London, Verso, 1991); and David Hawkes, *Ideology*, (London & New York, Routledge, 1996).

9   A text examining the relationship between art, social classes, ideology and style is Nicos Hadjinicolaou's *Art History and Class Struggle*, (London, Pluto Press, 1978). Hadjinicolaou argues that a style is a 'visual ideology' – an ideology in visible form. He then distinguishes between 'positive' and 'critical' visual ideologies.

10 On cultural appropriation, borrowings and cannibalism see: Steven Heller and Julie Lasky, *Borrowed Design: Use and Abuse of Historical Form*, (New York, Van Nostrand Reinhold, 1993); Deborah Root, *Cannibal Culture: Art, Appropriation, and the Commodification of Difference*, (Boulder, CO, Westview Press, 1996).

11 On shops and shopping see: John Ferry, *A History of the Department Store*, (New York, Macmillan, 1960); Dorothy Davis, *A History of Shopping*, (London, Routledge & Kegan Paul, 1966); Julie Sheppard and Carl Gardner, *Consuming Passion: The Rise of Retail Culture*, (London, Unwin Hyman, 1989); Rob Shields (ed.), *Lifestyle Shopping: The Subject of Consumption*, (London, Routledge, 1992); William Lancaster, *The Department Store: A Social History*, (London, Pinter, 1995); *Shopping*, BBC-2 television, five-part series, July-August 1995. On museum-going

see: Pierre Bourdieu, A. Darbel and D. Schapper, *The Love of Art: European Art Museums and Their Public*, (Cambridge, Polity Press, 1991).

12 On consumption see: 'Consumer Culture', *Theory, Culture & Society*, 1:3 (1983); N. McKendrick and others, *The Birth of the Consumer Society*, (London, Hutchinson, 1985); Alan Tomlinson, (ed.), *Consumption, Identity and Style: Marketing, Meanings, and the Packaging of Pleasure*, (London & New York, Comedia/Routledge, 1990); Martyn J. Lee, *Consumer Culture Reborn: The Cultural Politics of Consumption*, (London, Routledge, 1992); John Brewer and Roy Porter (eds), *Consumption and the World of Goods*, (London, Routledge, 1994); Robert Bocock, *Consumption*, (London, Routledge, 1993); Daniel Miller (ed.), *Acknowledging Consumption: A Review of New Studies*, (London & New York, Routledge, 1996); Frank Mort, *Cultures of Consumption: Masculinities and Social Spaces in Late Twentieth Century Britain*, (London & New York, Routledge, 1996).

13 On Reception Aesthetics see: P. Hohendahl, 'Introduction to Reception Aesthetics', *New German Critique*, 10 (Winter 1977), 29–63; H. Jauss, *Toward an Aesthetic of Reception*, (Brighton, Sussex, Harvester Press, 1982); R. Holub, *Reception Theory: A Critical Introduction*, (London, Methuen, 1984).

14 Nathalie Heinich has written a particularly illuminating study of this cult: *The Glory of Van Gogh: An Anthropology of Admiration*, (Princeton, NJ, Princeton University Press, 1996).

15 David Freedberg, *The Power of Images: Studies in the History and Theory of Response*, (Chicago & London, University of Chicago Press, 1989).

16 See the entry 'Customising and Custom Painting' in John A. Walker's *Glossary of Art, Architecture and Design since 1945*, (London, Library Association/Boston, MA, G. K. Hall, 3rd edn 1992), entry number 197. A bibliography is appended.

17 P. Boudon, *Lived-in Architecture: Le Corbusier's Pessac Revisited*, (London, Lund Humphries, 1972);

18 Recent texts on taste include: S. Bayley (ed.), *Taste: An Exhibition about Values in Design*, (London, Victoria & Albert Museum/Boilerhouse Project, 1983); S. Bayley, *Taste: The Secret Meaning of Things*, (London, Faber, 1991); Peter Lloyd Jones, *Taste Today: The Role of Appreciation in Consumerism and Design*, (Oxford, Pergamon Press, 1991); and Gary S. Becker, *Accounting for Tastes*, (Princeton, NJ, Harvard University Press, 1996).

19 Pierre Bourdieu, *Distinction: A Social Critique of the Judgement of Taste*, (London, Routledge & Kegan Paul, 1984); French edn 1979.

20 See David Edgar, 'How *Live Aid* Revived the Sixties Message', *The Guardian*, (2 September 1985), 9, and letters in the same newspaper on 4, 5, and 9 September.

21 Gianni Vattimo, *The End of Modernity: Nihilism and Hermeneutics in Post-Modern Culture*, (Cambridge, Polity Press, 1988), p. 7.

6   Institutions

> Literature, art and their respective producers do not exist independently
> of a complex institutional framework which authorises, enables, empow-
> ers and legitimises them. This framework must be incorporated into any
> analysis that pretends to provide a thorough understanding of cultural
> goods and practices. (Randal Johnson)[1]

A COMMON MEANING of the word 'institution' is: 'an organised pattern
of group behaviour, well established and accepted as a fundamental part of
culture'. In this sense, the family and slavery are social institutions.
Following this precedent, we can say that art, design, photography,
cinema[2] and so on are also social institutions. In the case of art, for instance,
it is whatever society defines as art at a particular time. The advantage of
the so-called 'institutional theory of art' is that it avoids the problems of
trying to define art in terms of a checklist of essential characteristics; it also
permits an open-ended, expansive concept of art – new objects and events
can be proposed as art and either accepted or rejected by the social institution.[3]

However, power is not evenly distributed within society: consequently
the power to define what is art, and who is an artist, is concentrated in the
art world, a subculture consisting of people with specialist knowledge of
art – artists, critics, curators, dealers, collectors, etc. – and a constellation
of arts institutions.[4] (The art world can also be described as an international network whose headquarters for most of the past five decades has
been New York.) The situation is summed up in figure 7.

A second, narrower meaning of the word 'institution' is: 'an organisation or establishment for the promotion of a particular object, usually one
for some public, educational, charitable or similar purpose . . . a building
used for such work'. (One of the defining characteristics of a modern
society is bureaucracy, and institutions are the natural habitats of bureau-
crats.) The rest of this chapter is concerned with the second meaning. The
term 'institution' will also be used to encompass associations, companies,
co-operatives, councils, foundations, organisations, societies and unions.

To some students, learning about arts and media institutions may appear
dry and academic, but they are too important to be ignored. There is also
a pragmatic reason why students should take an interest in them: future
employment opportunities.

Creative individuals are still vital to visual culture and they tend to hog the limelight, but this should not be allowed to obscure the fact that institutions are crucial too. Of course, some wealthy individuals establish institutions; for example, the American collector Paul Getty established the Getty Foundation; the British designer Sir Terence Conran founded shop/design company Habitat and, later on, the Conran Foundation and the Design Museum in London.

There are thousands of institutions and many different types fulfilling a wide variety of functions. Some are small operations, registered charities, employing a handful of people; others are enormous, powerful, international conglomerates earning and spending huge sums of money. Some – like the Independent Group – are informal think-tanks, while others – like government agencies and quangos – occupy prestigious offices and employ many full-time officers. Clearly, there will not be space here to describe or even to list them all. Brief accounts will be given of selected examples to illustrate the different kinds that exist and the various roles they play.

Media theorists have divided institutions into two broad categories – commercial and public service – but Raymond Williams distinguished four categories: authoritarian, paternalistic, commercial and democratic.[5] A further possible distinction is between official, conservative institutions and alternative, radical ones. Lord Young of Dartington, a founder of the Open University, also forwarded the idea of 'intermediate' institutions.

Some theorists (and artists) are critical of institutions because of the power and control they exercise over people. Doctors employed in mental hospitals, for example, have the power to decide whether or not patients are sane or insane, and, if the latter, to confine them against their wills. For these reasons, the French philosophers Althusser and Foucault stressed the repressive nature of institutions such as hospitals, prisons and universities (Althusser renamed the latter: 'Ideological State Apparatuses'). Apropos arts institutions, Michael Phillipson observes: 'Art is some-thing to be managed, to be accommodated to the needs of the institutional machinery that must continually reprocess and transform its objects of knowledge to provide for and secure the future of its own practices'.[6] However that may be, contemporary society is unimaginable without institutions (though we can imagine new, different ones) and, whatever their negative characteristics, they can, and do, play positive/enabling roles as well. Furthermore, although institutions may seem all-powerful, they fall as well as rise; many are regularly reported in the news media to be 'in crisis'.

The production/consumption sequence will be used as a structure for the rest of this chapter but, given the fact that some institutions perform a number of functions simultaneously, the same body could well appear under several headings. Another point of importance is that institutions are often interconnected – they exist in networks and systems. For example, the Arts Council of England distributes funds to regional branches and to other, smaller arts agencies.[7] Another example: Rupert Murdoch, the media tycoon with a global reach, owns or has interests in a host of newspapers, broadcasting/television networks, sporting events, phone/telecommunication businesses and film libraries around the world. Journalists have speculated that Murdoch's plan is to establish a consortium of complementary, interlinked media organisations, delivery systems and databases so that he can take advantage of the information/multimedia revolution to become 'the first emperor of the information superhighway'.

Certain commercial advantages accrue from owning several different but related media companies, namely horizontal integration and *synergy*, that is, combined energy/mutual reinforcement. For instance, those who own film and record companies can ensure that a pop music group such as Wet Wet Wet produces a hit record such as *Love is All Around* that provides the background music on the soundtrack for a popular movie such as *Four Weddings and Funeral* (1994); thus the record boosts the film and vice versa.

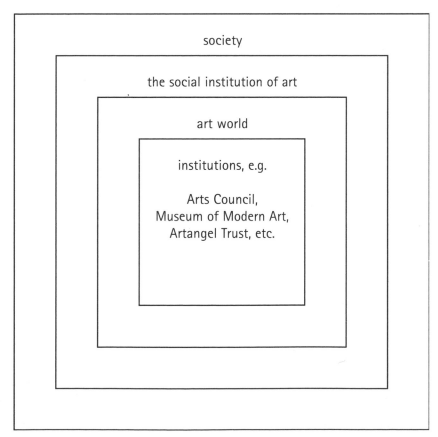

7 Arts institutions.

Production

There are many institutions whose role is to fund or sponsor the production of visual culture either for commercial or public service reasons. In societies dominated by religious ideologies, institutions such as the Catholic Church were major patrons of the arts for centuries. In today's more secular societies the role of patron is exercised by television companies and networks, BBC, NBC, etc. (both public and private), by film studios and companies, ministries of culture and arts councils (both national and local), publishers, fashion houses, record companies, etc., etc. These institutions supply the funds and resources that make cultural production possible but, since they are the paymasters, they generally control and influence what artists and designers produce by setting budgets and briefs, by imposing conditions, deadlines and so forth. If they are not satisfied with what they receive, then they may censor, change or ban it altogether.

Some institutions commission work from self-employed, freelance artists and from independent agencies and small film and video production companies. The commissioning institutions act as patrons but also as gatekeepers: only a few applications and proposals for projects are accepted. If cash from alternative sources cannot be found for the rejected projects, then they never reach fruition. (The economic, in this case, being determinant in the *first* rather than the *last* instance!) Freelance artists and designers who accept commissions from institutions and sign contracts with them enter into complex relations – social, economic and legal – with their employers which, if things go wrong, may result in bitter, costly disputes.

Artists, designers and film-makers who work within institutions and companies on a regular basis – normally described as 'in house' – have less freedom of action but more security of employment than freelancers. Raymond Williams has characterised such individuals as 'instituted artists'.[8] Examples range from the court artists of the medieval period, who were members of Royal households, to the car designers and stylists employed by modern car manufacturers. In the case of major Hollywood film studios, they will control the budget, hire and fire scriptwriters, actors and directors, re-edit films, and control the release and publicity a film receives. One has only to think of the lengthy credits that roll at the end of current movies to realise the size of the production crews. During their heyday the studios became noted for certain kinds of films, they had 'house styles'; consequently, in the eyes of some theorists, the studios came to be regarded as 'the authors' of the movies.

Large media companies are significant not only because they pay for the generation of 'software', but also because they invest in 'hardware', that is, the new technologies that make possible such innovations as the addition of sound and colour to silent films, new film formats such as Cinerama, Cinemascope and 3-D cinema, fantastic special effects, cable networks and so on. (For more on new technology, see Chapter 13.)

Agencies and practices

In contrast to the individualism associated with bohemian painters living in nineteenth-century Parisian garrets, others have seen the benefit of co-operation, collaboration and mutual aid. Architects, artists, graphic designers routinely band together to form teams, agencies or practices (in the sense of an architectural practice) in order to tout for business, share overheads and offer a range of skills to potential clients. In Italy during the Renaissance, bottegas – workshops in which apprentices learnt skills from a master – were commonplace. The French Impressionists formed their own exhibiting society because official venues were reluctant to show their paintings. In London in 1966 a group of radical artists formed the Artist Placement Group with the intention of placing artists as catalysts inside businesses, organisations and government departments.[9] Pentagram – a well-known London design partnership founded by five leading designers in 1972 – is just one of hundreds of design agencies that could have been cited.

Whenever teams or groups are responsible for the production of murals, movies, etc., the traditional, art-historical question of attribution – 'Who exactly did what?' – arises.

Educational institutions

While there are a few creative individuals who have succeeded without the benefit of a formal training, the vast majority have been trained in schools of art, design and film-making. Educational institutions such as the Bauhaus, Ecole de Beaux Arts, the Royal Academy, the Royal College of Art, Ulm (Hochschule für Gestaltung, Ulm), the VKhUTEMAS (1920s, Moscow school of design), the National Film and Television School (Beaconsfield) and Cal Arts have become famous. The influence of British art schools on the character and development of British pop/rock music has been documented by several scholars.[10] It follows that an adequate under-standing of visual culture requires knowledge of the various kinds of edu-cation that cultural producers have received over the centuries in different countries. In the content of the curricula, teaching and assessment methods, values and principles of educational institutions at particular times are to be found, in a condensed and vivid fashion, the dominant par-adigms and contradictions of specific cultural practices.[11]

Educational institutions have also acted as unacknowledged patrons: American and European art schools, for example, have employed fine artists as teachers, either full- or part-time, for many decades, thus enabling them to survive and subsidise their studio-work.

Trade unions and professional organisations

Workers employed in the visual culture industries have often formed or joined trade unions in order to protect their rights and to fight for better conditions and higher wages. Fine artists in various countries have founded artists' unions but the artists' isolated, individualistic, 'on spec' production methods meant that such unions proved hard to sustain. (Fine artists often have no employers to negotiate with or to strike against!)

At the beginning of their careers, entertainers are at the mercy of managers and business enterprises. There are many instances of even famous and wealthy film and pop music stars who discovered that the contracts they signed with studios and media corporations were exploitative and restrictive, and who then resorted to the law in order to extricate themselves. George Michael's 1994 court action against the mighty Sony Corporation is just one example. (Michael lost the case.) If a pop musician and the employer cannot reach an agreement, and the singer refuses to make another album, and the company refuses to promote existing records, then a situation of deadlock, censorship and suppression exists. The musician's creative freedom is restricted.

Large teams of instituted producers employed by powerful media corporations in industrial-type environments with a high division of labour are clearly much more likely to form unions and to support them than isolated fine artists. Because of the millions of separate cells required for animated films, Walt Disney's Hollywood studios became like a factory. As a consequence, the animators founded a trade union and in 1941 there was a bitter strike.

Less militant than trade unions are professional associations. Groups of artists and architects have often banded together in order to control entry into their professions, to regulate and maintain standards, and to ensure that the public receives a high-quality service. British artists, for instance, founded the Royal Academy in 1768. The RA has imposing premises in Piccadilly, London which are used to mount an annual summer exhibition in which the work of members of the Academy and other artists are displayed. This building also houses a school for training future artists. Despite its high public profile, the RA is a private institution; therefore, it continually has to raise funds to sustain itself. This is why it mounts a succession of popular, blockbuster exhibitions (some shows are more scholarly) which have to be commercially successful: they have to attract thousands of paying visitors and business sponsorship money. In 1995 it was reported that the RA had made a loss of £647,000 in the previous year, mainly owing to a decline in corporate sponsorship of its exhibitions.

Academies exist or have existed in most developed nations and are, or have been, very influential: no historian of nineteenth-century French art can ignore the role of the French Academy and the institution of the Salon (a huge, annual exhibition). Harrison and Cynthia White are the authors of a notable study of institutional change – the decline of the academic system and the rise of the dealer-critic system associated with the Impressionists – in the French art world during the late nineteenth century.[12]

The RIBA

In the field of British architecture the Royal Institute of British Architects is a long-established professional body. It was founded by Royal Charter in 1837 and today two-thirds of Britain's thirty-thousand architects are members. The RIBA has a monumental headquarters building in Portland Place, London, which was designed by Grey Wornum in 1934. During the 1980s the RIBA and its officials were subject to criticism as a consequence of Prince Charles's attacks on modern architecture. In the following decade further criticism came from within the profession: Reginald Grover launched a rival organisation entitled Association of Accredited Architects, and Richard Burdett headed the Architecture Foundation. The latter's aim was to promote architecture rather than architects.

Display, distribution, marketing and promotion

While it is possible for lone producers with minimal resources to generate artefacts, it is not normally possible for them to undertake the arduous, expensive and time-consuming labour of displaying, publicising, distributing and selling those products. Hence the existence of private art galleries and dealers, film distribution companies and cinema chains, book distributors and bookshops/clubs, shops and stores selling designed goods, advertising agencies, artists' and press agents, marketing companies, trade fairs and promotional festivals (such as the annual film festival held at Cannes) and auction houses such as Christie's and Sotheby's.

In the British rock music business there are companies such as the Mean Fiddler and Tribute who rent or run clubs and other venues both small and large, and who organise concerts and tours for bands and performers. However, income is derived not simply from the fans who pay entrance charges but also from the generation of 'intellectual property rights'; for instance, those pertaining to recordings, the transmission of shows via television and miscellaneous merchandise.

Since the goals of these institutions are to deliver and sell cultural products and events to customers, the associated publicity which they devise is invariably positive. More independent, critical evaluations can be found, of course, in newspapers and magazines that review new products.

But even here commercial pressures may exert a restraining influence. For example, some glossy art and fashion magazines are financially dependent on advertising more than sales; if they are too critical of the products being advertised, their advertising revenue may well diminish. Then, no matter how useful and high-quality their editorial content, they may fold.

Arts councils

Most developed nations have established state-funded bodies concerned with the funding and promotion of visual culture within their own borders: for example, in Britain there is the Arts Council and in the United States the National Endowment for the Arts. The constitution, internal organisation, allocation of funds, policies and performance of such bodies are frequently controversial and often give rise to heated debates in legislatures and in the press. In theory politicians favour 'the arm's length principle' in respect of such bodies, but in practice they seek to bring them to heel whenever they are outraged by some blatant 'waste of public money on worthless avant-garde antics' or on 'obscene or blasphemous art'. Witness the 1980s' attacks by American Right-wing politicians on the NEA for supporting exhibitions by the photographers Andres Serrano and Robert Mapplethorpe. A Cincinnati museum director even found himself in court defending a Mapplethorpe show he had mounted. Fortunately, he was acquitted.

The Crafts Council

In some cases an institution exists whose purpose is to promote a particular medium or an area of creative work. An example is the Crafts Council, a national organisation for promoting Britain's contemporary crafts, decorative and applied arts (calligraphy, ceramics, furniture, jewellery, lettering, metalwork, mosaics, textiles, etc.). It has two main aims: first, 'to advance and encourage the creation of works of fine craftsmanship', and second, 'to foster, promote and increase the interest of the public in the works of craftspeople' (Royal Charter, 1982). The Council was founded in 1974 and is described as an 'independent' organisation even though it is funded by the government. It has premises in Pentonville Road, London and a shop inside the Victoria and Albert Museum. It undertakes an impressive range of activities: gives grants to craftsmen and craftswomen; mounts exhibitions in its gallery; offers work for sale via its shop; organises the annual Chelsea Crafts Fair; maintains a collection of examples of craft; publishes a specialist magazine entitled *Crafts* (1973–); provides reference books and picture libraries; undertakes educational work; and compiles a national register of craftspeople.

In the past twenty years the craft economy and the public interest in craft in Britain has grown significantly. Evidently, the Crafts Council has had a share in fostering these developments. Paradoxically, craft, a pre-industrial form of production, has survived the age of industry and now finds a niche in the post-industrial society.

National and international bodies

Other state-funded institutions exist whose brief is to promote the nation's culture abroad. For Britain this task is performed by the British Council, which regularly mounts exhibitions of British art that travel abroad.[13] Naturally, the purpose of such bodies is to present a positive image of the home nation to foreigners. In other words, culture blurs into propaganda. Sometimes intelligence agencies play a sinister role; for example, the Central Intelligence Agency of the United States secretly funded the British magazine *Encounter* for a time. Visitors to exhibitions of foreign art may be blissfully unaware of their hidden ideological agendas. A notorious example, well documented by art historians, was the 1959 exhibition of American Abstract Expressionist painting that toured Europe during the Cold War period. One aim of this show was to prove the superiority of American culture when compared to Soviet culture: 'Our artists enjoy greater artistic freedom than their Soviet counterparts; as art Abstract Expressionism is superior to Socialist Realism; ergo, democratic, free-market capitalism is better than totalitarian, planned-economy communism.'

International institutions concerned with the promotion of culture are fewer than national organisations, but they do exist: UNESCO (United Nations Educational, Scientific and Cultural Organisation), for example (see Figure 8).

Multi-purpose institutions

As indicated earlier, some institutions perform multiple functions. Channel 4 television, for instance, commissions programmes and feature films, and it also transmits and sells them. In addition it sponsors the Turner Prize, a sum of money – £20,000 – awarded to 'the best' British artist (selected from four artists in competition with one another) at an annual promotional event hosted by the Tate Gallery and covered by Channel 4. In the eyes of some critics, the Turner Prize is a publicity gimmick that demeans the artists who agree to take part. This social institution has given rise to an anti-institution known as the K Foundation.[14] The latter's spoiling tactic has been to offer double the money to 'the worst' artist in the Turner Prize competition. In 1994 the British sculptor Rachel Whiteread enjoyed the dubious honour of winning both awards!

Retail chains such as Marks & Spencer do not merely sell goods designed and manufactured by others – their purchasing power is such that they can control and determine the nature and quality of goods being manufactured by suppliers. Students interested in designed goods will find that there are histories of major companies and brands such as Coca-Cola and General Motors in book form. Some histories are paid for by the companies themselves – and so should be treated with scepticism – but there are also independent critiques.

Alternative and anti-institutions

The existence of state-funded and/or dominant institutions often prompts groups critical of them to establish alternatives, some of which are called 'anti-institutions'.[15] (The word 'institution' is so redolent of conservative values that it seems contradictory to speak of radical or subversive institutions. Anti-institutions are paradoxical because they are still institutions.) Examples are the Anti-University that existed in London during the late 1960s and the Situationist International that existed from 1957 to 1972. During the 1970s and 1980s, feminists blamed patriarchy for their exclusion from so many existing cultural institutions. Some feminists banged on the doors demanding entry while others founded separate, women-only publishing companies, magazines (such as *Spare Rib*, *Heresies* and the *Feminist Art Journal*), exhibiting societies, archives (such as the Women's Artists' Slide Library in London; in 1993 it was renamed The Women's Art Library), galleries and museums (such as the National Museum of Women in the Arts, Washington, DC, founded by Wilhelmina Holladay). Thus a parallel set of institutions came into being.

   Clearly, the advantage of such alternative institutions is that they directly meet the needs of excluded groups but the disadvantage is that they can become special-interest ghettos struggling in the margins of mainstream culture. They may also serve a safety-valve role that allows the dominant institutions to avoid reform. Three fates await alternative institutions: first, they may succeed and continue; second, they may fail and disappear; third, they may apply for support from official sources and thus become dependent or incorporated bodies.

Regulatory and censorship institutions

The gatekeeper role of institutions has already been mentioned. Also acting as gatekeepers or filters are official, paternalistic, censorship organisations which claim to serve society as a whole; for instance, the British Board of Film Classification which grants or refuses certificates to new films and videotapes. Violent, sexual and blasphemous materials pose constant problems and extreme examples are regularly banned (if only for a time). Absurd situations arise in which a supposedly violent film can be seen in

8 Henry Moore, *UNESCO Reclining Figure* (1957–8), Roman Travertine Marble, length 507 cm, with the UNESCO Headquarters Building, Paris, in the background.

UNESCO was founded in 1946 for the purpose of 'advancing, through the educational, scientific and cultural relations of the peoples of the world, the objectives of international peace and the common welfare of mankind'. It has a budget of several hundred million dollars, some of which is spent on a cultural heritage programme aimed at protecting and conserving historic sites and landmarks such as the temples at Abu Simbel, Egypt, and Chartres Cathedral, France. UNESCO is also concerned with non-physical heritage such as oral traditions, music and dance. It subsidises travelling exhibitions and the publication of literary and historical texts, and translations. UNESCO encourages the enforcement of international legislation on copyright; it also publishes various journals, books, statistics, maps and atlases.

Such institutions can themselves act as patrons of the arts. UNESCO's 1958 headquarters building in Paris, for instance, was designed by a team of leading modern architects which included Marcel Breuer and Pier Luigi Nervi. For the inside a mural was commissioned from Picasso and for the outside sculptures were commissioned from Henry Moore, Hans Arp and Alexander Calder. This patronage of the arts reinforced UNESCO's credibility as a cultural organisation; however, its role as a world institution was somewhat undermined by the Euro-centric nature of its location and commissions.[16] At the time of writing, Britain and the United States are both refusing to pay any contributions to UNESCO.

one country but not in another, or can be seen in the cinema but not on video. Having had their curiosity aroused by press publicity and controversy, the public are keen to obtain illegal, bootleg copies of banned movies. Today, international communication systems such as satellite television and the Internet increasingly challenge or circumvent national, control and censorship authorities. At the time of writing, the availability of child porn on the Internet is causing great public concern.

In addition to the regulatory organs of the state there are private pressure groups such as viewers' and listeners' organisations, concerned with protecting children and preserving standards of public decency. Critics of these organisations object that they do not trust adults to make up their own minds. Furthermore, they regularly try to ban films and television programmes before they have been screened! If such priggish, puritanical people were to be successful then a bland, conformist, middle-brow culture would be imposed on everyone. The constant public arguments about what should or should not be banned are signs of a divided society in which different values and moralities uneasily co-exist. The disputes can also be regarded as a tribute to the power of cultural products to challenge and disturb audiences.

Museums and galleries

Out of the billions of artefacts produced annually, only a select few enter the institutions dedicated to collecting, conservation and preservation. Examples of the latter include galleries and museums such as the Prado in Madrid, the Museum of Modern Art in New York, the Museum of the Moving Image and the Design Museum in London, and film archives such as that maintained by the BFI. The decisions made by trustees and curators regarding acquisitions, their arrangement and display are clearly of vital importance to the reception of works of art, and to the establishment of historical lineages and canons of masterworks. The contents of museums, galleries and their associated temporary exhibitions are also studied and copied by art students and so they repeatedly exert an influence upon new visual culture.

Most museums and galleries are fairly recent – they date from the nineteenth and twentieth centuries. Today, however, the field of visual culture is virtually inconceivable without them. With their programmes of exhibitions, their millions of tourists and school parties, their merchandise/shops and 'ace' cafés, their populist policies, museums have become a kind of mass medium/leisure industry. While most contemporary artists regard museums and galleries as essential, there are some who have taken a different view. The Italian Futurists, for instance, wanted to reject the past and so called for the destruction of museums. Since Futurist paintings and sculptures are now on display in museums, it is clear who won the battle.

The literature on museums is now extensive. It includes books on the so-called 'New Museology'.[17] (This term dates from the late 1980s. It signified a radical questioning of the ideologies, values and methodologies of existing museums.) Illuminating studies have been written by Michael Baldwin, Pierre Bourdieu, Annie Combes, Carol Duncan, Donald Horne, Marcia Pointon and Alan Wallach.

Today, there are examples of politically motivated artists – Hans Haacke, Daniel Buren, Art & Language – who make use of art institutions but at the same time subject them to a critique. During the 1970s, community artists avoided museums and galleries because they considered them tombs of dead art used by the middle class. Community muralists placed their work in the street and housing estates in order to communicate directly with particular groups of people living in particular neighbourhoods. In the following decade a vogue for public art and events developed and a number of organisations were founded to encourage and sponsor work of this kind: for example, the Public Art Development Trust (1983–) and the Artangel Trust (1985–).

Heritage institutions

Most nations value their cultural heritage, but to varying degrees according to their age, wealth and national pride. As visual culture is man-ufactured in ever-increasing quantities, and as time elapses more and more of it accumulates: the task of deciding what to retain and what to discard or 'de-accession' becomes ever more pressing. (It has been reported that the new British Library that has been under construction in Euston Road, London for decades will be full – indeed ten miles short of shelf space – when it opens.) Maintaining the past also becomes more and more expen-sive and more of a burden. Two questions arise: 'What proportion of the annual gross national product is it reasonable to spend on preserving the culture of the past? Should ancient or living culture have priority in funding?' Some politicians regard national lotteries as one painless way of raising extra money for cultural institutions and projects.

In Britain an obsession with the past has given rise to the expression 'the heritage industry'. The cultural critics/historians Robert Hewison and Patrick Wright employed this expression in the mid–1980s to describe a movement associated with the decline of British manufacturing industry: instead of goods Britain produced a commodity called 'heritage' for sale to tourists.[18] Conservation, preservation and heritage organisations flourished: the National Trust, English Heritage, etc. (At the time of writing the British government includes a Department of National Heritage.) More and more museums (including open-air and working museums), theme parks and heritage centres (such as the Jorvik Viking Centre in York) were opened until Britain was in danger of becoming one vast, open-air museum. Hewison argued that a sanitised image of the past was being retailed for the benefit of citizens and tourists. He advocated a critical culture rather than a closed culture, history instead of heritage, a spirit of renewal in place of nostalgia for a bogus past.

In 1993 similar criticisms were levelled against the Disney Corporation in the United States because of its plans to build a $650 million American History amusement park near Washington, DC.

Summary

Strictly speaking, empirical studies of cultural institutions are part of the discipline of sociology (there is already a body of literature designated 'the sociology of art'[19]), or, in the case of media organisations, they are part of Media Studies.[20] But students of visual culture also need to grasp the facilitating, controlling and mediating roles institutions in general play. In the case of particular examples, students need to trace the institution's origins and history, to consider its aims, internal structure, operation and place in the art/media systems, and in the society of which it is a part.

From the perspective of Visual Culture Studies, a key reason for such research is to discover the ways in which institutions determine or influence images and artefacts. In the case of a simple, well-documented relationship such as that between a patron and a painter, the patron's influence on the work of art may be easy to discern. (One of Ford Madox Brown's patrons asked for a portrait of his wife to be included in a figure composition, that is, a smaller version of the painting *Work*. Brown duly obliged.) But in the case of large, complexly structured arts and media institutions employing or commissioning teams of specialists to produce films, television programmes, etc., the influence of the institutions on the content, form and ideological agenda of the final product is likely to be harder to judge because of the many functionaries and levels of mediation involved.

Notes and further reading

1   Randal Johnson, editor's 'Introduction' to Pierre Bourdieu's *The Field of Cultural Production: Essays on Art and Literature*, (Cambridge, Polity Press, 1993), p. 10.

2   The words 'film' and 'cinema' are often used as synonyms but, although they overlap, they are not identical in meaning. According to Christian Metz, the cinematic institution is 'not just the cinema industry (which works to fill cinemas, not to empty them). It is also the mental machinery – another industry – which spectators "accustomed to cinema" have internalised historically and which has adapted them to the consumption of films. (The institution is outside us and inside us, indistinctly collective and intimate, sociological and psychoanalytic . . .)': 'The Imaginary Signifier', *Screen*, 16:2 (Summer 1975), 18–19. Metz mentions the specially designed buildings in which films are projected. Today, because of technological developments, films can be appreciated apart from cinemas: some films go straight to video for home viewing on television monitors.

3 For more on this theory see: Milton C. Albrecht, 'Art as an Institution', *The Sociology of Art and Literature: A Reader*, eds M. C. Albrecht, J. H. Barnett and M. Griff, (London, Duckworth, 1970), pp. 1–26; George Dickie, *Art and the Aesthetic: An Institutional Analysis*, (Ithaca, NY, Cornell University Press, 1974); Noel Carroll, 'Film History and Film Theory: An Outline for an Institutional Theory of Film', *Film Reader 4: Point of View, Metahistory of Film*, (1979), 81–96. It should be acknowledged that this theory has its critics.

4 On the art world see: A. Danto, 'The Art World' *Journal of Philosophy*, 6 (1964), 571–84; A. Silvers, 'Art World Discarded', *Journal of Aesthetics & Art Criticism*, 34:4 (Summer 1976), 441–54; H. Becker, Art Worlds, (Berkeley, CA, University of California Press, 1982); L. Alloway, *Network*, (Ann Arbor, MI, University of Michigan Research Press, 1984); R. Hagenberg, *Untitled '84: The Art World of the '80s*, (New York, Pelham Press, 1984); D. Crane, *Transformation of the Avant-Garde: The New York Artworld 1940–85*, (Chicago, University of Chicago Press, 1987); H. Pindell, 'Art (World) and Racism', *Third Text*, 3/4 (Spring-Summer 1988), 157–90.

5 R. Williams, *Communications*, (Harmondsworth, Middlesex, Penguin Books, 1976).

6 M. Phillipson, 'Managing "Tradition" . . .', *Visual Culture*, ed. C. Jenks, (London & New York, Routledge, 1995), p. 207.

7 There are several histories of the Arts Council. For a recent account see: Andrew Sinclair, *Arts and Culture: The History of the 50 Years of the Arts Council of Great Britain*, (London, Sinclair-Stevenson, 1995).

8 R. Williams, *Culture*, (London, Fontana, 1981). See especially chapters two and three: 'Institutions', 'Formations'.

9 For more on APG see: John A. Walker, *John Latham – The Incidental Person – His Art and Ideas*, (London, Middlesex University Press, 1995), pp. 97–101.

10 On the role of art schools see chapter one – 'The Art School Connection' – of John A. Walker's *Cross-overs: Art into Pop/Pop into Art*, (London & New York, Comedia/Methuen, 1987), pp. 14–36, and Simon Frith's and Howard Horne's, *Art into Pop*, (London & New York, Methuen, 1987).

11 A history of Europe's art academies is provided by Nikolaus Pevsner's *Academies of Art, Past and Present*, (Cambridge, Cambridge University Press, 1940). For a useful series of articles on the paradigms and contradictions operative in modern art schools see: *The Artist and the Academy: Issues in Fine Art Education and the Wider Cultural Context*, eds Nicholas de Ville and Stephen Foster, (Southampton, John Hansard Gallery, 1994).

12 H. C. and C. A. White, *Canvases and Careers: Institutional Change in the French Painting World*, (New York, London, Sydney, John Wiley & Sons, 1965).

13 For a history of the British Council see: Frances Donaldson, *The British Council: The First Fifty Years*, (London, J. Cape, 1984).

14 On the K Foundation see: Alix Sharkey, 'Trash, Art and Kreation', *The Guardian Weekend*, (21 May 1994), 24–6, 29, 52; Jim Reid, 'Money to Burn', *Life, The Observer Magazine*, (25 September 1994), 28–33. See also the television programme directed by Kevin Hull, *Omnibus*, (BBC–1, 6 November 1995).

15 For information on so-called alternative spaces in the fine art field see entry 27 in John A. Walker's *Glossary of Art, Architecture and Design Since 1945*, (London, Library Association/Boston MA, G. K. Hall, 3rd edn 1992).

16 For more about UNESCO see: Richard Hoggart, *An Idea and its Servants: UNESCO from Within*, (London, Chatto & Windus, 1978). On the art of UNESCO see: W. J. Strachan, 'Henry Moore's UNESCO Statue', *The Studio*, 156:789 (December 1958), 170–5, and Alain Jouffrey, 'UNESCO . . .', *Graphis*, 15:82 (March–April 1959), pp. 138–45, 171.

17   Peter Vergo (ed.), *The New Museology*, (London, Reaktion Books, 1989).
18   P. Wright, *On Living in an Old Country: The National Past in Contemporary Britain*, (London, Verso, 1985); R. Hewison, *The Heritage Industry: Britain in a Climate of Decline*, (London, Methuen, 1987).
19   See, for example, M. C. Albrecht, J. H. Barnett and M. Griff (eds), *The Sociology of Art and Literature: A Reader* (London, Duckworth, 1970); I. C. Jarvie, *Towards a Sociology of the Cinema: A Comparative Essay in the Structure and Functioning of a Major Entertainment Industry*, (London, Routledge & Kegan Paul, 1970). See also books by Pierre Bourdieu.
20   Most books on teaching and studying the mass media have chapters devoted to media institutions. For a study of institutions in relation to one mass medium see Simon Watney, 'On the Institutions of Photography', *Photography Politics: Two*, eds P. Holland, J. Spence and S. Watney, (London, Comedia, 1986), pp. 187–97; Stevie Bezencenet and Philip Corrigan (eds), *Photographic Practices: Towards a Different Image*, (London, Comedia, 1986).

7   Looks, the gaze and surveillance

THIS CHAPTER seeks to extend understanding of 'the visual' by examining the notion of the gaze and the various kinds of look associated with pictorial representation. Most of the examples considered are drawn from the history of painting but some are derived from the cinema. We also touch briefly upon the topics scopophilia and panopticism. Finally, we consider the way cameras are increasingly being used to observe and record human behaviour, thereby helping to bring about what some writers call 'a surveillance society'.

The eye and the gaze

The eye exerts an influence over a distance; consequently powers for good and ill have been attributed to it. A fourteenth-century book by Peter of Limoges – *On the Moral and Spiritual Eye* – discussed 'thirteen marvellous things about the vision of the eye which contain spiritual information'; in 1972 Stuart Hall published an article about the famous British magazine *Picture Post* (1938–57) in which he argued that it had 'a social eye' because it supported progressive social policies.[1] For centuries there has been a superstitious belief in 'the evil eye'. The continuing potency of the latter was demonstrated in 1996 when the ruling British Conservative Party issued negative political propaganda showing the face of Tony Blair (the Labour Opposition Party leader) with a strip across his face upon which 'demon eyes' had been superimposed. A caption below the image warned: 'New Labour, New Danger'.

Optical power has been amplified by such technological inventions as microscopes, telescopes and cameras (still-photo, moving-picture and real-time closed-circuit surveillance cameras). Cameras are especially important of course, because they record what they 'see' on film and videotape.

Gazes are dependent upon eyes but some theorists distinguish between 'the eye' and 'the gaze': 'the eye', for them, refers to the viewer gazing upon the world, while 'the gaze' refers to the fact that we are all subject to the gazes of others.[2] Being gazed upon can be pleasurable or painful: there are times when we enjoy being watched or photographed or filmed by others, but there are also times when being watched or recorded makes us feel acutely embarrassed, persecuted even.

Looks in pictures

The role of the scopic drive in the creation and appreciation of visual culture is clearly crucial. Being a viewer or spectator is central to the consumption of images, and this is why it has prompted so much analysis, especially by film theorists.[3] But looking is also part of the content and formal structure of many still and moving pictures.

Theorists have identified four basic looks in relation to images:

1 the look of artists, and photographers/film-makers and their cameras, towards the motif or scene to be recorded;
2 the looks exchanged by depicted characters within pictures or films.
3 the look of the spectator towards the image;
4 the looks exchanged between depicted characters and spectators.

Before considering the four looks in more detail, an aside on the word 'look' (in French, 'le regard'). To look is to fix one's eyes on a certain object; however, paradoxically 'a look' can also refer to the appearance of an object; for example, a particular fashion is called 'a look'. A fashion look is intended to attract and please the gazes of others. Since clothes and cosmetics conceal the wearer's body to some extent, the fashion look can be thought of as a mask or shield that reflects the viewer's look back.

Jewellery, metalwork and precious stones, worn mainly by women (especially Hollywood film stars), reflect light particularly well and so act as magnets for sight. Their use was analysed by the German sociologist Georg Simmel (1858–1918).[4] Gleams and glitter enable the wearer to be a centre of emanation, to extend the self beyond bodily limits, and to attract the gazes of others. Carrie Asman comments: 'The borrowed ray of light, which the precious stones catches from an external source and sends out again, is finally returned to its indirect origin through the reflective gaze of the beholder who views the wearer from a changed perspective.'[5]

Look 1, then, encompasses the looks of all those artists who have scrutinised nature in order to make representational images.

Artists also look at their canvases and sketchpads, so there is a back-and-forth process of looking at the motif, then looking at the canvas and making a mark, then looking at the motif again, and so on. (In *Art and Illusion* Gombrich called this process 'making and matching' and asked 'Which comes first?'.) To ensure greater accuracy, artists often take measurements with the aid of a pencil and some also frame the scene with their hands or with the aid of a wooden perspective device (Van Gogh used one), or a camera obscura. (In cameras a framing device is built-in by means of the viewfinder and the rectangular shape of the film frame.) Observations are translated into bodily actions using the tools and materials of the medium to compose and construct a picture. The artists' empirical observations will be informed by their whole histories and personalities, by their previous practice and their knowledge of the art of the past. Although Cézanne scrutinised the motifs in front of him with extraordinary zeal, he also stated that he wanted 'to do Poussin again after nature'; in other words, his looking was modulated by an awareness of Poussin's carefully composed, ideal, classical-style landscapes.

An insight into the visual habits of a leading twentieth-century artist – Willem de Kooning – can be gained by considering his own statements and a catalogue essay by the critic Richard Schiff.[6] In 1960 de Kooning remarked that for him content was 'a glimpse of something, an encounter like a flash'. Fleeting sensations and observations were perceived via glimpses and glances; for instance, things seen briefly from a moving car. Although de Kooning was dubbed an *Abstract* Expressionist, many of his paintings were *figurative* – woman was a favourite theme. However, de Kooning maintained that his 'content' was 'tiny'; for example, the light reflected from a puddle of water. He described himself as 'a slipping glimpser' because his perceptions were most acute when he was slipping, that is, off balance. The fleeting character of de Kooning's visual sensations was transmitted to canvas via fluent, gestural brushstrokes using paint that was fluid and slippery.

Since cameras can be regarded as mechanical eyes that automated the perspectival system of representation perfected in Renaissance Italy, look 1 also encompasses all still and moving pictures. Viewfinders make framing easy for photographers. What is before the camera – the so-called 'profilmic or pro-pictorial display or event' – can, of course, be natural or artificial. Painters and photographers can spend hours arranging a still life of apples or the pose of a model (hence the expression 'staged photography'); designers working for film studios build elaborate sets or models specifically for the purpose of being filmed.

Various film theorists have commented upon what they call 'the cinematic apparatus'.[7] In essence, they claim that the mechanical eye dominates the other senses; the perspectival system of representation it inherited has surpassed all other systems; it is an instrument that embodies bourgeois ideology. (According to Jean-Louis Comolli, cinema owes its existence to the ideological demand 'see life as it is'; and to the economic imperative 'make a profit'.) Feminists added a further charge: the ideology was patriarchal because it was designed by and for men. Theoretical accounts of the apparatus by male writers were also flawed because they ignored the issue of sexual difference, that is, the representation of women in movies and the responses of women to movies. By way of reply, Jacqueline Rose devoted a whole book to the subject of 'sexuality in the field of vision'.[8]

A more general question arises here: 'Is technology ethically and politically neutral?' We will defer considering this question until Chapter 13.

We move on to look 2: the looks exchanged between depicted characters within the narrative of a picture or film, as in Vermeer's paintings where meaningful exchanges of looks occur between maidservants and their mistresses when love letters are handed over. Vermeer's *Lady with a Guitar* (c. 1670) shows a woman looking towards someone standing outside the picture space. (Her look activates what in film theory is called 'off-screen space'.) It is a means of 'breaking frame', of rupturing the hermetic character of the painting. Christian Metz has noted that off-screen characters and spectators have two things in common: both are out-of-frame and both are looking at the screen image.

During the Italian Renaissance some murals were constructed around a complex interaction of looks. Jean Paris, a theorist whose research has been informed by Noam Chomsky's linguistics, has analysed Giotto's frescos and shown how their compositions are built around 'invisible' geometric forms such as triangles, and around the eyebeams of the depicted characters.[9] Paris has also studied Madonna and infant Jesus images over several centuries and claims that there was a gradual metamorphosis from a sacred to a profane image. At first, in Byzantine art, Madonna and Child representations were set against flat gold backgrounds and conformed to a stiff, frontal, symmetrical schema. Slowly, the mother–child relationship became more natural. By the time of Duccio, a shallow depth had appeared and Mary had been permitted to sit down. Variations of the gaze between mother and child proliferated: Paris cites fifteen combinations of looks between Virgin, child, angels and the spectator. Finally, Italian painters like Andrea Solario depicted an ordinary-looking woman suckling an ordinary-looking baby in a naturalistic landscape setting.

Paris concludes that the 'progressive degradation of the Madonnas . . . conceals in fact a visual struggle, a deliberate invasion of God's territory . . . perspective is nothing but a 180 degree reversal of divine space'. In confirmation he quotes Alberti's remark: 'At long last perspective makes us see the world as God saw it.' Hence the complete inversion of space and God's regard signals the triumph of Renaissance humanism. Despite the Christian subject matter of so much Renaissance painting, the mastery of perspective indicated the supersession of God by Man.

Look 3 is the look of the spectator towards the image. Individuals will vary, of course, in how they perceive and react to images – but this is a matter for Reception History and Audience Studies. Every representational image provides a viewing or vantage point for the spectator to occupy. Still pictures normally provide just one viewpoint but in the case of Picasso's and Braque's Cubist paintings, and Hannah Höch's photomontages, many viewpoints were incorporated into the same composition.

We will come back to look 4 later.

Voyeurism

Images are made to be seen but in the majority of cases they do not acknowledge the presence of the viewer. This, and the fact that the people in images are not literally present, is what enables us to enjoy images voyeuristically: we can look at a scene as if we were peering into a room through a one-way mirror. Fundamental to the appeal of visual media is the fact that we can watch to our heart's content without ourselves being observed.

'Scopophilia' is the technical term Freud and other psychoanalysts use to describe the erotic gratification derived from looking.[10] ('Scopophobia' is the fear of being looked at.) We are all familiar with the pleasures of being peepers or voyeurs, of seeing without being seen. In *Ways of Seeing* (1972) John Berger cited Jacopo Tintoretto's painting *Susannah and the Elders* (c. 1560) as a prime example of pictorial voyeurism. Its theme, derived from an Old Testament tale about two elderly men spying on Susannah while she bathed naked, provided male artists with the perfect excuse for satisfying men's desire to enjoy female nudity. Tintoretto shows Susannah gazing into a mirror, so she is also taking pleasure in looking, but, because of her self-regard, men are likely to accuse her of vanity and narcissism.

According to the Bible, the 'dirty' old men were punished for their presumption but when a modern man stands in front of this painting he sees both Susannah and the peeping Elders. The viewer is thus placed in a superior, hypocritical position: he can enjoy what the old men enjoyed while at same time condemning them. He knows that he will not be punished for gazing at Susannah's body. We have assumed the viewer is male because paintings of naked women were and are generally produced for, and purchased by, men. The general point here is that the positions constructed by pictures for the spectator may be gendered.

Another painting catering for the optical appetite of heterosexual males is Jean-Auguste Dominique Ingres's *Bain Turc* (1862–3). Since this picture is circular in shape, it resembles a large spyhole. It shows the naked inmates of an Oriental harem. There is an unparalleled display of voluptuously curved flesh. It was Ingres's custom, in his odalisques, to celebrate all the five senses; consequently in *Bain Turc* the pleasures of touch are depicted via the women who caress one another, the pleasures of smell via the perfumes from the incense burners, the pleasures of taste via the sweets and coffee being consumed, and the pleasures of sound via the music of mandolin and tambourine. Of course, viewers can enjoy these four sensory experiences only by proxy, but they can enjoy the final one – vision – directly. *Bain Turc*, as John L. Connolly puts it, is 'an allegory of the senses wherein the spectator is the living personification of sight'.[11]

Marcel Duchamp's last major work, *Etant Donnés . . .* (1946–66), was a three-dimensional tableau with the figure of a nude woman hidden behind an old wooden door. The installation can be viewed only by one person at a time through two holes punched in the door. In this work the viewing position is literally prescribed and its 'peeping Tom' character is foregrounded.

One of the most controversial films that made voyeurism its explicit subject was called *Peeping Tom* (directed by Michael Powell, 1959). Reynold Humphries comments: 'The entire film revolves around vision in one form or another. The first shot is a huge close-up of a closed eye that suddenly opens and stares at the spectator.'[12] The main character is a perverted photographer and film-maker who films women while he murders them in order to record the terror on their faces. He even attaches a mirror to his camera so that his victims can witness their own fear. He then enjoys watching the films he has made. Finally, as the police close in, he documents his own suicide.

It seems obvious now that one of the reasons this film was greeted with a storm of abuse on its release was that the film-making within the film called attention to the voyeuristic, sadistic 'perversions' of cinema audiences. They also enjoy seeing people being murdered in crime and horror movies, and they enjoy the fear such movies can generate.

In the case of paintings, it might be argued that the viewer takes up the vantage point of the artist and therefore sees what he or she saw. However, this is too simplistic. The disturbed vision of the world portrayed in Edvard Munch's famous Expressionist painting and print *The Scream* (1893) is surely being experienced by the main depicted character. (Munch recounts that he did have such an experience, but he could also have imagined it.) Of course, the viewer can empathise with the plight of depicted, fictional characters.

Viewpoint in film

Viewpoint (or point-of-view) is most clearly evident in film and television because of the mobility of the camera (pans, tracking shots, zooms, etc.) and because editing (cuts from one camera position to another, etc.) constantly shifts the viewer's point-of-view. In a sense, the viewer's eyes are sucked from the body into the camera and are then taken on an exciting, weightless journey. (This is especially evident in high-speed, aerial sequences.) Film theorists distinguish between *objective* and *subjective* camera shots. An objective shot will show two people looking at one another and conversing, that is, the camera adopts a third-person vantage point (the position of an invisible narrator). Subjective shots normally follow in which the camera assumes the position of first one character and then the other (so-called 'reverse-shot structure'). By this means the viewer is made to identify with the camera and the characters in question, thus becoming involved in the emotional drama. A more intense subjective shot occurs when the screen image is marked or distorted in some way to signify the mental state of the character; for example, if a character is given drugs or knocked out, the screen image often becomes blurred.

James Monaco, in his helpful book *How to Read a Film* (rev. edn 1981), cites the film *Lady in the Lake* (directed by Robert Montgomery, 1946) as a rare experiment in linking narration and camerawork. In this film the camera is identified exclusively with the hero's viewpoint. We, the cinema audience, see only what he sees. His appearance is thus visible only when he stands in front of a mirror. The film-makers were attempting to imitate the first-person narration familiar to us from many novels and autobiographies.

Mirrors

When individuals look into mirrors their faces and gazes are reflected back: consequently mirror images are unusual in that they do acknowledge the spectator's presence and his or her environment. The Conceptual artist Martin Craig-Martin once constructed a work from an arrangement of interlinked mirrors mounted in several booths that was quite disturbing: when one looked into a mirror what one saw was not one's own face but that of a stranger's located in a nearby booth. (*Faces*, (1971), shown as part of *Seven Exhibitions*, (London, Tate Gallery, 1972)). An intimate, private moment rudely became a public one. At other times the kind of mirroring that occurs when we gaze into another's eyes can be a source of exquisite erotic pleasure – think of the locked eye contact between two lovers.

Jacques Lacan, the French psychoanalyst, called an important moment in infant development 'the mirror stage or phase'.[13] This is the moment when infants recognise their bodies in mirrors and realise that they are whole beings independent of their parents. (This perception is complicated by the fact that the image is both the child and not the child – that is, it is only a reflection.) Lacan's mirror-phase concept became immensely important to many film theorists because it appeared to be a fundamental moment of identification with an image and seemed to throw light on the unconscious psychic processes involved in the adult experience of the cinematic apparatus.[14]

Many advertisements self-reflexively draw attention to the act of looking involved in perceiving visual images. In one billboard advert for the Silk Cut brand of cigarettes the image consisted of a huge eye: consequently the advert was like a reflection of our eye if we peered closely into a mirror. A 'mosaic' effect was used to fragment the depicted eye in order to delay perception and thus prolong visual pleasure – an idea reinforced by the caption invitation: 'Take the time to enjoy Silk Cut'. The product itself – a carton of cigarettes – was fully integrated into the image and the act of vision by being part of the pupil of the depicted eye. The advertisement's designers solved their brief with brilliance and economy.

Whenever, therefore, we encounter an eye in an image or a film we experience a mirror-like effect and are reminded that our own eyes are engaging in an act of looking. This surely accounts for the powerful shock effect of the woman's eye (actually a dead cow's eye) slit open with a razor in Luis Buñuel's and Salvador Dalí's Surrealist film *Un Chien Andalou* (1929). This gruesome cut is also a metaphor for the act of cutting in editing film that is fundamental to montage.[15]

The number of mirrors that appear in paintings and movies is too large to examine in detail here. Of course, depicted mirrors do not reflect what exists in front of the painting or screen. However, some contemporary artists have made works from reflective materials precisely in order to achieve this. The Italian artist Michelangelo Pistoletto (b. 1933), for instance, made a series of pieces from polished steel plates from 1962 onwards. They were as tall as a human being and rested on the gallery floor; images of anonymous human beings were attached or silk-screened to their surfaces. From a distance the works looked like open doorways. As spectators approached, their images were reflected in the surfaces alongside the anonymous figures. Images of spectators were thus incorporated into the content of the works. Pistoletto succeeded in blurring the distinction between outside and inside, real and fictional spaces.

Finally, look 4, which is that 'exchanged' between depicted characters and spectators. This occurs whenever a depicted character looks directly out of the image towards the viewer, and is frequently found in the genre of portraiture because so many portraits show a person with a full or three-quarter face. An illusion associated with such portraits is that the eyes of the depicted subject seem to follow the viewer when he or she moves. This endows portraits with a quasi-supernatural or uncanny power. When a single viewer confronts a large group portrait in which figures stare out of the canvas, he or she is outnumbered. (Posters and publicity photos of Punk rock bands frequently showed them glaring aggressively at the viewer. Photographs of the British artist Damien Hirst also show him glaring at the viewer.) The cumulative effect of the group's gaze can be quite intimidating.

One of the reasons Manet's painting *Olympia* (1863) aroused such a furore in Paris when it was first exhibited is the frank stare which the naked prostitute gives the presumed male customer.[16] Olympia lies motionless on her bed but, unlike Giorgione's *Sleeping Venus* (c. 1505–10), she is not prepared to close her eyes in order to become a passive object for the male gaze, nor to pretend that the sexual service on offer is anything but a mundane commercial transaction.

During times of war, recruitment posters frequently depict a military man – Lord Kitchener, for instance – with a piercing look reinforced by a pointing arm and finger. There is usually a caption saying 'Your Country Needs You!'. Such aggressive propaganda is a visual example of what Louis Althusser – in his analysis of ideology – called 'interpellation', that is, the subject is being hailed by the power of the state.[17]

In large figure compositions most of the cast of characters interact with one another; in other words, they appear oblivious to the presence of the spectator. European painters often included at least one figure, usually at the margin, who looked out of the picture in order to mediate between those inside and those outside. Velázquez's painting *Surrender at Breda* (1634–5) is an example. Again there is a Manet which makes use of this device: *Déjeuner sur l'Herbe* (1863). On the left is a nude woman who looks out at the viewer while her two fully-dressed male companions are engrossed in conversation. In many adverts and pornographic images a woman being embraced by a man looks not at him but at the viewer as if to say: 'It is you I really prefer.'

As Michael Baxandall has explained, choric figures – minor actors – called 'festaiuolo' performed the same function in Renaissance plays.[18] A direct address to the viewer often occurs in modern plays too – Pirandello's *Six Characters in Search of an Author* (1921) is a case in point – and in Woody Allen's films, and in fictional television series such as the British drama *Lovejoy* (BBC–1), starring Ian McShane as an antique dealer. From time to time the main character faces the camera and comments on the action as a private aside to the viewer. Many people find this device pleasurable because it creates a sense of intimacy between the hero and the viewer, and because it momentarily disrupts the flow and naturalism of the drama.

Las Meninas

A more complex situation arises in the case of Velázquez's *Las Meninas* (1656). The artist has depicted himself at work but looking out of the picture space. We see part of the back of the large canvas which he is paint-ing but we can never be certain what it depicts. (It could either be a por-trait of the King and Queen of Spain or *Las Meninas* itself.) To paint himself Velázquez must have used a mirror and so when we look at *Las Meninas* we stand in the position of artist's mirror reflection which is, in fact, also the position the real Velázquez must have stood to paint *Las Meninas*. However, the viewer is also invited to stand in the shoes of the King Philip IV of Spain and his Queen because they are having their portraits painted. We know this because their reflections appear in a mirror on a far wall behind the artist.

Las Meninas is one of the most ambitious and complex paintings in the whole history of European art. Indeed, it is a 'meta-painting', that is, a painting about the art of painting, a representation about representation.

It has been the subject of a famous analysis by Michel Foucault.[19] In his book *The Order of Things* (1966, French edn; translation London, Tavistock, 1970), an investigation into the human sciences, Foucault argues that 'Man' as an object of knowledge emerged quite late in the development of human thought. During the era of classical culture, pictures did not acknowledge the presence of the person for whom they were made. *Las Meninas*, he considered, exemplified the era of classical representation. That era was surely ending because Velázquez was showing an awareness of the subject standing in front of his picture.

To sum up: the effect of the fourth look is to dissolve, to some extent, the division between the imaginary space inside the image and real space outside. As we have seen, the fourth look can also activate the space in front of the image and make viewers more conscious of the positions they take up.

Surveillance

In societies dominated by religious ideologies, control of the population's behaviour was facilitated by the idea that God was watching and judging everyone all the time. The Christian God's scrutiny was assisted by painted icons, murals and mosaic images showing God or his son Jesus. Icons were present in churches and in virtually all homes. As explained earlier, the eyes in full-face portraits seem to follow viewers when they move. This visual effect reinforced the omniscience of God's gaze. Jean Paris has also pointed out that the gold haloes and backgrounds of these icons reflected the light, thereby dazzling the viewer. The gold surface prevented the viewer from seeing into three-dimensional depth; instead, the real space in front of the icon was activated. Paris writes:

> the third dimension is not to be found at the background of the image but *in front* of it, protruding straightforward as the very Regard of Transcendence itself: we are the third dimension, we are the picture! How to paint God? asked the Byzantines . . . the solution is . . . by inverting the relation between the observer and the observed. By imposing God as an eye, that is, not as an object to be looked at, but as a Subject watching us.[20]

In totalitarian societies dominated by dictators such as Hitler, Stalin, Chairman Mao and Saddam Hussein, the leader's portrait replaced religious icons in homes and schools. Such mass-produced portraits were/are a cheap form of representational surveillance. Governments of liberal, democratic nations are not exempt from the need to monitor and control their populations – particularly groups such as criminals, spies, political dissidents and terrorists. A famous example of this was Jeremy Bentham's 1791 proposal for a prison called 'the Panopticon' (from the Greek word 'panoptes' meaning 'all-seeing'). Prison cells were to be arranged in a circular structure inside which was a central tower for the warders who could observe all the prisoners without themselves being seen. (The Isle of Pines, near Cuba, had a Panopticon-style prison (1932–67) in which Fidel Castro was imprisoned.) During the 1970s Foucault undertook a historical and theoretical study of the type of power, which he called 'panopticism', in a variety of institutions.[21] His bleak conclusion was that a system of surveillance had been established via 'an inspecting gaze', and that individuals would internalise that gaze until they became their own supervisors.

During the nineteenth century the invention and documentary character of photography greatly assisted the authorities in the power they exercised over criminals, revolutionaries and members of the underclass. Photographs were taken of those arrested and filed for later use. The ability of the photograph to be mass-produced eventually resulted in the 'wanted man' poster. Crime scenes and murder victims are now routinely photographed in order to provide evidence for trials.

Today, monitoring of public spaces is assisted by electronic eyes (closed-circuit cameras and video-recorders). The aims are to deter crime and to catch criminals. Television programmes about crime feature video-recordings of robbers caught on camera. The fact that criminals are often identified as a result, surely confirms the correspondence theory of truth. If a person can be recognised from a photograph, then there must be some isomorphism – similarity of form – between the representation and the referent.

In capitalist states, privately owned newspapers and other mass media companies employ hundreds of journalists and photographers who engage in a frenetic pursuit and surveillance of famous people. Many of those subjected to such attention have their lives spoiled. (Of course, some seek publicity and use the magnifying ability of the mass media to become famous.) John Lennon and Yoko Ono were well aware of the intrusive power of the media and so, in 1968, they commissioned Nick Knowland to make a colour film illustrating the process and its effects. Entitled *Rape* (or *Chase*), the film tells the story of an innocent young German woman who is selected at random in London by a film crew, who then follow her relentlessly for three days until she becomes distressed and hysterical.

New forms of technology such as telephoto lenses and Earth-orbiting satellites enhance and mechanise surveillance. In addition, huge quantities of visual information can now be recorded and stored on video, or compact discs or in computer memories. Such data banks can also be accessed over distance by means of communication networks. Radar and other instruments aboard satellites convey millions of bits of information to the ground every second from which beautiful colour images are assembled. The instruments are so sensitive that ocean wave heights and different crops can be detected. Like all technology, satellites can serve positive or negative ends: they can warn about changes in the Earth's atmosphere, help

9 Jamie Wagg, *History Painting: Shopping Mall, 15:42:32, 12/2/93.* Computer-generated electro-static print, 6′ × 4′, (1993–94). Artist's collection. (Print damaged by a scratch.)

In February 1993 the British people were shocked by the brutal murder of the toddler James Bulger by two ten-year-old boys. James's abduction from a shopping mall was recorded on a security videotape. This did not save him but it did help detectives to trace his killers. Jamie Wagg (b. 1958), a British artist who has re-worked media imagery for many years, appropriated the image – it had been reproduced in the mass media countless times – and, after altering it in various ways via computers, he made a large ink-jet, laminated print of it. In May 1994 it was displayed in a mixed exhibition at the Whitechapel Art Gallery. Tabloid press reporters made the work notorious and claimed that Wagg was seeking fame and money. (This charge was the height of hypocrisy because the print media had exploited the abduction image for profit for months.) In fact, Wagg's motive was to make art in the history-painting tradition of Manet and Géricault, that is, art that responds to events of contemporary history rather than events of the distant past.

Given the hysterical reaction of the press to Wagg's print, it seems that it is not acceptable for contemporary artists to make art about contemporary events. His intention was also to use the art gallery context to prompt a slower, more considered reading of the image and what it revealed about British society in the 1990s. In the mass media images appear and disappear with extraordinary rapidity; there is thus little time for reflection. As result of being targeted by the tabloids, Wagg became a figure of hate and received death threats. His print was also vandalised.

Wagg simplified the shopping mall scene to make it even more graphic and iconic, and the lighter areas around the figures of the children were tinged with the colours orange and yellow. A viewer who had no knowledge of the killing that followed the abduction would probably regard the mall picture as very innocuous. Its power to fascinate is surely due to the fact that the three figures seen from the rear walking towards the top edge of the picture are suffused by light. In other words, it has a transcendental quality typical of religious or spiritual paintings in which figures face a heavenly prospect. Implicitly, therefore, it was already an image of death. Wagg's transformations served to enhance this signification.[22]

seafarers, detect fraud by European farmers, assist the military in the prosecution of wars . . .

We are now all watched by electronic eyes to such an extent that some
theorists believe 'a surveillance society' has come into being.[23] While
surveillance has some beneficial social uses, it also makes an Orwellian *1984*,
'Big Brother is Watching You', type of regime a more practical possibility.

Summary

This chapter first discusses the constitution of the various looks and gazes.
Taking 'look' as both a noun and as a verb, it is possible to distinguish
between the notion of an integrated visual appearance, and the construction of different acts of looking.

The chapter touches on voyeurism and narcissism, picking up on the
Lacanian mirror stage, whereby a complex looking at the self is articulated
as an important moment in the development of a child's visuality.

The tensions and anxieties which surround issues to do with the gaze
and the look have nowhere been more apparent than in recent debates
about whether or not we are being turned into a surveillance society,
watched constantly in city centres by closed circuit television, a look
which is ultimately intended to produce docile, self-policing people,
according to Foucault's predictions regarding the Panopticon.

The aim of this chapter, then, is to demonstrate that no act of looking is
innocent, and the student of visual culture should be aware of all the connotations and implications involved.

Notes and further reading

1   S. Hall, 'The Social Eye of *Picture Post*', *Working Papers in Cultural Studies*, 2
    (Spring 1972), 71–120.
2   The main theorist in question is Jacques Lacan. See: *The Four Fundamental
    Concepts of Psychoanalysis*, (New York, Norton, 1978).
3   See writings by Noel Burch, Stephen Heath, Laura Mulvey, Jean Paris and Paul
    Williemen.
4   See G. Simmel, 'Adornment', *Sociology* (1908), reprinted in *The Sociology of Georg
    Simmel*, (New York, Free Press/Macmillan, 1950), pp. 338–44.
5   Unpublished conference paper, Amsterdam School for Cultural Analysis, 1995.
6   R. Schiff, 'Water and Lipstick: De Kooning in Transition', *Willem de Kooning
    Paintings*, essays by David Sylvester and Richard Schiff, catalogue by Marla
    Prather, (Washington, DC, National Gallery of Art/New Haven & London, Yale
    University Press, 1994), pp. 33–73.
7   See: Teresa de Lauretis and Stephen Heath (eds), *The Cinematic Apparatus*,
    (London, Macmillan, 1980). For an overview of film theory about the gaze see:
    Robert Stam and others, *New Vocabularies in Film Semiotics: Structuralism, Post-
    Structuralism and Beyond*, (London & New York, Routledge, 1990), pp. 162–74.
8   J. Rose, *Sexuality in the Field of Vision*, (London, Verso, 1986).
9   J. Paris, *Painting and Linguistics*, (Pittsburgh, PA, Carnegie Mellon University,
    1975).

10   S. Freud, 'Three Essays on Sexuality', in vol. 7 of *The Complete Psychological Works of Sigmund Freud*, (London, Hogarth Press & The Institute of Psychoanalysis, 1953), pp. 156–7; L. Eidelberg, *Encyclopedia of Psychoanalysis*, (New York, Free Press, 1968); G. Malanga (ed.), *Scopophilia: The Love of Looking*, (New York, Van der Marck Editions, 1985).

11   J. L. Connolly, 'Ingres and the Erotic Intellect', *Woman as Sex Object: Studies in Erotic Art 1730–1970*, eds T. B. Hess and L. Nochlin, (London, Allen Lane, 1973), pp. 16–31.

12   R. Humphries, '*Peeping Tom*: Voyeurism, the Camera, and the Spectator', *Film Reader 4: Point of View, Metahistory of Film*, (Evanston, IL, Northwestern University, 1979), pp. 193–200.

13   See: J. Lacan, 'The Mirror Stage as Formative of the Function of the I', *Ecrits: A Selection*, (London, Tavistock, 1977).

14   A succinct summary is supplied by Susan Hayward in *Key Concepts in Cinema Studies*, (London & New York, Routledge, 1996), pp. 149–52, 185–90.

15   A detailed but very difficult analysis of *Un Chien Andalou* is provided by Phillip Drummond, 'Textual Space in *Un Chien Andalou*', *Screen*, 18:3 (Autumn 1977), 55–119.

16   T. J. Clark has given an extended analysis of *Olympia*, the genre of the nude and prostitution in nineteenth-century Paris. He describes Olympia's look as 'candid but guarded . . . blatant and particular' but strangely he also says it is 'unreadable'. *The Painting of Modern Life: Paris in the Art of Manet and His Followers*, (London, Thames & Hudson, 1985), p. 133.

17   L. Althusser, 'Ideology and Ideological State Apparatuses', *Lenin and Philosophy and Other Essays*, (London, New Left Books, 1971), pp. 121–73.

18   M. Baxandall, *Painting and Experience in Fifteenth Century Italy: A Primer in the Social History of Pictorial Style*, (London, Oxford & New York, Oxford University Press, 1972), pp. 72–5.

19   M. Foucault, *The Order of Things: An Archaeology of the Human Sciences*, (London, Tavistock, 1970), pp. 3–16.

20   Paris, *Painting and Linguistics*, p. 39.

21   M. Foucault, *Discipline and Punish*, (Harmondsworth, Middlesex, Penguin Books, 1977).

22   For more on the Bulger case see: Alan Travis, 'Bulger Family Demands Gallery Boycott', *The Guardian*, (26 May 1994), 8; Mark Thomas, *Every Mother's Nightmare: The Killing of James Bulger*, (London, Pan Books, 1993) (this paperback by a Press Association journalist features the shopping mall image on its cover – no one has protested about this use); Sarah Kember, 'Surveillance, Technology and Crime: The James Bulger Case', *The Photographic Image in Digital Culture*, ed. Martin Lister, (London & New York, Routledge, 1995), pp. 115–26.

23   See, for instance, Christopher Dandeker, *Surveillance, Power and Modernity: Bureaucracy and Discipline from 1700 to the Present Day*, (Cambridge, Polity Press, 1990); Oscar Gandy, *The Panoptic Sort: A Political Economy of Personal Information*, (Boulder, CO, Westview Press, 1993); D. Lyon, *The Electronic Eye: The Rise of the Surveillance Society*, (Cambridge, Polity Press, 1994); and Simon Davies, *Big Brother*, (London, Pan Books, 1996).

8 Visual literacy and visual poetics

We believe that visual communication is coming to be less and less the domain of specialists, and more and more crucial in the domains of public communication. Inevitably this will lead to new, and more rules, and to more formal, normative teaching. Not being 'visually literate' will begin to attract social sanctions. 'Visual literacy' will begin to be a matter of survival, especially in the workplace.
(Gunther Kress and Theo van Leeuwen)[1]

Literacy

TO BE LITERATE means being able to read and write; more generally, it means being an educated or learned person. Literacy, therefore, is not an innate ability — it is something children have to be taught over a number of years by parents and teachers. Tests have been devised to measure children's literacy, but what of their *visual* literacy? Is it taught or tested? In Britain it is one of the educational goals of the National Curriculum taught in secondary schools but it seems to have a low priority. In British schools the study of media and fine art occurs in different departments: according to the National Curriculum, media belongs to English and visual literacy to Art.

In Britain visual literacy is not regarded as important as literary literacy. For example, television viewing is routinely blamed for causing a decline in literacy amongst children.[2] The charge reveals that television is deemed inferior to books, and that the ability to 'read' images is valued less than the ability to read words. Television is now the primary medium of mass entertainment in developed nations, and it is also an educational aid in many schools and universities. Logically, therefore, schools should be testing visual skills alongside reading ability.

Watching television is often characterised as a passive activity compared to reading, but the sequences of images on television and in films involve gaps, condensations of time, shifts of location and viewpoint, parallel narratives, etc., that require mental work on the part of the viewer if sense is to be made of them. Again, the relentless flow of television is said to militate against pauses for reflection and the re-reading that books permit. This charge was valid before the invention of the home video-recorder, but now the latter machine enables viewers to replay programmes over and over again, and to 'freeze' images by pressing the pause button.

Books are also said to stimulate the imagination because the reader has to flesh out the words with images. Is this received wisdom correct? Surely it is possible that the images provided by the best television series are superior to those supplied by readers with feeble imaginations? (In any case, the more subtle directors of horror or crime movies and television series do not show everything – they too leave room for the viewer's imagination.) In certain instances the priority given to literary texts results in a distortion of history and art: Shakespeare's plays, for example, were meant to be experienced as live theatre not as words on the page. When performed, the plays provide visual as well as aural pleasures.

Multimedia

The opposition between words and images implied by the difference between literary literacy and visual literacy needs to be questioned. As explained earlier, most contemporary mass media employ more than one medium. During the 1950s American crime and horror comics were criticised for their supposed negative effects on British children. Because these comics were pictorial, they were said to be contributing to illiteracy but, as Martin Barker later pointed out in a book about this moral panic, some of the comic-strip stories contained as many as two thousand words![3] Watching television may not involve much reading of words but it certainly involves exposure to linguistic (and musical) expression. Suppose the worst happened and reading died out altogether. Would this mean a time without culture? No, because there have been many cultures in the history of the world that have been oral. In such cultures memory and story-telling become highly developed.

From the perspective of semiotics – the science of signs – languages and pictures are simply two kinds of sign. Although different in certain respects – readers of English texts have to be content with the colour-word 'orange' whereas viewers of a painting can experience the colour orange – to an extent they overlap. For instance, poetic or rhetorical devices are common to both. Various examples will be considered shortly, but to indicate the way equivalent phenomena can occur in different media we will cite visual effects in pop music videos. These videos are now a familiar example of the combination of words, music and imagery. Advances in video-editing technology during the 1970s and 1980s enabled images to be transformed and manipulated in ways comparable to sounds. Many pop videos provide visual effects that seek to rival musical effects; for instance, a musical echo is a sound that is repeated while reducing in volume. The matching video effect would be an image of, say, a face that was duplicated over and over again while shrinking in size. This particular example occurred in the pop video (directed by Bruce Gowers for Jon Roseman Productions) that promoted Queen's 1975 hit *Bohemian Rhapsody*.[4]

It follows from the above that the study of visual signs can be just as instructive as the study of poetic signs. However, it is not really a question of privileging one or the other because, since the dominant forms of communication are multimedia, it is appropriate to study them in combination.

Contextual knowledge

The visual dimension of visual culture is probably the reason for the low status of visual literacy in our society. Images – particularly photographs – are thought to be easier to assimilate and to be more universal than words in one of humanity's six thousand languages. There is some truth in this view but it does not automatically follow that just because people can see an image they can understand its meaning. This is because codes, conventions and symbols are used in the making of visual artefacts which may not be familiar to the viewers, and because viewers may lack the contextual – cultural and historical – knowledge that is generally required before the subject and content of images can be grasped.[5]

Our lack of contextual knowledge in regard to images is most often exposed when we encounter examples from ancient or foreign cultures, or those made by artists from an ethnic minority to which we do not belong. The more remote the culture, the more learning will be required. However, the acquisition of knowledge necessary to comprehension does not always demand months or years of study. Indeed, it can be acquired quite quickly; for instance, a running joke in a film or a play can easily be learnt during the opening frames or scenes. Or, in the case of a painting or cartoon, by the repetition of a certain motif, device or mannerism across a range of examples (Steve Bell's use of a pair of underpants in his newspaper cartoons of the British Prime Minister John Major is a case in point), or simply by means of information supplied by a caption or in a catalogue essay.

Visual literacy and skills

It is time to distinguish visual skills and literacy from cultural/historical literacy. Most children draw, paint and model consequently they gain some years of experience of making visual artefacts. The early art of children is figurative but does not employ a coherent system of spatial representation such as perspective. Older children are encouraged to make more objective, naturalistic representations by observing and recording a motif, and they are taught perspective. At this point, or shortly afterwards, most teenagers cease to draw and paint.

While children are growing up they are exposed to millions of still and moving images supplied by the mass media. Since the majority of children soon derive meaning from these images, they must have acquired a degree of visual literacy by means of looking. Paul Messaris, the author of a thorough study of visual literacy, argues convincingly that since children learn to see the world before they learn to see images (or in parallel), their ability to interpret images is based on skills derived from real-life visual perception.[6] Although images are two- rather than three-dimensional, and are therefore reductive in terms of the information they supply compared to perceptions of reality, as representations of reality they are not so arbitrary as words (semioticians have distinguished between 'arbitrary' and 'motivated' signs). This is because figurative images are *iconic*: they *resemble* their referents to some extent. Messaris concludes that the ability to see and understand images does not require so much teaching and learning as reading and writing.

According to Messaris, there are four widely held views about visual literary:

1 visual literacy is generally considered to be a prerequisite for comprehending visual media. Paradoxically, it is normally acquired via cumulative exposure to visual media;
2 improving visual literacy is believed to enhance the general cognitive abilities of children, thus helping them to solve other intellectual tasks;
3 improving visual literacy should increase pupils' understanding of the mechanisms of mental and emotional manipulation via visual media, thereby making them more resistant to the persuasive power of political propaganda and commercial advertising;
4 improving visual literacy should deepen aesthetic appreciation. Even though knowledge of how certain visual effects are achieved may dispel their mystery, such knowledge is clearly essential if one wishes to evaluate the artistic skill involved.

One can add a fifth point: improving the visual literacy of students pursuing practical, studio-based degree courses will help them to become more effective professionals. For example, those training to be architects need to become expert in 'reading' plans, sections and elevations, and other systems of projection.

Improving visual literacy

If students are already visually literate when they arrive at university, is there any point in teaching them anything more? The answer is 'yes' because students are unlikely to have a deep understanding of the mechanisms by which meaning is communicated in art and mass media: hence the need for explanations of codes, symbolism, cinematography, montage, editing techniques and pictorial rhetoric.

The need for all of us to learn about new image-making/transforming techniques was demonstrated by the digital revolution. Still and moving pictures can now be reduced to a series of pixels, recorded on CD-roms or scanned into the memory banks of computers and then altered at will to produce seamless, illusionistic results. Of course, it has always been possible to alter photographs by retouching them, but digitisation makes possible pictorial invention on an unprecedented scale. A knowledge of such techniques should make all viewers sceptical of the truth-claims of press photos and of filmed reports on television news programmes.

Most students will be more familiar with the mass media than with avant-garde art. They are likely to need particular help with the visual character of the latter because the content of such art is often deliberately complex and obscure, and because it frequently avoids the use of widely known codes and conventions (that is, those typical of mass culture). In other words, rather than use *public* codes, fine artists often invent *personal* ones. In the case of the art of Joseph Beuys for instance, viewers will need to learn from the artist's biography the particular significance and meaning of the materials fat and felt which featured in his performances and installations. In some instances, artists are unwilling to explain their pictorial symbols: Australian aboriginal artists, for example, have refused to disclose the meaning of all their symbols to outsiders in order to keep some of their tribal culture secret.

Visual literacy involves lifelong learning because radical artists in all media are continually questioning existing codes and conventions, and struggling to invent new ones to communicate new insights. A commonplace visual convention is that humans depicted in pictures are shown the same way up as viewers. An artist who has contradicted this general rule is the German painter Georg Baselitz (b. 1938): since 1969 he has painted his motifs upside-down (a making-strange tactic) and displayed them this way too.

First year students will vary in their existing knowledge and in their visual competence, consequently some initial tests and questionnaires are desirable to discover the extent of their abilities. A series of film clips can be used, for instance, to find out what students already know about film rhetoric and movie-making techniques.

Slide tests

In order to measure improvements in visual literacy as a consequence of their teaching, art historians often set their students slide tests. While being shown slide-images of paintings, sculptures and buildings, students are asked to identify such things as the name and nationality of the creator, date or period of production, medium, art movement, style and genre. Slide tests are thus concerned with the rudiments of connoisseurship – training the eye and honing the skill of attribution. Such tests reveal what students have committed to memory during illustrated lectures and they are, to some extent, tests of visual literacy. However, they are very basic. Asking students to analyse and explain the methods of signification used in an magazine advertisement or a movie extract is probably a more demanding and useful exercise. In the latter case, recent technology is of great value: video playback machines now enable students to view repeatedly a clip from a feature film recorded on video, and to slow it down so that the camera movements and sequence of shots can be closely observed.

Practical exercises

A key objective of Visual Culture Studies is to raise the level of all students' visual literacy. One of the best ways of achieving this is through 'hands-on' practical exercises – for example, operating a film or video camera – and some colleges and universities do provide such practical sessions. However, many do not because they lack equipment and studio facilities in sufficient quantities to meet student demand. Increasingly universities are establishing learning centres (often attached to libraries) which give students access to computers, and visual imagery is more and more to be found on computer screens. Computers are also becoming more interactive so students are able to scan in images and transform them in various ways at the touch of a button.

Even if expensive technology is unavailable, there are still many practical exercises students can undertake at low cost. Everyone has access to paper and pencil and to illustrated magazines, and many have access to still photography cameras, so there is no reason why students should not further their understanding of visual representation and montage by making drawings from nature, by copying existing works of art in galleries, by constructing photomontages, and by taking photographs. Feature films are usually based on scripts but to show the proposed visual sequence of camera shots story-boards are created which consist of a series of drawings or sketches. So, students could try their hand at producing a story-board based on a script or a short story.

'Reading' images

Reading is a mental activity normally associated with the comprehension of written language/printed matter. It is an extended, temporal process: a book can take several hours to read, and understanding the whole will not be possible until the final page has been turned. However, the term 'reading' hardly seems applicable to seeing and understanding a still image because we seem to have the ability to take in the whole of an image in a moment, in a single glance. (Museum visitors are reported to spend only a few seconds looking at each object.) This is certainly true in terms of a simple design such as the swastika flag but in the case of a highly detailed picture, such as Hans Holbein's *Ambassadors* (1533), there is so much to see that a viewer needs to spend far more time than a moment. Furthermore, when a viewer is confronted by multi-panel schemes such as those decorating the interior walls of Italian Renaissance churches, then much time is needed to study the various individual scenes, to connect the sequences of panels that constitute mini-narratives, and finally to relate all the parts to the whole.[7] The same applies to comic strips and graphic novels, and to films and television programmes: a temporal, mental process akin to reading long texts is clearly required.

Of course, not all cultures employ the same order in terms of their arrangement of words or characters on the page. In Western cultures printed words are arranged in horizontal rows and are intended to be read from left to right. Asian calligraphic ideograms and pictograms, in contrast, are arranged in vertical columns and are intended to be read from top to bottom, then right to left. Western comic strips adopt the same left-to-right, horizontal convention of reading typical of lines of type, but Japanese Manga reverse this. In the case of Renaissance church murals with many panels, a left-to-right, horizontal reading order is generally employed but panels are also connected in vertical, diagonal or, in the case of domes, concentric directions. The ability to present spatial connections in any direction simultaneously is one advantage visual art has over literature.

How people look at individual still images has been considered by art historians and scientists. Art historians have been concerned with left and right in pictures (do the eyes enter via the left or the right hand side of pictures?) and they have analysed compositions in order to discover how the viewer's eye is directed around the picture space. Scientists have been able to track the eye movements of people when looking at images. To see at all our eyes have to move constantly (the so-called saccadic eye movements of which we are not conscious) and from time to time they dwell on prominent features of the image such as faces or edges. A viewer's knowledge of a picture is thus built up from a succession of glances which, in part, are determined by the image's forms. So, while no single linear order of reading is imposed upon the viewer, the presence of dominant features will attract the eyes.

In addition, we can consciously direct our gaze. Standing in front of a painting we feel sure we have the freedom to explore it at will. We can stand back to study it as a whole and then focus on one part and then another. Alternatively, we can move closer in order to study details and brushwork. In the case of a long mural or tapestry we have to walk along its length to see it in its entirety and, in the case of sculptures, we have to circle them in order to view them from all sides. However, when we watch films and television we are compelled to surrender our freedom of movement to the camera – we have to go where it goes; we can only look at something for the length of time the camera dwells upon it. This explains why the movements of a rostrum camera – a camera on a stand that is used to explore still images – often irritate viewers of television arts documentaries: the camera meanders in ways we would not have done had we been looking at the original; also, it does not allow us the time we would like to study the image for ourselves.[8]

From work to text

Owing to the strong influence of literary theory and criticism in recent decades, the terms 'reading' and 'texts' have been applied to visual signs in preference to 'seeing' and 'works'.[9] (To some extent this has been unhelpful because of the differences between linguistic and pictorial signs.) Following the supposed 'death of the author', theorists shifted their attention away from writers and their intended meanings towards readers and the meanings they derived from texts. According to Barthes, the text is 'a methodological field . . . the work can be held in the hand, the text is held in language . . . *the Text is experienced only in an activity of production* . . . the Text does not stop at (good) Literature . . . the Text practices the infinite deferment of the signifier . . . the Text is plural . . . the metaphor of the Text is that of *network*'.[10] He also distinguishes between 'readable' and 'unreadable' texts, that is, classic, traditional texts and radical, experimental texts.

A literary text, therefore, is print that has been actualised through the act of reading. All items of visual culture no matter what their medium or aesthetic quality can be considered to be 'texts' that are subject to an endless series of 'readings' on the part of the public, critics and theorists. Reception theorists have expended much effort trying to understand the ideal or implied readers constructed by texts, while empirical researchers have studied how real people read texts, how actual audiences respond to films or television.

Often, when theorists refer to 'a reading' they do not mean reading in the straightforward sense of a person privately assimilating what an author has written but rather a special interpretation of a text by a scholar who then makes it public. Such a reading generally involves analysis via the application of external perspectives such as psychoanalysis, feminism or Marxism.

Ariel Dorfman's and Armand Mattelart's book *How to Read Donald Duck: Imperialist Ideology in the Disney Comic* can serve as an example.[11] It is a powerful indictment of the capitalist, imperialist ideology propagated by Disney comics distributed in South America. The book was first published in Chile in 1971; the authors had to flee the country when the 1973 military coup occurred. Their political critique of Disney stemmed from Marxist and underdeveloped nations' perspectives. (Since their interpretation departs so drastically from what most readers derive from Disney comics, it can be characterised as a 'critical' reading or 'aberrant' or 'oppositional' decoding. We presume the book was intended to benefit teachers and parents of the children who would have been the main consumers of the comics.) One complaint that could be made about their analysis, from a Visual Culture Studies standpoint, is that it focused on content and therefore paid little heed to the specifically visual, formal aspects – drawing style, composition, etc. – of the comics.

Stephen Jay Gould is a biologist who has analysed the appearance of Disney characters over time. Following Konrad Lorenz, he has argued that baby-like features trigger innate releasing mechanisms in viewers designed to make them feel affection for babies. In the case of Mickey Mouse, Gould showed that his appearance became progressively infantile as his character evolved and was softened.[12] In the 1995 Walt Disney Corporation animated feature about the real Native-American princess Pocahontas, not only was history distorted but also the heroine's face was absurdly idealised and cutesified. By such visual means, Disney animators seek to mobilise deep-seated psychic mechanisms in the audience and disarm their critical faculties.

A psychoanalytic 'reading' of Disney productions would no doubt generate yet another interpretation. In the case of a famous visual 'text' that has prompted a series of 'readings' over time, later scholars can profit from the insights, blindness and 'misreadings' of pioneers; they can develop or disagree with what their predecessors have written.[13] It may be that the various 'readings' complement rather than contradict one another. However, when mutually contradictory interpretations occur, the reader is faced by the question: 'Which one is correct, or the most plausible?'

Pictorial rhetoric and visual poetics

Rhetorical devices or 'figures of speech' or 'tropes' are to be found in both poetry and pictures (aside, that is, from abstract works of art).[14] Visual Poetics is one name that has been given to that branch of Visual Culture Studies which examines visual or pictorial rhetoric.[15] Such rhetoric can be found in virtually all kinds of figurative imagery but it is especially evident in publicity, caricatures and political propaganda/photo-montages.

Rhetoric is an ancient type of speech designed to move audiences and to persuade them to accept certain ideas. Today, politicians, advertisers and pressure groups are the main producers of rhetoric. To engage the interest of the public, rhetoricians use language in a non-literal manner. They employ a range of poetic devices – alliteration, metaphors, personifications, hyperbole, etc. – in order to make their ideas vivid and memorable. A number of examples, both verbal and visual, will now be cited.

Simile: in a verbal simile one thing is likened to another: 'My love is *like* a red, red rose.' This figure of thought is extremely common in advertising photography and generally operates within a single frame image via a juxtaposition of two items in such a way that a likeness between them is implied. For example, a cup of coffee and jars of coffee were shown in the foreground of an advert while in the background there were several famous works of art. This arrangement was a visual version of the proposition: 'Our brand of coffee is like a work of art.' The interpretation was confirmed by the accompanying caption. (See also figure 10.)

Metaphor: a stronger form of simile. An identity is asserted between two different things: 'King Richard was a lion in battle'. In an image the identity between two disparate things can be communicated by means of superimposition: the assertion 'Man is a wolf' can be represented by merging a photo of a man with a photo of a wolf. In terms of fashion and comics, a human/animal synthesis is communicated via costumes such as the ones worn by Batman and Catwoman. Contemporary movies often reveal the bestiality of a character by using special effects to show the metamorphosis of a human being into an animal. Light and dark in images are often metaphors for good and evil. The streamlining of forms of designed goods not intended to travel fast is a metaphor for efficiency and modernity.

In films metaphors often occur as a result of viewers perceiving a link between two successive scenes; for example, in the final moments of Hitchcock's *North by North West* (1959) the hero and heroine are about to consummate their marriage in a train couchette. Hitchcock does not show their sexual union directly, instead he cuts from the train's interior to an exterior shot showing the train entering a tunnel. The idea of sexual penetration is thus communicated metaphorically.

Metonymy: change of name: when London was a smoky city people sometimes called it 'The Smoke'; also, cause for effect: smoke as an indication of fire; also, substitution: hippies used to ask: 'I need bread, man' ('bread' being a substitute for 'money' because money could buy bread). In an advertisement for marmalade, slices of orange were piled on top of one another to form the shape of a jar, hence the raw material was substituted for the final product. Van Gogh's painting *Open Bible* (1885) depicts two books: a large Bible and a smaller French novel with a yellow cover. The books stand in for the Christian religion and modern secularism. Those who know the painter's biography will also realise that the Bible stands in for Van Gogh's father and the novel for Vincent himself. Later, in Arles, Van Gogh painted pictures of two differently shaped chairs which served as 'portraits' of their respective users – himself and Paul Gauguin.

Synecdoche: parts that stand for the whole: 'the crown' meaning king-ship; factory workers described as 'hands'. In advertisements for drinks, a bottle is often indicated merely by a cork or bottletop. Cubist paintings are full of pictorial synecdoches because fragments stand in for whole objects; for example, a press clipping or masthead represents the whole newspaper. In paintings like Ford Madox Brown's *Work* one or a few human figures stand as tokens for a type or a social class: three navvies standing in for all manual labourers (they also personify the idea of work); a well-dressed man and woman on horseback standing for the English aristocracy, two intellectuals signifying brainworkers, and so on.

Hyperbole: excesses, exaggerations not intended to be taken literally: 'the basketball star was as tall as a skyscraper'. In advertisements giantism (a huge figure dominates smaller figures) and miniaturisation (a group of tiny people being swept along by a huge yardbrush) are often employed. Exaggeration is a common characteristic of recent automobile television commercials: cars are shown falling from tall buildings and landing undamaged.

Personification: abstract ideas represented in terms of animals or people: 'Theory' represented by Reynolds via a draped woman has already been cited; or capitalism represented by a fat, ugly man with a cigar, wearing a top hat and black frock coat. The gods and goddesses of classical myths were endowed with human qualities, and female figures have repeatedly been used to personify such concepts as liberty, war, peace, the dawn, the nation and the muse of painting. (The answer to the question: 'Why have females been used so much more than males?' is, according to Gombrich, due to a peculiarity of the Greek language. A woman scholar such as Marina Warner may think of other reasons for such a gender bias.[16]) Animism is the primitive belief that all things have their own souls or spirits. Animated cartoon films bring to life all kinds of inanimate objects − toys, trains, etc. − and endow them with energy, and with animal and human personalities.

Symbols: signs or objects that have acquired, through much usage, fixed secondary meanings; for example, the image of a wooden cross shows a Roman tool of execution, but, because Jesus died on one, the cross later became an emblem of Christianity; the skull as an emblem of death. The deities of Greece and Rome were identified by means of particular objects or attributes: thus Cupid is recognisable because of his babyish or boyish body, wings, and his bow and arrows. (There are some symbols that have different meanings in different cultures: the swastika for instance.) Thousands of such symbols exist and there are dictionaries that define and illustrate them.[17] Today many businesses commission designers to invent symbols or 'logos' for the purpose of corporate identity − for example, a stylised figure of Mercury − messenger for the Roman gods − as the emblem of British Telecom. The Scottish artist Ian Hamilton Finlay has pointed out the irony of BT's choice: Mercury is the name of one of its principal competitors!

Allegory: according to a dictionary: 'a figurative treatment of one subject under the guise of another; a presentation of an abstract or spiritual meaning under concrete or material forms; a symbolic narrative'. Thus a painting or a film may tell a story containing a number of related symbols and personifications which together constitute a second, semi-disguised meaning or moral message. Agnolo Bronzino's mannerist masterpiece *Allegory with Venus and Cupid* (1540s) has been interpreted as 'luxury, its disadvantages revealed by time and truth' and also as a warning that the pleasures of love may result in the pain of sexual disease. (For more on this picture see the next chapter.)

In repressive societies artists sometimes resort to allegory as a means of circumventing censorship. Gustave Courbet's huge painting *The Painter's Studio: A Real Allegory Summing up Seven Years of My Artistic Life* (1855) employed disguised symbolism for precisely this reason. However, Courbet's allegory proved to be so obscure that it was not fully decoded until the 1970s.[18]

Although rhetorical figures have been discussed above one at a time, in practice of course most images contain a number of them.

Other poetic devices

In addition to figures of speech, poets and writers employ patterns of sounds and arrangements of words designed to enhance the impact of language. For example: alliteration, antithesis, assonance, quotation,

---

10 [facing page] John Heartfield, *The Gallows Salute*, photomontage published in *Allgemeine Illustrierte Zeitung*, 12:38 (28 September 1933), 643.

Heartfield (1891–1968), a member of the German Communist Party, was on a Nazi death list because of his savage pictorial attacks upon their leaders and movement. During the 1930s his photomontages were published weekly in mass-circulation, Left-wing illustrated magazines printed by means of copperplate photogravure. The original image was sepia in colour not black and white and was produced while Heartfield was in exile in Prague. This particular montage is an example of *visual simile*. The juxtaposition of Hermann Goering giving the Nazi salute and a gallows implies that the salute equals death. What makes the statement visually persuasive is the similarity of the two inverted L-shaped forms. The text on the montage reads: 'In the Hitler salute he raises his arm, Goering, Prussia's top gendarme. His arm is like a gallows, the gallows like his arm, black from fire and stained with blood stretching across Germany. But a court will one day from the highest gibbet hang this gangster!' Goering instigated the Reichstag fire – it is seen burning in the background – as a pretext for outlawing communist rivals. After the Second World War he was tried for war crimes and found guilty, but in the end he cheated the gallows by taking poison in prison in 1946.

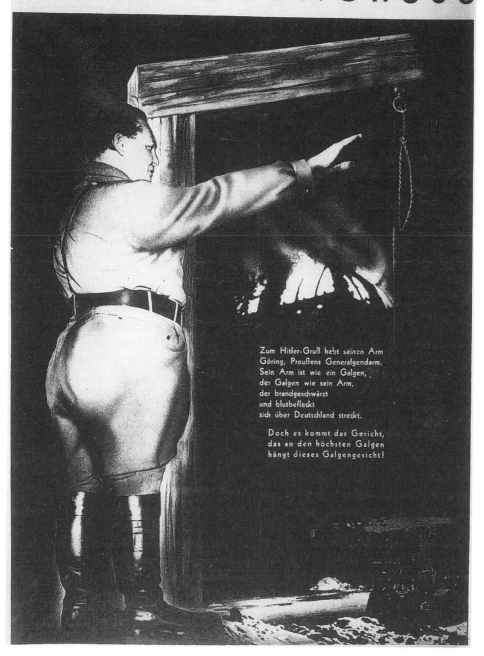

rhyme and paraphrase. For explanations of these and other terms, see hand books on rhetoric such as that by Richard A. Lanham (note 14).

Alliteration, assonance and rhymes involve repetitions of the same or similar sounds which serve to link the various parts of the text together and to endow it with musical rhythms and qualities. Their equivalent in pictures are repetitions or patterns of colours, forms, shapes and brush-marks. In a Walker Evans' photograph of an American petrol station, three men sit in chairs next to three gas pumps: this repetition can be considered to be a visual rhyme.

Antithesis means 'opposition, contrast'. Margaret Bourke-White's famous photograph *At the Time of the Louisville Flood* (1937) showing a line of Afro-Americans waiting for food and water in front of a billboard image of a happy white family in a car is remarkable for the number of contrasts it contains: blacks/whites, individuals/family, poor/affluent, passive/active, careworn/carefree, pedestrians/car owners, facing to the side/facing to the front, below/above, documentary-genre photo/advertising genre photo.[19]

Chiasmus means 'crossing'. Two phrases are juxtaposed; the order of words in the first is reversed in the second: 'It's not the men in my life that count – it's the life in my men' (Mae West). According to Hammond and Hughes, Magritte's painting *Maternity* (c. 1935) is an example of visual chiasmus. The picture shows a mother and child but their heads have been transposed, they have crossed over on to the wrong bodies.

Other literary techniques such as quotation and paraphrase are also commonplace in the visual arts. For example, Van Gogh 'paraphrased' Rembrandt's *The Raising of Lazarus* when, in 1890, he rendered it in his own style; the Italian neo-realist painter Renato Guttuso directly 'quoted' paintings by Mondrian and Van Gogh in some of his pictures. Manet's references to earlier pictures were generally more subtle: he borrowed compositions from the past as a sly way of paying homage to tradition while simultaneously legitimating the modern elements he was also introducing. Quotes and allusions to other images all fall under the general rubric of *intertexuality*. Contemporary popular movies such as *Independence Day* (1996) are generally full of borrowings and references to other films belonging to the same genre, in this case science fiction. Intertextuality increases audiences' enjoyment by mobilising their existing knowledge, by treating them as sophisticated viewers.

Double meanings

Humans use plain language for mundane, utilitarian purposes but they also treat language in a creative, light-hearted way by inventing words, stories and jokes, and by making plays on words. Because words can be read by the eyes and heard by the ears, various kinds of double meanings can arise, for example, puns, homophones, homonyms and double entendres. As Paul Hammond and Patrick Hughes have demonstrated, equivalent double meanings can be found in images and sculptures.[20] Artists achieve double meanings by such methods as superimposition or overlapping (two men greet a young woman; the anonymous artist places them so that their bald heads seen from the rear occupy the position of the woman's breasts); by juxtaposition (in a Thomas Rowlandson drawing a cannon's barrel is placed next to a man's crotch so that it protrudes like an enormous penis); by constructing one figure from many smaller figures (Giuseppe Arcimboldo's well-known paintings of librarians made from books, peasants made from fruit and vegetables, etc.). A sculpture can be thought of as having a front and a back: this means that a carving can be a female goddess from the front and a phallus from the back.

Images have been devised that are ambiguous because they have two referents; for instance, the same drawing can be interpreted as either a rabbit or a duck. (The viewer oscillates between the two readings.) In some instances, the second meaning of such figures can be seen only if the image is inverted or turned on its side.

Summary

Exposure to the mass media means that most adults possess a measure of visual literacy; consequently there might seem to be no need for them to try and improve it. Yet the practised and informed eye will see more. Readers and viewers do not need to be able to name rhetorical figures in order to gain meaning and enjoyment from texts and pictures; nevertheless, such knowledge enhances appreciation and is of value to writers and artists because it gives them greater awareness of, and command over, their creative resources.

By referring students to dictionaries of rhetoric and visual symbols we may have given the impression that understanding an image is simply a question of making a list and looking them up, but matters are rarely so straightforward because of the way artists inflect and combine different symbols. A 1996 television documentary concerning the meaning of Botticelli's famous *Primavera* (painted between 1470 and 1490) – about whose origins little is known – revealed that a range of art historians disagreed about the content and meaning of the picture.[21] There were several, possible explanations: first, contemporary art historians are visually incompetent; second, Botticelli was a poor communicator; and third, the painting is an 'open' text in the sense that its contents are undecidable.

Notes and further reading

1   Gunther Kress and Theo van Leeuwen, *Reading Images: The Grammar of Visual Design*, (London & New York, Routledge, 1996), pp. 2–3.

2   If the advent of television has caused a decline in reading, one wonders why there are now more new book titles published annually in Britain and the United States than ever before (in 1995 the figure for new titles in Britain was 80,000 and the figure for English-language book titles in print was 675,000), and why there are now so many books tied to television series? There is evidence that television stimulates reading: the appearance of Kenneth Clark's 1969 *Civilisation* series in the United States prompted sales of at least a million copies of his book with the same title. Since John Berger's BBC series *Ways of Seeing* appeared in 1972, the paperback associated with the programmes has sold nearly half a million copies and it is still in print. Since the 1950s British television has encouraged people to read about archaeology, astronomy, cookery, gardening, history, technology and the arts.

3   M. Barker, *A Haunt of Fears: The Strange History of the British Horror Comics Campaign*, (London & Sydney, Pluto Press, 1984).

4   Michael Shore, *The Rolling Stone Book of Rock Video*, (London, Sidgwick & Jackson, 1985), p. 56.

5   Richard Andrews writes: 'meaning in fact derives from the whole composition with a social context. There is a danger that a visual literacy based on a syntax of art will look only within the frame, not at the nature of the frame and what that suggests about the relationship of signs within the frame to those without it.' *The Nature of 'Visual Literacy': Contiguities and Convergence between Art, English and IT* (unpublished paper, 1995), p. 3. See also his article: 'Visual Literacy in Question', 20:20, 4 (Spring 1996), pp. 17–20.

6   P. Messaris, *Visual 'Literacy': Image, Mind, and Reality*, (Boulder, CO, Westview Press, 1994). See also David Allen, 'Teaching Visual Literacy – Some Reflections on the Term', *Journal of Art & Design Education*, 13:2 (1994), 133–43. Allen reports giving a paper to the 'International Visual Literacy Association' in 1990.

7   Illuminating analyses of multi-panel murals in Italian Renaissance churches are given by Catherine King and Charles Harrison in television arts programmes made for the Open University.

8   On the workings of the rostrum camera see: John A. Walker, *Arts TV: A History of Arts Television in Britain*, (London, Paris & Rome, Arts Council & John Libbey, 1993), pp. 62–5.

9   On reading see: John Fiske and John Hartley, *Reading Television*, (London, Methuen, 1978); Wolfgang Iser, *The Act of Reading: A Theory of Aesthetic Response*, (Baltimore, Johns Hopkins University Press/London & Henley, Routledge & Kegan Paul, 1979); U. Eco, *The Role of the Reader: Explorations in the Semiotics of Texts*, (London, Hutchinson, 1981); E. Freund, *The Return of the Reader: Reader-Response Criticism*, (London, Methuen, 1987); Neil Cummings (ed.), *Reading Things*, (London, Chance Books, 1993).

10   R. Barthes, 'From Work to Text' (1971), *Image–Music–Text*, (London, Fontana/Collins, 1977), pp. 155–64.

11   A. Dorfman and A. Mattelart, *How to Read Donald Duck: Imperialist Ideology in the Disney Comic*, (New York, International General, 1975).

12   S. J. Gould, 'A Biological Homage to Mickey Mouse', *The Panda's Thumb: More Reflections in Natural History*, (New York & London, Norton, 1982), pp. 95–107; see also: Oliver Bennett, 'Dark Side of the Toon', *Observer Review*, (10 September 1995), p. 8.

13   See, for example, John A. Walker's essay 'Art History versus Philosophy: The Enigma of the Old Shoes', *Van Gogh Studies: Five Critical Essays*, (London, JAW Publications, 1980), pp. 61–71. This essay was a contribution to a discussion about the content of a painting by Van Gogh following interpretations by Martin Heidegger, Meyer Schapiro and Jacques Derrida.

14 For a list of rhetorical figures see: Richard A. Lanham, *A Handlist of Rhetorical Terms: A Guide for Students of English Literature*, (Berkeley & Los Angeles, University of California Press, 1969).

15 See: Stephen Bann (ed.), 'Visual Poetics', *20th Century Studies*, 15/16 (December, 1976); B. A. Uspensky, 'Structural Isomorphism of Verbal and Visual Art', *Poetics*, 5 (1972), 5–39; Meyer Schapiro, *Words and Pictures: On the Literal and Symbolic in the Illustration of a Text*, (The Hague & Paris, Mouton, 1973). On pictorial rhetoric see: Gui Bonsiepe, 'Persuasive Communication: Toward a Visual Rhetoric', *Uppercase*, 5 (1961), 19–34; E. H. Gombrich, 'Visual Metaphors of Value in Art', *Meditations on a Hobby Horse, and Other Essays on the Theory of Art*, (London, Phaidon Press, 1963), pp. 12–29; Gui Bonsiepe, 'Semantic Analysis', *Ulm*, 21 (April 1968), 33–7; Victor Burgin, 'Art, Common Sense and Photography', *Camerawork*, 3 (1976), 1–2; R. Barthes, 'Rhetoric of the Image', *Image–Music–Text*, (London, Fontana/Collins, 1977), pp. 32–51; Harold Evans, *Pictures on the Page: Photo-Journalism, Graphics and Picture Editing*, (London, Heinemann, 1978); W. J. T. Mitchell, *Picture Theory: Essays on Verbal and Visual Representation*, (Chicago, University of Chicago Press, 1994).

16 E. H. Gombrich, 'Personification', *Classical Influences on European Culture AD 500–1500*, ed. R. R. Bulger, (Cambridge, Cambridge University Press, 1971), pp. 247–57. See also: M. Warner, *Monuments and Maidens: The Allegory of the Female Form*, (London, Weidenfeld & Nicolson, 1985).

17 On symbols see: George Ferguson, *Signs and Symbols in Christian Art*, (New York, Oxford University Press, 1954); Arnold Whittick, *Symbols, Signs and their Meaning*, (London, Leonard Hill, 1960); J. E. Cirlot, *A Dictionary of Symbols*, (London, Routledge & Kegan Paul, 1962); C. G. Jung (ed.), *Man and His Symbols*, (London, Aldus Books, 1964); Philip Thompson & Peter Davenport, *A Dictionary of Graphic Clichés*, (London, Pentagram Design, 1977); James Hall, *Dictionary of Subjects and Symbols in Art*, (London, John Murray, rev. edn 1979); Barbara G. Walker, *The Woman's Dictionary of Symbols and Sacred Objects*, (San Franciso, CA & London, Harper & Row, 1988); James Hall, *Illustrated Dictionary of Symbols in Eastern and Western Art*, (London, John Murray, 1994); Jennifer Speake, *The Dent Dictionary of Symbols in Christian Art*, (London, Dent, 1995).

18 See Hélène Toussaint, 'The Dossier on *The Studio* by Courbet', *Gustave Courbet 1819–1877*, (London, Arts Council of Great Britain/Royal Academy of Arts, 1978), pp. 249–85.

19 For a more detailed analysis of this photograph see: John A. Walker, 'Reflections on a Photograph by Margaret Bourke-White', *Creative Camera*, 167 (May 1978), 148–9.

20 P. Hammond and P. Hughes, *Upon the Pun: Dual Meaning in Words and Pictures*, (London, W. H. Allen, 1978). See also: Patrick Hughes and George Brecht, *Vicious Circles and Infinity: An Anthology of Paradoxes*, (London, J. Cape, 1976); and Eli Kince, *Visual Puns in Design: The Pun used as a Communication Tool*, (New York, Watson Guptill, 1982).

21 Agnieszka Piotrowska, *Primavera, Myths or Fingerprints*, (Channel 4 television, 14 September 1996). See also: Veronica Horwell, 'Oh No it Isn't', *The Guardian*, (14 September 1996), 6.

9   Modes of analysis

TO ASSIST the interpretation of the meanings of images and other cultural products, theorists have developed various modes of analysis, some of which this chapter will summarise. While certain analyses focus upon the internal structure of a single object or 'text', others involve examining many similar examples, that is, they are *comparative* in character. Amongst the latter are studies of influence and genre.

City dwellers daily encounter a plethora of visual signs which, in the main, they can decipher. (This does not mean, of course, that their reactions to signs will be identical. Many black viewers watching a video-recording of white police beating a black suspect will respond differently from many white viewers.) Since many of these signs are part of their own culture, there is no need to subject them to 'a close reading', to a *conscious*, *systematic* analysis. However, the existence of books with titles like *Decoding Advertisements* and *Interpreting Contemporary Art* indicates that there are certain signs which do require deliberate analysis.

Form and content

Modes of analysis can be divided into two kinds: those that focus upon *content* and those that focus upon *form*. (This distinction is a long-standing but problematical one. A representational work of art is a synthesis of both form and content consequently they can only be separated in the realms of thought and criticism.) A picture, we say, is *of* something, therefore, content is the substance or purport contained within a representation. There are two, principal sources for content: first, real events, scenes and people (fact); and second, the human imagination (fiction); mixtures of the two are sometimes referred to as 'faction' and 'drama-documentaries'.

The words 'content' and 'subject matter' are often used interchangeably, but a difference between them can be discerned: the subject matter of the art collection of the Imperial War Museum, London, is war in general; the content of individual pictures is more specific; for example, the Battle of the Somme. Many art history books collocate imagery according to subject matter: there are volumes on animals in art, violence in the movies and so forth. One danger of this approach is that authors write about the images as if they were transparent windows on the world. In other words, there is a danger of ignoring the role of form, technique and the medium of representation. There are other books which collocate examples according to formal characteristics; for example, John Gage's *Colour and Culture: Practice and Meaning from Antiquity to Abstraction* (London, Thames & Hudson, 1993).

Some buildings and designed goods are representational – a church whose plan is the shape of a cross, a cheese dish in the shape of a country cottage, for example – but the majority are not. In the case of architecture and design, therefore, the equivalent of content is *function* (hence the slogan 'form follows function').

Most content analysts distinguish between *manifest* and *latent* content. The former refers to the depiction of objects – shoes, for example – that are recognised by the majority of viewers. Shoes perform everyday, practical functions, but they can also serve as sexual symbols and fetish objects. If a shoe-drawing conveys the latter meanings, then this is latent content. Roland Barthes coined the terms 'denotation' and 'connotation' to distinguish between first-level (literal) and second-level (associational) meanings. (The number of personal associations an image or object can evoke is such that no theorist can account for them all.) These in turn gave rise to a third level of meaning Barthes called 'myth'. As we shall discover shortly, there is a close parallel between Barthes's ideas and the art-historical mode of analysis called iconography and iconology.

Content analysis

This is an empirical, quasi-scientific procedure, popular with mass media theorists, which is essentially a quantitative operation involving measuring and counting.[1] Measurement can be undertaken by very simple means: a media analyst who wished to discover the importance the daily press gave to a particular event (that is, its news-value) could take a ruler and measure the column inches the event was allocated in various newspapers. Of course, such measurements would give no indication of the *quality* of comment in the articles concerned. To measure quality a scale of values would have to be drawn up and then applied.

A series of pictorial advertisements for kitchens could be gathered from American magazines published during 1996 – an initial problem is determining the size of the sample to be analysed – and then the questions posed: 'How often are women featured compared to men? In pictures showing both sexes which is dominant? Who is shown doing the cooking and washing up? How often is a nuclear family shown? How often are members of ethnic minorities represented?' Countable units have to be identified which other researchers could use to repeat the test and check the validity of the findings.

In the case of an illustrated history of fashion the following question could be asked: 'What nations' clothes are represented and in what proportions?' The question could be answered by counting the number of pictures that showed Italian clothes, Japanese clothes, etc., and then arranging the resulting figures in a most-to-least table. Once such data has been gathered it still needs to be interpreted: if French fashion was 'top of the league' this could have been due to the fact that the author was French or that France dominates the fashion industry. A 'symptomatic' reading of the book, that is, one that searches for gaps and absences, would reveal those nations whose fashions were excluded.

Feminist artists, in order to discover the extent of their exclusion from the male-dominated art world, have counted the number of women artists represented in museum collections, in the 'stables' of private galleries, and in group exhibitions. Guerrilla Girls (1984–), an American band of feminist artists/activists who wear gorilla masks in order to remain anonymous, have often employed statistics derived from such content analyses. For example: 'Only 4 of the 42 artists in the Carnegie International exhibition are women. Why in 1987 is Documenta [a massive international exhibition held in Kassel, Germany] 95% white and 83% male? Less than 5% of the artists in the Metropolitan Museum's Modern art sections are women, but 85% of the nudes are female.' Such information has been of value in supporting the arguments of feminist artists and in reducing discrimination against them.

While the results of content analysis often confirm existing intuitive impressions, they have the advantages of objectivity, precision and verifiablity. Comparisons made between statistics derived from content analyses of the mass media and statistics derived from real life have often exposed striking differences. For example, on television far more murders are depicted than actually take place. Content analysis is thus one way of revealing the distortions of reality found in media representations.

Iconography and iconology

Both these words begin with the word 'icon', which is derived from a Greek term meaning 'likeness', 'image' or 'picture'. 'Graphy' means 'writing', so iconography is literally 'writing about images'. 'Ology' means 'science', consequently 'iconology' is 'the science of images'. Erwin Panofsky claimed that the difference between the two is that iconography is 'descriptive and classificatory', whilst iconology is 'interpretative'. He further defined iconography as 'that branch of the history of art which concerns itself with the subject matter or meaning of works of art, as opposed to their form'.[3] Since Panofsky was concerned with *figurative* images, iconographic analysis seems inapplicable to abstract art and to most architecture (only a minority of buildings resemble something).

When art critics refer to an artist's iconography, they mean the motifs that habitually recur in his or her work. In the case of Francis Bacon's paintings we can list metal cages, dangling tassels, screaming heads and splatters of blood. We have only to think of the role that guns, horses, cattle-drives, cowboy and Native-American dress, saloons and so on play in Westerns to realise how significant iconography in this sense can be.

Iconographic analysis is practised by most living art historians and film critics but it is a method particularly associated with such European scholars as Emile Mâle, Aby Warburg, Panofsky, Fritz Saxl, Edgar Wind and Ernst Gombrich. (See also Pamela Tudor-Craig's television series: *The Secret Life of Paintings*, BBC-2, 1986.) Historically, iconographic analysis developed during the nineteenth and twentieth centuries as a corrective to the formalist approach to art. Panofsky is the art historian who has explained the method most fully, in a famous 1939 essay, so his ideas are summarised here.

Panofsky identified three levels or kinds of content: first, primary or natural subject matter; second, secondary or conventional subject matter; and third, intrinsic meaning or content. So, there is a movement from surface appearances to depth understandings. At the first level viewers recognise that configurations of line and colour on a canvas depict human beings, animals, houses and so forth. Panofsky contended that all observers needed to understand level one was practical experience of the world: a picture was comprehensible because it depicted things already familiar to us. (Sometimes in old paintings there are utensils which are no longer in use and therefore we do not recognise them.)

Level one Panofsky subdivided into A, 'factual', and B, 'expressional'. By 'factual' he meant the recognition that a painted apple was indeed an apple, and by 'expressional' he meant the way it was painted. Here Panofsky acknowledged the part played by handling, technique or style in the communication of meaning. (In some modern paintings by Frank Auerbach and Leon Kossoff the pigment is so thick and the brushwork so emphatic that objects and figures are hard to discern.)

For Panofsky, the relation between pictorial representations and an external reality was not a matter of much concern because his main interest was in the meanings of images not their realism or truth. Of course, for analysts of realist artworks, documentary photographs, films and television programmes, the question of truth is important. One reason why Panofsky was not interested in the representation/reality issue was that his focus was Renaissance art, and this kind of art was primarily inspired by literary texts. Renaissance artists did draw from life and painted portraits of their contemporaries, but mostly their themes derived from the Bible, classical history and myth. Often, patrons devised 'programmes' for the artists to work from. Confronted by pictures whose theme is unfamiliar, the iconographer's instinct is to search for the text or programme that the artist used.

Iconography proper begins with level two, secondary or conventional subject matter, that is, the realisation that the female figure holding the golden apple (an attribute) in Bronzino's *Allegory with Venus and Cupid* (figure 11) is not just any woman but a personification of Venus, the Roman goddess of love and beauty; that the young boy kissing her with wings sprouting from his back and a quiver of arrows is her son Cupid, another Roman god of love; that the old man pulling back a curtain is a personification of Father Time; and so on.[4]

The first requirement of iconography, therefore, is accurate identification of such personifications and attributes. If they are wrongly identified then the picture's meaning will be misunderstood. (We have all had the experience of misreading something and then discovering our mistake, hence the validity of the distinction between 'correct' and 'incorrect' readings.) In some old reproductions of the Bronzino there is a plant obscuring the buttocks of Cupid and a cloth covering the genitals of Venus. The danger of relying on iconographic analysis alone is demonstrated by the fact that the plant was a later addition designed to reduce the eroticism of the image (it was removed in 1958 when the painting was cleaned). Art historians who did not realise the plant was a later addition might have tried to identify it and interpret it as part of Bronzino's allegory. Iconographic analysis needs, therefore, to be supplemented by other techniques such as dating, X-raying and pigment analysis.

What then do modern viewers need in order to grasp the content of the Bronzino? A knowledge of classical mythology, plus the intellectual topics discussed in the immediate circle of the artist in question. Bronzino scholars believe the painter was friendly with a poet, philosopher and historian called Benedetto Varchi who is known to have written and lectured on the pleasures and pains of love consequently it may have been one of Varchi's texts which constituted the programme for Bronzino's painting.

Panofsky's third level – intrinsic meaning or content – was defined as 'those underlying principles which reveal the basic attitude of a nation, a period, a class, a religious or philosophical persuasion'. Whereas iconography was *analytic*, iconology was *synthetic*. It considered the work of art as a whole and as a symptom of the personality of its creator and/or as a historical document of the culture or civilisation of which it was a manifestation. For example, in relation to the Bronzino, Panofsky wrote: 'That alluring sexual voluptuousness rather than other forms of evil should be selected at this particular date to symbolise vice, is perfectly in harmony with the spirit of Counter Reformation.' So, he interpreted the artistic meaning of this non-Christian image as a symptom of Catholic religious attitudes at a certain period in history.

The iconologist must be able, therefore, to bring to bear knowledge derived from other fields of enquiry – social history, religion, philosophy and politics – in order to treat it as a symptom of the wider culture. As

11 Agnolo Bronzino, *Allegory with Venus and Cupid* (1540s), Oil on panel, 146 × 116 cm. London, National Gallery.

As the eye penetrates the space of this luxurious and seductive painting there is a transition from light to dark, from pleasure to pain. Discarded masks signify a process of unmasking. Two nude, mythical gods of love dominate the foreground: Venus is shown disarming her son Cupid. Although a number of scholars have researched this painting, the precise meaning of its allegory remains uncertain because of disagreements concerning the identity of some of the marginal figures, especially the screaming female figure behind Cupid. One historian has claimed that she personifies jealousy. Another says she symbolises syphilis and that therefore the picture was a kind of health warning: time (Father Time, top right) reveals that the sweetness of love and sex is following by suffering.

Panofsky put it: 'It is in the search for intrinsic meanings or content that the various humanistic disciplines meet on a common plane.'

Iconologists tend to assume that artists were unaware of the larger meanings and significances of their work at the time they made it. Panofsky wrote: 'The discovery and interpretation of these "symbolical" values (which are often unknown to the artist himself and may even emphatically differ from what he consciously intended to express) is the object of what we may call "iconology" as opposed to "iconography".' Difficult theoretical issues arise in relation to artistic intention. (Literary theorists speak of the 'intentional fallacy'.[5]) There may be no information external to the work available as to intention because, in many instances, the makers of artefacts are unknown. (Of course, in the case of living artists, intentions can be ascertained via interviews.) Viewers may try to deduce the artists' intentions from the works themselves, but this is problematic because the artists may have failed to realise their intentions.

Panofsky's method was multi-layered and complex because this accorded with the character of the paintings he studied. High Renaissance paintings such as Bronzino's *Allegory* were not simple images with crude messages addressed to a popular audience; they were complicated communications designed for the educated humanists who belonged to the ruling strata of European society. Bronzino, for instance, worked for the Florentine court of Cosimo I, and the latter sent the *Allegory* to the King of France as a diplomatic gift.

So, the methods of iconography and iconology need to be supplemented by historical research that considers patronage, intellectual milieu and audience. Scholars need to ask: 'What meanings and social functions did the pictorial signs have for the public at the time they were produced?' The Bronzino still exists today and so its warnings about the pleasures and pains of love and sex may still be relevant to modern viewers. The sexual disease to worry about now, of course, is AIDS rather than syphilis.

Mythologies

Roland Barthes's celebrated collection of essays *Mythologies* (1972) contains an analysis of a magazine cover photograph. Like Panofsky's, Barthes's decoding procedure also moves from surface to depth, and it too may be said to engage in the practice of iconology in the sense that it treats the photo's meaning as a symptom of French society.[6] The magazine in question was *Paris-Match* 326 (25 June–2 July 1955) and the cover photo showed a young black soldier wearing a French uniform saluting with his eyes uplifted. This description of manifest content is the *denotational* level of the image. According to Barthes, the *connotational* meanings that it evoked were: 'France is a great empire . . . all its sons, without any colour discrimination, faithfully serve under its flag . . . there is no better answer to the detractors of an alleged colonialism than the zeal shown by this Negro in serving his so-called oppressors'. For Barthes, the photograph embodied a myth which repressed the historical truth of French imperialism and racism, and which surreptitiously served Right-wing propaganda purposes. Myth, Barthes argued, transformed history into nature; he described it as 'depoliticised speech'. In the 1950s Barthes thought it was the duty of critical theorists to analyse and denounce such myths.

Both Panofsky and Barthes wanted to uncover the latent or 'unconscious' meanings of images. However, while Panofsky, the apolitical art historian, sought to recover the meanings of historic paintings for the enlightenment of modern viewers, Barthes, the politically motivated semiologist, sought to expose the reactionary messages of mass communications in order to counter dominant ideology. Neither theorist was concerned about the aesthetic quality of the images they scrutinised.

Genre and type analyses

'Genre' is a French word meaning 'species, kind or sort'. A genre is a classification or grouping of artworks that share certain iconographic elements, themes and stylistic conventions.[7] It provides an artistic context within which the meanings of works can be understood and compared. However, genre is not merely an analytical category of value to critics and audiences, it is also a creative resource as far as artists are concerned.

Genres occur in various art forms – literature, painting and the cinema. Those of painting include history-pictures, the nude, portraiture, animal pictures, landscapes and still lives (this sequence constitutes a hierarchy because some subjects were deemed more important than others). Within the discourse on painting, the term 'genre' also has a more specialised meaning, that is, paintings – usually Dutch seventeenth-century – depicting humble or low-life scenes.

Familiar cinematic genres are: film noir, the Western, musical, horror and melodrama. As the name 'film noir' indicates, some genres are marked by formal/stylistic characteristics; in this instance, crime movies shot in black-and-white in such a way as to stress shadows, blackness or darkness. Film theorists maintain that certain genres are gendered in their appeal for instance, Westerns are masculine and melodramas are feminine. Like natural species, genres have life cycles: they emerge and evolve; they can also lose credibility and even disappear altogether. Once established, genres are subject to self-reference and parody; and when a number of genres exists they can be combined: the musical/Western for instance. Theorists discuss the character, origins and evolution of genres in general and the relation of individual works to the genre to which they belong.

In the case of architecture and design, the equivalent to genre is *type*, that is, building-types such as airports, hospitals, bungalows, museums, and product-types such as cars, chairs and telephones.[8]

Form and style analyses

The term 'form' generally encompasses such phenomena as materials, colours, lines, lighting, tonal values, forms or shapes, space, structures, textures, techniques and composition. Formalist art historians concentrate on these phenomena.[9] Some reduce complex paintings to simple diagrams in order to clarify compositional dynamics. Such analyses are essential to the appreciation of works of art, but critics who ignore content altogether provide only partial accounts.

Some theorists claim that content determines form, and that form changes over time as a result of social changes. (Technological developments also facilitate formal innovation.) Others argue for a unity or harmony of form and content.[10] An example of the *interdependence* of form and content can be found in the art of Van Gogh: when painting peasants digging and ploughing he used thick brown pigment with emphatic brushmarks on the 'field' of his canvas to echo the earth and the furrows of the fields the peasants were cultivating.[11] Thus the material and manner of execution reinforced the picture's content and the artist's labour was equated with that of the peasantry.

Film theorists have paid much attention to cinematography and the use of lighting and colour in the cinema. Some mass media analysts have also investigated such formal matters as camera angles by empirical means. They have, for example, studied – via questionnaires – the responses of viewers to a television presenter speaking direct to camera and the same person seen from a three-quarter viewpoint. Somewhat surprisingly, viewers found the three-quarter viewpoint made the presenter seem more trustworthy.[12]

Graphic signs such as maps and diagrams have real referents but, in addition, their formal characteristics are capable of communicating a set of values in a manner comparable to the abstract paintings of Mondrian. For instance, the geometric network of lines with hard edges and saturated colours in Harry Beck's design for the London Underground Diagram embodies such values as clarity, order, rationality, purity, and economy.[13] Such values surely derive from the realities of visual perception.

Consideration of handling, technique, manner of expression, that is to say *how* something is said rather than *what* is said, brings us to the contentious notion of style. Some scholars define a style in terms of a set of formal characteristics but others argue that a style is always a specific combination of content and form. In certain instances style has been defined as a spiritual force. Styles cut across the differences between art forms and media: a wide variety of artefacts/buildings can be grouped together according to shared styles such as the Baroque and Art Nouveau. Like genres, styles are historical phenomena and have limited lifespans. Exceptionally, some styles are imitated and revived so regularly that they never seem to die. (Classicism is a case in point.) Some scholars assume there is one style per age and they write histories of art consisting of a sequence of styles. Other scholars argue that, normally, several styles co-exist within one culture. Marxist art historians like Frederick Antal have explained the co-existence of different styles by pointing to the presence of different factions within dominant social classes.[14] Nicos Hadjinicolaou has claimed that styles are the 'visual ideologies' of particular classes.[15]

Style is such a complex concept that it has prompted many theoretical debates concerning its nature, the causes of stylistic change and the relationships between style and fashion, styles and societies. The more recent term 'lifestyle' is also much discussed in texts on design, subcultures and consumer culture.[16]

Semiotic analysis

The science of semiotics has a much wider scope than other modes of analysis because it studies the life of all signs within society. It became fashionable (along with structuralism) in academic circles during the 1960s and 1970s, especially in France and Italy.[17] An International Association of Semiotics was founded in 1969 and several scholarly journals were established including *Semiotica*, *Versus* and the *American Journal of Semiotics*. Other magazines featuring articles applying semiotics to different kinds of material were *Communications*, *Tel Quel* (Paris), *Cultural Studies* (Birmingham) and *Screen* (London).

The word 'semiotic' derives from the Greek 'semeion' meaning 'sign'. Initially, on the continent of Europe, 'semiology' was preferred to 'semiotic' but international agreement was later reached in favour of the latter term. Various thinkers have made use of the term: John Locke in the seventeenth century, Charles S. Peirce and Ferdinand de Saussure in the late nineteenth century. However, the majority of semiotic studies date from the second half of the twentieth century. Peirce defined a sign as 'something which stands to somebody for something in some respect or capacity'. Hence a sign can stand for something which exists but which is absent, that is, a real referent (for example a photograph of a living person), or something which exists only in the human mind (fairies, for example). All sign systems can be used to make truthful statements but they can also be used to lie or to construct fictional worlds.

Any process of communication or experience of meaning involves signs; consequently semiotic research encompasses such diverse phenomena as gestures and facial expressions, clothes, diagrams, comics, films, photographs, buildings, etc., etc. As a result, some theorists have maintained that semiotics is the 'science' best qualified to disclose 'the logic of culture'.

Human language has been the sign system most studied during recent centuries; consequently linguistics has tended to serve as the model for all other branches of semiotics, even those concerned with visual signs. Saussure was the linguist who introduced the terms 'signifier' and 'signified' (the two constituent elements of a sign). The signifier is the material dimension of a sign, for example, the sound of the word 'cat' or the printed letters of the word 'cat' on the page. The signified is the conceptual dimension of a sign; in the case of cat, 'a certain species of animal'. Most signs in language are arbitrary – languages other than English will use different words and sounds for cat. In contrast, a photograph of a cat is 'motivated' and 'iconic'; it is also more specific: it depicts one particular animal which exists or has existed in the world.

During the 1960s Joseph Kosuth, an American Conceptual artist, made works that were almost illustrations of semiotic theory. For instance, *One and Three Chairs* (1965) consisted of three items: a photograph of a chair; a dictionary definition of the word 'chair' – both displayed on a gallery wall; and a real chair standing on the gallery floor. Arguably, the photo functioned as signifier, the definition as signified; together they made up a sign whose referent was the real chair. Alternatively, one could say that Kosuth's presentation contrasted visual and linguistic signs for chair and then invited viewers to compare them with an example of the real thing.

Various scholars have undertaken semiotic analyses of visual signs: Umberto Eco – architecture, comics and television; Jacques Bertin – diagrams; John A. Walker – the London Underground Diagram; Barthes – photography and fashion; Christian Metz – the cinema; Judith Williamson – advertising; and P. Fresnault-Deruelle – comics.

Many art historians and critics welcomed semiotics because it provided them with a sophisticated method for decoding images. The British artist Victor Burgin found it valuable because it increased his understanding of the mechanisms of photographic signs and the pictorial rhetoric of advertising, thus enabling him to analyse and construct signs for educational, critical and aesthetic purposes. Semiotics has also been considered a tool of value to trainee designers: it was once part of the curriculum of the noted German school of design known as Ulm.[18]

Charles Sanders Peirce (1839–1914) was an American philosopher who classified and named dozens of different kinds of sign, but the best known are index, icon and symbol. Peirce's terms are more useful to Visual Culture Studies than Saussure's because they explain visual images better.[19] A footprint in the sand is an example of an indexical sign, so is the trace left by a pen or brush on a flat surface: there is a direct, causal connection between what made the mark and the mark itself. Photographs too have been considered indexical because during exposure light falls on the film inside the camera and causes chemical changes in an automatic fashion.

Iconic signs are those which resemble or look like what they depict in some respects if not in all respects: a mirror-image has many of the qualities of what it reflects; a bronze sculpture of a cat may be the same size and shape as a real cat but it is does not have the same physical material or colour of a live cat.

Symbolic signs are those which are arbitrary or conventional in respect of their referents, that is, there is simply an agreement amongst a group of people that such and such a mark, sound or object stands for something else.

These three signs can occur not just in isolation but in combination, in a sedimented manner. For example, in Jackson Pollock's 'abstract' paintings made with poured paint, indexical signs are evident: the lines of pigment as traces of the artist's bodily movements, plus handprints. Iconic signs also occur: in some late canvases the lines of pigment form faces. A photographic portrait is both indexical and iconic. An artist can make certain pencil marks (indexical signs) which gradually form a configuration that resembles a known building, say The White House (iconic sign); but if that drawing then serves as a substitute for 'The President of the United States' then the sign is being used symbolically. (The building can stand for the person/presidential office because there is a contiguous or metonymic relationship between them.)

Semiotics is of value to Visual Culture Studies because it enables different kinds of signs to be distinguished and named, and because it makes possible a systematic analysis of images and communication processes. However, many theorists are more interested in the general laws of semiotics than in the semiotic analysis of specific examples of visual culture.

Structuralism

Structural anthropology – a discipline indebted to structural linguistics – treats human culture and social behaviour as if they were articulated like a language (with surface and deep structures). Hence it studies human kinship systems, legends, myths, sign systems and so on, in order to reveal their hidden structures, social functions and the rules of transformation which govern their metamorphoses. As in the work of Saussure, relations and differences between the various elements of a system count rather than the particular character of the individual elements. The doyen of structuralism was the French scholar Claude Lévi-Strauss (b. 1908–). His writings were extremely influential during the 1960s and 1970s and had a significant impact on theorists in the spheres of advertising, art, architecture, art history, fashion and popular culture.[20]

Since there is not room to provide a full account of structuralism and visual culture, we will simply list some noted applications. In his book *Tristes Tropiques* (1955; English translation with same title London, Jonathan Cape, 1973), Lévi-Strauss analysed the facial paintings of the South American Caduveo Indians in relation to symmetry and asymmetry. Pierre Bourdieu elucidated the meanings of the layout of a Berber peasant dwelling in Algeria via a series of binary oppositions such as inside/outside, male/female, day/night (structuralists are extremely fond of binary oppositions).[21] In 1975 Varda Leymore applied structuralist theory to advertising campaigns to clarify their myths and symbolism,[22] and in 1977 Edmund Leach provided a structural analysis of Michelangelo's Sistine Chapel ceiling painting.[23]

Within structuralism the relationship between structure and event/history is problematic. Structuralists tend to stress the synchronic rather than the diachronic; for example, Bourdieu's study of the Berber house was 'timeless', it paid no heed to the social changes taking place in Algeria. Consequently, structuralism as a mode of analysis, has severe limitations as far as historians of visual culture are concerned.[24]

Deconstruction

This is a philosophical and literary term associated with the post-structuralist writings of the French scholars Jacques Derrida, Jean-François Lyotard and their followers.[25] Deconstruction, it has been claimed, is not a method, critique, analysis, theory or practice. Like anti-art art, it appears to be a type of philosophising continually at war with the very possibility of philosophy.

Deconstructionists are extreme sceptics who refuse to accept the truth and knowledge claims of existing philosophical systems. They undertake 'readings' of texts in order to show that they are ultimately illogical and self-contradictory. Binary oppositions such as nature/culture favoured by structuralists are attacked to release what they repress. However, it has been argued that deconstruction is not a dismantling of a system but a demonstration of the fact that it has already dismantled itself. Deconstructionists themselves produce texts which are hard to evaluate because they are as much creative literature as rational discourse. Their use of language is said to be marked by 'productivity' and 'free play'. Sceptics have accused deconstruction of nihilism and claim it produces political paralysis.

Literary texts are said to undermine their own claims to have determinate meanings. Analysis of the meanings of pictures cannot be confined to what is within a frame because the 'inside' is always contaminated by the 'outside', for example, by intertexuality and contexts (see below). Works of art always have a surplus of meaning and resist attempts to fix meaning;

therefore, deconstructionists stress indeterminacy and undecidability rather than closure. However, they do admit that books and paintings still generate 'meaning effects'. Presumably, if they did not, then deconstructionist writings themselves would be without meaning!

Whereas Saussure gave speech priority over written language, Derrida stressed the importance of written language and drew attention to its visual or graphic characteristics, that is, typography, page layout, spacing and punctuation – hence the interest some graphic designers have shown in deconstruction.[26]

The main value of deconstruction is the radical questioning of established modes of thought and academic disciplines which it has instituted. Also, the attention it has drawn to apparently marginal phenomena such as frames. Deconstructionists have evinced considerable interest in the visual arts. For example, in 1989 Derrida curated an exhibition at the Louvre in Paris entitled *Memories of the Blind*. Most of the works featured were self-portraits, and the theme of this visual show was, paradoxically, blindness. Painters cited in the writings of Derrida include Goya, Van Gogh, Magritte, Valerio Adami and Gérard Titus-Carmel. He has also written about architecture in relation to Bernard Tschumi and the Parisian Parc de la Villette project. However, works of art tend to be used in order to serve Derrida's critical and literary ends rather than treated as intentional, meaningful and historical artefacts in their own right.[27]

Three of Derrida's books were published in the 1960s but it was over a decade before deconstruction became fashionable in the art world. With doubtful justification, the term and ideas of deconstruction were embraced by various artists, architects, fashion and graphic designers during the late 1980s and applied to their own practices.[28] Similarly, deconstruction influenced the thinking and practice of several art historians and critics.[29]

Physical context

As we all know, one word can be polysemic (have several meanings). Which meaning a speaker intends is normally indicated by the sentence – the context – in which the word is used. Similarly, in the visual arts display context is a crucial determinant of meaning especially for sculpture and 'site-specific art'.[30] The New York Harbour setting is clearly a vital signifying factor in the case of Auguste Bartholdi's *Statue of Liberty* (1886). An altarpiece viewed in a church rather than in a museum clearly gains from its sacred ambience. In the case of modern works of art such as Carl Andre's arrangements of bricks, the gallery context may be the only clue that the items in question are indeed works of art.

Intertextuality

As indicated earlier, virtually all images 'quote' from, borrow from, allude to, other images either historic or contemporary. Text-to-text connections literary theorists call 'intertextuality'. Cartoonists employed by the daily press borrow a great deal from the history of painting and they often credit their sources with inscriptions like 'After . . .', 'With apologies to . . .'. The French painter Manet was fond of using the compositions of earlier masters for his shocking, new pictures as a way of bemusing critics and viewers. A person who views a Manet and does not pick up the intertextual references because of a lack of cultural capital will miss a key ingredient of his paintings. Post-modern architecture has been described as 'double-coded' because it has been designed to appeal to two kinds of audience: those ignorant of architectural history and those whose knowledge of architectural history permits them to enjoy additional levels of meaning.

Certain images and personifications have very long histories and have migrated across many lands.[31] A consequence, for art historians, is that they can trace the origins and evolution of a representation, say, the figure of Liberty, from Roman sculptures to Renaissance emblem books, to Delacroix's canvas *Liberty Leading the People* (1830), to the *Statue of Liberty* (1886), to contemporary swimwear or corset advertisements showing women carrying banners labelled 'freedom'. Tracing such chains of images over time, mapping their migration across space, their transmission from culture to culture, is a fascinating pursuit. Of particular interest to scholars is 'contamination', that is, the gradual mutations caused by artists copying an image and making small errors as they did so. Some art and design historians have considered that such historical developments can be elucidated by reference to the biological theory of natural selection/evolution.[32]

For the sake of convenience, tracing and comparing images is usually done via photographs or reproductions. There are several dangers to this approach which need to be borne in mind: the images discussed will probably be drawn from diverse sources and cultural categories, from popular culture as well as high art, whose differences the analyst may well ignore. Questions of medium, material, scale, artistic quality may also be overlooked. Regarding artistic value for instance, Bartholdi's *Statue of Liberty* is a huge, popular, symbolic monument but as a work of art it is puerile.

Hermeneutics

In the realm of philosophy, the art or 'science' of interpreting and understanding texts and works of art is called 'hermeneutics'. (Originally this term referred to interpretations of Scripture which were accompanied by 'exegesis', that is, explanations, commentaries.) Reflections upon the theoretical problems of hermeneutics were undertaken in the nineteenth century by the Germans Friedrich Schleiermacher and Wilhelm Dilthey, and in the twentieth century by Hans-Georg Gadamer, author of *Truth and Method* (German edn 1965), a thinker influenced by Martin Heidegger's ideas concerning *Being and Time*.[33] These philosophers considered such issues as: the meaning and significance of works of art; the internal, parts-to-whole relations within a work; the artist's intended meaning (in so far as this can be ascertained); what viewers bring to a work – their prejudices and expectations; questions such as: 'How universal is an individual's interpretation? Are there correct and incorrect readings of an image? Are there determinate and stable meanings or are meanings indeterminate and unstable?' Gadamer stressed the situated and historical character of acts of interpretation. For instance, a surviving ancient work of art derives from a past historical moment but we experience it at another historical moment – the present. Comprehension requires a fusion of past and present 'horizons'. It may also involve a knowledge of all previous interpretations of the work in question. These and other issues are discussed further in books on reception theory and history.[34]

The aim of hermeneutics is to make works of art intelligible. Theodor Adorno dissented: he once remarked 'What at present needs to be grasped is their unintelligibility'.[35] Similarly, in 1964 Susan Sontag wrote a famous polemic against interpretation in which she claimed that it was 'the revenge of the intellect upon art', that 'the effusion of interpretations of art today poisons our sensibilities', and that interpretation 'tames the work of art . . . makes art manageable'! Her conclusion was: 'In place of a hermeneutics we need an erotics of art.'[36]

Summary

Even the abbreviated discussion contained in this chapter has shown that the question of the meaning of visual culture – especially that of the past and of foreign peoples – is complex and problematic. The various modes of analysis reviewed indicate that extracting meaning can involve considerable mental labour and interpretative skills.

Despite the above, the majority of viewers – who do not consciously apply such methods – continue to derive meanings from contemporary visual signs every day. The ability and necessity to read and interpret signs is surely of biological origin and serves vital survival functions for our species. The human need for meaning, significance and truth cannot be gainsaid. When Umberto Eco was asked by a television interviewer to explain the popular appeal of 'Who dunnit?' murder mysteries/detective stories, he replied by saying that 'Who dunnit?' (that is, 'Who made the cosmos?') was the fundamental question all religions and philosophies seek to answer.

Notes and further reading

1   For more on content analysis see: B. Berelson, *Content Analysis in Communication Research*, (New York, Haftner, 1952); G. Gerbner and others, *The Analysis of Communication Content: Developments in Scientific Theories and Computer Techniques*, (New York, John Wiley, 1969); O. R. Holsti, *Content Analysis for the Social Sciences and Humanities*, (Reading, MA, Addison-Wesley, 1969); K. Krippendorff, *Content Analysis: An Introduction to its Methodology*, (Beverly Hills & London, Sage Publications, 1980); R. P. Weber, *Basic Content Analysis*, (London, Sage Publications, 1985).

2   Guerrilla Girls (whoever they really are) and Whitney Chadwick, *Confessions of the Guerrilla Girls*, (London, Pandora, 1995).

3   E. Panofsky, 'Iconography and Iconology: An Introduction to the Study of Renaissance Art', *Meaning in the Visual Arts*, (Harmondsworth, Middlesex, Penguin Books, 1970), pp. 51–81. Other texts include: Jan Bialostocki, 'Iconography and Iconology', *Encyclopedia of World Art*, vol. 7, (New York, McGraw-Hill, 1958, cols 769–85); Göran Hermerén, *Representation and Meaning in the Visual Arts: A Study in the Methodology of Iconography and Iconology*, (Lund, Berlingska, Boktryckeriet, 1969); Lawrence Alloway, 'The Iconography of the Movies', *Movie*, 7 (February–March 1973), 4–6; W. J. T. Mitchell, *Iconology, Image, Text, Ideology*, (Chicago & London, University of Chicago Press, 1986); Roelof van Straten, *An Introduction to Iconography: Symbols, Allusions and Meanings in the Visual Arts*, (London, Harvey Miller Publishers, 1994); Mary Gedo, *Looking at Art from the Inside Out: The Psychoiconographic Approach to Modern Art*, (Cambridge, Cambridge University Press, 1994).

4   Articles on the Bronzino include: Graham Smith, 'Jealousy, Pleasure and Pain in Agnolo Bronzino's *Allegory of Venus and Cupid*', *Pantheon*, 39 (July–Summer 1981), 250–9; J. F. Conway, 'Syphilis and Bronzino's London *Allegory*', *Journal of the Warburg and Courtauld Institutes*, 49 (1986), 250–5.

5   The intentional fallacy, that is, the 'error' of explaining works by reference to the author's intentions, was named by W. K. Wimsatt and Monroe C. Beardsley in a 1946 paper. It is reprinted in Wimsatt's *The Verbal Icon: Studies in the Meaning of Poetry*, (London, Methuen, 1970).

6   R. Barthes, 'Myth Today', *Mythologies* (French edn 1957), (London, J. Cape, 1972), pp. 109–59.

7   On genre see: M. J. Friedlander, *Landscape, Portrait, Still-Life: Their Origin and Development*, (New York, Schocken, 1963); Barry Grant (ed.), *Film Genre: Theory and Criticism*, (Metuchen, NJ, Scarecrow Press, 1977); Steve Neale, *Genre*, (London, British Film Institute, 1980); Jim Collins, 'Genericity in the '90s: Eclectic Irony and the New Sincerity', *Film Theory Goes to the Movies*, eds J. Collins and others (New York, Routledge, 1993), pp. 242–63.

8   For more on types see: N. Pevsner, *A History of Building Types*, (London, Thames & Hudson, 1976); John A. Walker, *Design History and the History of Design*, (London, Pluto Press, 1989), pp. 110–18.

9   Writers who have foregrounded form include: Adolf von Hildebrandt, Wilhelm Wörringer, Clive Bell, Heinrich Wölfflin, Henri Focillon and Clement Greenberg.

10 For a thoughtful discussion of form and content see: T. Eagleton, 'Form and Content', *Marxism and Literary Criticism*, (London, Methuen, 1976), pp. 20–36.

11 For more on Van Gogh's techniques see: John A. Walker's *Van Gogh Studies: Five Critical Essays*, (London, JAW Publications, 1981) and his article 'Van Gogh's Drawing of La Crau from Mont Majour', *Master Drawings*, 20:4 (Winter 1982), 380–5.

12   This example is cited by John Fiske in *Introduction to Communication Studies*, (London & New York, Routledge, 2nd edn, 1990).

13   For more on Beck's diagram see: John A. Walker, 'The London Underground Diagram', *Icographic*, 14/15 (1979), 2–4; Ken Garland, *Mr Beck's Underground Map: A History*, (Harrow Weald, Middlesex, Capital Transport Publishing, 1994).

14   F. Antal, *Florentine Painting and its Social Background*, (London, Routledge & Kegan Paul, 1948).

15   N. Hadjinicolaou, *Art History and Class Struggle*, (London, Pluto Press, 1978).

16   On style see: Meyer Schapiro, 'Style', *Anthropology Today*, ed. A. Kroeber (Chicago, University of Chicago Press, 1953), pp. 287–312; J. Genova, 'The Significance of Style', *Journal of Aesthetics and Art Criticism*, 37:3 (Spring 1979), 315–24; B. Lang (ed.), *The Concept of Style*, (Philadelphia, University of Pennsylvania, rev. edn 1987); Mike Featherstone, 'Lifestyle and Consumer Culture', *Theory Culture and Society*, 4 (1987), 55–70; John A. Walker, 'Style, Styling and Lifestyle', *Design History and the History of Design*, (London, Pluto Press, 1989), pp. 153–73.

17   Introductions to the subjects of semiotics and structuralism are provided by T. Hawkes, *Structuralism and Semiotics*, (London, Methuen, 1977) and R. Stam and others, *New Vocabularies in Film Semiotics: Structuralism, Post-Structuralism and Beyond*, (London & New York, Routledge, 1992). Books on semiotics include: R. Barthes, *Elements of Semiology*, (London, J. Cape, 1967); F. de Saussure, *Course in General Linguistics*, (London, Fontana, 1974); C. Metz, *Film Language: A Semiotics of the Cinema*, (New York, Oxford University Press, 1974); C. Metz, *Cinema and Language*, (The Hague & Paris, Mouton, 1974); U. Eco, *A Theory of Semiotics*, (Bloomington, IN & London, Indiana University Press, 1976); L. Matejka and I. Titunik (eds), *Semiotics of Art: Prague School Contributions*, (Cambridge, MA, MIT Press, 1976); G. Broadbent and others, (eds), *Signs, Symbols and Architecture*, (Chichester, John Wiley, 1980); R. Innis (ed.) *Semiotics: An Introductory Anthology*, (London, Hutchinson, 1986); W. Noth, *Handbook of Semiotics*, (Bloomington & Indianapolis, IN, Indiana University Press, 1990); M. Bal and N. Bryson, 'Semiotics and Art History', *Art Bulletin*, 73:2 (June 1991), 174–208.

18   See: Theo Crosby (ed.), 'HfG ULM', *Uppercase*, 5 (1961).

19   C. S. Peirce, *Collected Papers*, 8 vols, (Cambridge MA, Belknap Press of Harvard University Press, 1931–58); Douglas Greenlee, *Peirce's Concept of the Sign*, (The Hague & Paris, Mouton, 1973); J. Hope (ed.), *Peirce on Signs: Writings on Semiotics by Charles Sanders Peirce*, (Chapel Hill, NC & London, University of North Carolina Press, 1991).

20   C. Lévi-Strauss, *Tristes Tropiques* (1955), (London, J. Cape, 1973); *Structural Anthropology* (1958), (London, Allen Lane, 1968); G. Dorfles, 'Structuralism and Semiology in Architecture', *Meaning in Architecture*, eds C. Jencks and G. Baird, (London, Barrie & Rockliff, 1969), pp. 38–49; S. Nodelman, 'Structural Analysis in Art and Anthropology', *Structuralism*, ed. J. Ehrmann, (New York, Doubleday, 1970), pp. 79–93; J. Burnham, *The Structure of Art*, (New York, Braziller, 1971).

21   P. Bourdieu, 'The Berber House', *Rules and Meanings: The Anthropology of Everyday Knowledge*, ed. M. Douglas (Harmondsworth, Middlesex, Penguin Books, 1973), pp. 98–110.

22   Varda L. Leymore, *Hidden Myth: Structure and Symbolism in Advertising*, (London, Heinemann, 1975).

23   E. Leach, 'Michelangelo's *Genesis*: Structuralist Comments on the Sistine Chapel Ceiling', *Times Literary Supplement*, (18 March 1977), 311–13.

24   For a critique of structuralism see: D. Francis, 'Advertising and Structuralism: The Myth of Formality', *International Journal of Advertising*, 5 (1986), 197–214.

25 Books on deconstruction include: J. Derrida, *Of Grammatology* (1967), (Baltimore, MD & London, John Hopkins University Press, 1976); J.-F. Lyotard, *The Postmodern Condition: A Report on Knowledge* (1979), (Manchester, Manchester University Press, 1984); J. Culler, *On Deconstruction: Theory and Criticism after Structuralism*, (Ithaca, NY, Cornell University Press, 1982); C. Norris, *Deconstruction: Theory and Practice*, (London & New York, Methuen, 1982); C. Norris and A. Benjamin, *What is Deconstruction?*, (London, Academy Editions, 1988); *Deconstruction: Omnibus Volume*, (London, Academy Editions, 1989); G. Broadbent, *Deconstruction: A Student Guide*, (London, Academy Editions, 1991).

26 For an overview of deconstruction and graphics see: Ellen Lupton and J. Abbott Miller, 'Deconstruction and Graphic Design: History Meets Theory', *Visible Language*, 28:4 (1994), 346–66.

27 Pierre Bourdieu has criticised Derrida's use of Kant's *Critique* as follows: 'in treating the third *Critique* as a work of art or a beautiful object, which it was not meant simply to be, I [Derrida] act as if the *existence* of the book were indifferent to me . . .', *Distinction: A Social Critique of the Judgement of Taste*, (London & New York, Routledge & Kegan Paul, 1984), p. 495. For J. Derrida's writings on painting see: *The Truth in Painting*, (Chicago, University of Chicago Press, 1987). For a discussion of the different approaches of art history and deconstruction see: John A. Walker, 'Art History versus Philosophy: The Enigma of the *Old Shoes*', *Block*, 2 (1980), 14–23.

28 An exhibition of so-called 'Deconstructivist' architecture was held at MoMA in New York in 1988. It featured the work of Peter Eisenman, Bernard Tschumi, Zaha Hadid, Coop. Himmelblau, Frank Gehry, Rem Koolhaas and Daniel Libeskind. (The show's title involved a play on the words 'deconstruction' and 'constructivism'.) See: Philip Johnson and Mark Wigley, *Deconstructivist Architecture*, (New York, Museum of Modern Art, 1988). An international symposium on Deconstruction and Architecture took place at the Tate Gallery in the same year. See also: Mark Wigley, *The Architecture of Deconstruction*, (Cambridge, MA & London, MIT Press, 1994).

29 Various articles on the relation between the fine arts and deconstruction appear in Andreas C. Papadakis (ed.), 'The New Modernism: Deconstructionist Tendencies in Art', *A.D. (Art & Design)*, 4:3/4 (1988), (London, Academy Editions), and in Peter Brunette and David Wills (eds), *Deconstruction and the Visual Arts: Art, Media, Architecture*, (Cambridge, Cambridge University Press, 1994).

30 For more on context see: John A. Walker, 'Context as a Determinant of Photographic Meaning', *Camerawork*, 19 (August 1980), 5–6; M. O'Toole, *The Language of Displayed Art*, (Leicester, Leicester University Press, 1994).

31 See: Rudolf Wittkower, *Allegory and the Migration of Symbols*, (London, Thames & Hudson, 1977).

32 See: Philip Steadman, *The Evolution of Designs: Biological Analogy in Architecture and the Applied Arts*, (Cambridge, Cambridge University Press, 1979).

33 H-G. Gadamer, *Truth and Method*, (New York, Crossroad Press, 2nd rev. edn 1990). See also: Janet Wolff, *Hermeneutic Philosophy and the Sociology of Art*, (London & Boston, MA, Routledge & Kegan Paul, 1975).

34 See, for example, the discussion of hermeneutics in Robert C. Holub, *Reception Theory: A Critical Introduction*, (London & New York, Methuen, 1984).

35 T. W. Adorno, *Aesthetic Theory*, (London, Routledge & Kegan Paul, 1984), p. 173.

36 S. Sontag, *Against Interpretation and Other Essays*, (London, Eyre & Spottiswoode, 1967), pp. 3–14.

10 The pleasures of visual culture

> The proper pleasure of art is an informed pleasure, and understands that its object – unlike the beauties of nature – is an artefact, has a history, and represents something done or achieved. (Jerrold Levinson)[1]

VISUAL CULTURE provides aesthetic pleasure and various other kinds of enjoyment. Humans would not pay it any attention, or indeed produce it, if it did not. (Displeasure too occurs when we encounter crass films and poorly designed goods.) Pleasure and value are closely related because high artistic values are generally assigned to those artefacts that provide us with enduring gratification, that is, a succession of pleasurable experiences. However, not all works of art are beautiful and pleasant; indeed some appear at first sight to be ugly. Furthermore, not all artefacts provide instant gratification. They may be so complex and demanding that we have to invest considerable time and mental effort before any pleasure is gained. And, in the case of Conceptual art, for instance, the appeal is to the intellect rather than to the senses.

Analysis versus pleasure

Reaching a conscious understanding of pleasure entails intellectual analysis, but many contend that pleasure is spoiled in the process.[2] A common assumption is that the mind is superior to the body, consequently the intellect is judged to be serious while pleasure – associated more with the body and the senses – is judged to be frivolous.[3]

There is a misunderstanding here, for, as Louis Althusser reminds us, 'knowledge of sugar is not sweet'. In other words, an intellectual understanding of pleasure will not provide the same kind of gratification as the experience itself. (Although scholars will confirm that there are pleasures associated with research, analysis and theory.)

Laura Mulvey, a British film-maker/theorist, is the author of an influential article – 'Visual Pleasure and Narrative Cinema' (1975) – which made a virtue of the destructive effect of analysis: 'It is said that analysing pleasure, or beauty, destroys it. That is the intention of this article. The satisfaction and reinforcement of the ego that represents the high point of film history must be attacked'.[4] Her motives derived from a feminist critique of cinematic pleasures in which the female body was a prime spectacle for the male gaze. She also sought 'a total negation of the ease and plenitude of the narrative fiction film'. (Theorists who dare to question or be critical of pleasure tend to arouse angry reactions and to be condemned as 'killjoys'.)

But can we be certain that analysis does destroy pleasure? After all, optical illusions persist even after they have been explained by psychologists of visual perception. Indeed, it could be argued that, since analysis deepens our understanding of art and aesthetic experience, it thereby enhances them. In any event, if we are to discuss the pleasures of visual culture at all, then we must risk spoiling them.

Pleasures of producing and consuming

Most discussions of pleasure focus on the experiences of viewers, on the *consumption* of visual culture, but pleasure is also crucial to the *making* of visual culture even though many professional artists complain that creation is hard work or even agony. The delight producers experienced when using their imaginations, tools and materials, in playing with visual media and conventions, can generally be deduced from their finished artefacts. (Films of artists at work are a further source of information.) When pleasure was absent, the results look constipated and lifeless.

While most artists enjoy their work, many factory, office and domestic workers do not. The latter, therefore, seek pleasures in consumption rather than in production at particular (leisure) times – evenings, weekends, vacations – and in particular places – arcades, bars, casinos, funfairs, nightclubs, theatres, sports stadia, holiday resorts, theme parks, red-light districts – dedicated to the pursuit of fun and pleasure. (In the modern world play and pleasure have become timetabled and millions feel a social obligation 'to have fun'. Holidays, travel and tourism are now duties because whole economies depend upon them.) Blackpool, Britain's most popular holiday resort, has an entertainments zone called *The Pleasure Beach*. The place or situation of encounter thus contributes significantly to the nature of the pleasure experienced.

The model of pleasure most theorists have in mind when they write is the experience of one person enjoying a single artefact. However, for millions of people pleasure occurs in group or mass situations such as cinemas, rock music concerts, sporting events and carnivals. (Writings on the subversive pleasures of carnival by the Russian theorist Mikhail Bakhtin are frequently cited in the literature on pleasure.) Such activities are thus more sociable than the contemplation of a picture. As we all know, feelings can be infectious in crowd situations. The sense of mergence with others all cheering for the same end may be a welcome release from the confines of the self, but such collective behaviour has its negative aspects – as the Nazi rallies held at Nuremberg in the 1930s demonstrated.

Varieties of pleasure

Works of art are extremely various, consequently the pleasures they provide are various too. Some, like the prints and sculptures of Käthe Kollwitz, are heart-rending and melancholic, while others, like the paintings of Raoul Dufy, are cheerful and exuberant. Movies too evoke a range of responses: awe and wonder, exhilaration and excitement, tears of laughter or sadness, fear and anger. Some films can arouse us sexually, others can even make us think. Movies, then, please more than the senses of sight and hearing – they engage our emotions and intellects too.

When viewing films and television the body is generally still, therefore optical and mental pleasures are paramount, but in the case of such physical activities as rides at funfairs and dancing, pleasure is more visceral than cerebral. In the case of dancing to the beat of loud music, sensations engulf the whole body and prolonged movement eventually produces chemical changes in the body that generate a sense of well-being. Hence the pleasures of the all-night, acid-house raves – enhanced by drugs and light patterns – of the late 1980s.

Designed goods also provide pleasure: think of the ego satisfactions associated with new garments that enhance the appearance, with new houses, furnishings, interior and garden design. Many men are obsessed by fast cars and motorbikes despite the ecological and health problems they cause. (It has been estimated that, since their invention a hundred years ago, cars have killed twenty-five million people!) These men delight in fine mechanical engineering, throaty exhausts, power, speed, sleek bodywork, the ownership of an expensive status and virility symbol; in short, the car as a visible, mobile proof of material success and personal identity.[5] In the documentary film *Fathers of Pop* (Arts Council, 1979) the British design historian Reyner Banham (1922–94) praised the sensual shapes, impressive design and styling of a 1953 Cadillac. In his opinion, the American car was as complex and important as any sculpture and thus equally worthy of serious inconographic analysis and aesthetic appreciation.

Wolfgang Fritz Haug, a German neo-Marxist philosopher, takes a more jaundiced view of designed goods. Since 1970 he has used the expression 'commodity aesthetics' to describe the aesthetic innovations capitalist firms regularly make in the appearance of their products in order to achieve new sales.[6] Aesthetic revamping of goods, Haug argues, is all too often accompanied by a deterioration in their basic use-values. He also cites 'the technocracy of sensuousness' and contends that 'the entire world of useful things is subjugated within its sensuous organisation to a permanent revolutionising which feeds back into the sensuous organisation of people themselves'. In other words, it is a form of social engineering.

Ornament

Patterns, repetitive motifs, movements and sounds may be summed up by the term 'ornament'.[7] It is a common feature of many arts and media: architecture and the decorative arts, tattooing and scarification, music and formation dancing, military marches and synchronised athletic displays. Ornament would not have existed for centuries unless it satisfied deep-seated needs of the human psyche and body. However, some modern architects and designers have opposed the popular passion for ornamentation by rejecting it – witness Adolf Loos's plain buildings and his famous critical essay 'Ornament as Crime' (1908). (Loos believed that fine art fulfilled the decorative needs of modern humans.)

In 1927 Siegfried Kracauer, the German film theorist, examined the appeal of what he called 'mass ornament' typical of dance troupes such as The Tiller Girls who moved in unison like 'an undulating snake'.[8] Later, in 1930s musicals choreographed by Busby Berkeley (1895–1976), lines of chorus girls formed ever-changing geometric patterns. Kracauer thought the appeal of such repetitive and synchronised movements was due to the masses' conditioning via their experience of repetition and regimentation during mass production in factories and offices. Places of amusement he dubbed 'distraction factories' and 'pleasure barracks'. The members of Nazi Party formations, he concluded, were 'living ornaments' organised into super-units – the instruments of Hitler's will. Leni Riefenstahl's celebratory films of Nazi rallies with their endless ranks of uniformed men marching in step had a powerful but eventually numbing, hypnotic effect. In a 1974 essay entitled 'Fascinating Fascism', Susan Sontag explored further the sinister aesthetic appeal of Riefenstahl's films and photographs.[9]

The functions of pleasure

Pleasure is a crucial part of the *experience* of visual culture, yet, arguably, it is not normally *the goal* of visual culture. It is a *means* rather than an *end*. The human species would not engage in sexual intercourse unless it was pleasurable, but orgasm is not the biological goal of intercourse, babies are; or, speaking more generally, the reproduction of the species. In most instances, the aims of visual culture are the communication of ideas, values, moral messages and stories. Pleasure is *the means* by which visual culture persuades and seduces us to look and listen while the ideas, etc. are delivered. During the seventeenth century Dutch artists produced veritable 'feasts for the eye' in the form of sumptuous still life paintings, but these so-called *vanitas* pictures also used symbolism to convey moral messages about the transience and vanity of human life. Today, messages and exhortations are most clearly evident in advertising and propaganda.

Furthermore, pleasure is essential to the functioning, the continuance, of the culture industries as profitable enterprises because it is the promise of more pleasure that makes viewers return time and time again to entertainment venues.

Pleasure, then, may be likened to sugar added to a medicine as a sweetener to disguise a horrid taste. The 'medicine', in the case of propaganda and advertising, is a commercial/ideological/political message or instruction. It is essential, therefore, to consider the social and political functions of pleasure. Freud's comments on jokes are pertinent: he argued that the pleasure of a joke derived from its *form* – the various poetic devices (such as puns) and the artist's playful use of language – but he also pointed out that jokes have a 'thought content':

> The thought seeks to *wrap* itself in a joke because in that way it recommends itself to our attention . . . above all because this *wrapping bribes our powers of criticism* and confuses them. We are inclined to give the *thought* the benefit of what has pleased us in the *form* of the joke; and we are no longer inclined to find anything wrong that has given us enjoyment and so spoil the source of the pleasure.[10]

Thus, for example, if we smile or laugh at a cartoon that pokes fun at avant-garde art, then we will be less inclined to criticise the conservativism, envy and philistinism that so often prompts cartoonists to satirise modern art.

Subjective or objective?

Pleasure is a *response* to visual culture, it is therefore an attribute of a viewer rather than an artefact. This raises again the theoretical problem cited earlier: can there really be a history of art or the cinema which is a history of millions of people's mental experiences over many cultures and centuries? This seems to be a research project more suited to psychologists, psychoanalysts and sociologists of taste. And there is a field of study called 'reception aesthetics' which considers audience responses, but surely this is only part of the history of the cinema or art.

A connected question concerns *the relationship between the work of art and the viewer*: to what extent is pleasure *caused* or determined by the work of art? We presume the artefact must possess certain objective properties which impact on the senses and mind of the viewer. And, despite the fact that individuals differ from one another, those responses must be widely shared, otherwise those watching a Charlie Chaplin comedy would not laugh in the same places. Laughter, incidentally, is an example of cathartic release from tension. (Catharsis: the effect of art in purging the emotions.) Doctors even maintain laughter is good for our health.

When individuals disagree about their experience of a work of art, this poses yet another problem for theorists. If we subscribe to the common view that 'there's no accounting for taste', then there's nothing more to be said – variations of taste will remain eternally mysterious. (Pierre Bourdieu disagrees.) Another example of folk wisdom is the view 'Beauty is in the eye of the beholder'. But is this really the case? Are not many film actors and fashion models stars precisely because they really are better-looking than the rest of us? What counts as beauty may be culturally inflected but social consensuses are reached as to who is beautiful and who is ugly, what is normal and abnormal in terms of the shape of the human body. Global beauty pageants such as the 'Miss World' and 'Mr Universe' contests, seem to indicate that standards of beauty are widely shared. Some theorists also maintain that the male perception of female beauty depends upon universal mechanisms shaped by natural selection, that men have 'evolved psychological mechanisms that selectively detect and respond to certain specific characteristics – such as smooth skin and bilateral symmetry – of women's bodies'.[11] Biologists claim that men and women with the most symmetrical bodies are fitter and more fertile, as well more attractive, than those whose bodies are not so well balanced.

In contrast to pleasure, beauty and ugliness are considered to be attributes of the thing itself rather than viewer. Some theorists seek to overcome this paradox by defining beauty as 'objectified pleasure'.

Aesthetic pleasure

It is time to distinguish aesthetic pleasure from other kinds of enjoyment. Some students appear not to know what aesthetic pleasure is – they claim never to have experienced it. Some signs of aesthetic pleasure are physiological: a tingling sensation along the spine, goosepimples, the hairs on the body stand up. There is also mental agitation, a sense of exquisite excitement prompted by the conviction that one is in the presence of an artefact or performance of major artistic value, significance and meaningfulness.[12] However, the feeling prompted by, say, a Cubist painting is of a different and more subtle kind than that aroused by, say, a sentimental, 'tearjerker' movie involving a dog called Lassie. (There are individuals who report that paintings have moved them to tears, but art galleries are not, in our experience, full of weeping or laughing people.) Some art critics have argued that this is because aesthetic pleasure is a response to form rather than to content. (See 'Formalism' below.)

Use of the word 'aesthetic' dates from the eighteenth century and it means 'pertaining to the sense of the beautiful'. Aesthetic experiences, therefore, are broader than the realm of visual culture – we can have aesthetic responses to such natural phenomena as sunsets, flowers, naked bodies and animals. In many instances, therefore, illusionistic media such as photography and the cinema *relay* or reproduce the appearances of those things that give us pleasure in everyday life – as in a pristine black-and-white photograph of a flower by Robert Mapplethorpe. Clearly, photography transforms the original to some extent but the medium is also capable of transmitting much of the natural beauty of the flower seen from one point of view. Colours that ravish us in reality can also ravish us in art. Thus the aesthetic pleasures of nature and art overlap.

The concern of art historians and critics, however, is to identify those experiences that are specific to art, because a sunset in a painting is not a real sunset. It is a sunset represented in a particular medium – oil paint on canvas – consequently our pleasure must also depend on the way in which it has been painted. In Van Gogh's Provençal landscapes, for example, the orb of the sun is often exaggerated in size and it is constructed from thick daubs of yellow pigment which stand proud from the surface of the canvas. Since pigment and brushstrokes are not part of the sun, art may be said to *add value* to natural appearances. So, representational paintings can be enjoyed on several levels: as schematic, intensified representations of natural scenes; as human fabrications involving skill and craft; as material objects with properties like textures which are additional to the motif.

Umberto Eco, the Italian semiotician and novelist, has argued that most works of art perform several functions simultaneously: referential, emotional, aesthetic, etc. According to Eco, the aesthetic or poetic function occurs when the language of a work is ambiguous or self-focusing.[13] As an example of the ambiguous he cites: 'green colourless ideas sleep furiously'. This sentence is grammatically correct but semantically ambiguous. The individual words are meaningful but the sentence as a whole does not make sense – it is 'surreal'; this causes readers to attend to it more closely than they would a normal statement. Self-focusing occurs when the work directs the viewer's attention to its own shape or sound: for example, in the statement 'I like Ike' (a slogan used in the American Presidential election campaign of General Eisenhower) the sound 'ike' is repeated twice; shape and sound are thus foregrounded.

Many theorists think the aesthetic dimension of art is its defining characteristic because it distinguishes art objects from non-art objects and from mass culture. However, matters are more complicated because aesthetic qualities are also found in media which are not generally classified as fine art – for example, advertising, design and television. Perhaps one can say that – as a general rule – the aesthetic dimension is stressed more in the fine arts than in, say, a television news programme or documentary. In the latter, the communication of factual information is given priority over aesthetic delight. Yet even documentaries could be characterised as well- or poorly crafted.

Some theorists regard aesthetic pleasure as a private, individual matter, but others take the view that individuals are social beings whose cultural habits and preferences are minute parts of a complex pattern that makes sense only when viewed as a totality. As explained earlier, the French sociologist Bourdieu used questionnaires and statistical records to map and analyse the patterns of taste and discrimination across the whole of French society during the 1960s and 1970s. He concluded that all taste differences can be explained by reference to the class divisions and unequal distribution of cultural capital across society, and that the aesthetic pleasures associated with the appreciation of high art are motivated by the need of the upper classes and intellectuals to maintain a difference/distance from the 'vulgar' enjoyments of the lower orders.[14]

Bourdieu's writings impress upon us the need to ask: 'What pleasures, enjoyed by whom, when and where?' The example of car culture reveals that social divisions give rise to different attitudes towards designed goods and therefore to different kinds of pleasure: the majority of car drivers are affluent, employed adults who take pride in the ownership and preservation of their vehicles. This contrasts sharply with the 'joyriding' of unemployed, disaffected youths who delight in stealing, racing and trashing cars.

Like Bourdieu, Terry Eagleton is conscious of the relation between culture and social class. In a book published in 1990 he argued that 'the aesthetic' was an 'ideology' associated with the rise of the bourgeoisie.[15] The aesthetic virtually replaced religion. It, like religion, supplied a refuge from the world of industry, ruthless commercialism and utilitarianism that the capitalist class had created.

Renaissance aesthetics

Ideas about aesthetic pleasure dating from the Renaissance were challenged by the advent of modernism. Between 1535 and 1536 the Italian artist and architect Leon Battista Alberti wrote a treatise on the art of painting – *Della Pictura*[16] – in which he argued that what gave pleasure in a painting was *copiousness or abundance, novelty and variety*; for example, a mixture and variety of figures. Variety was also to be achieved by using many dissimilar poses and contrasts (of light and dark, broad and narrow, high and low). Alberti believed 'all things are known by comparison'; consequently, the copiousness and variety of a painting's forms and contents stimulated the viewer's comparative faculty. Although Ford Madox Brown's *Work* (1852–63) is not a Renaissance period painting, it is a prime example of copiousness and variety. It is so full of figures and so detailed that it can engage the eyes for hours.

Alberti also believed that the painter's task was to 'move the soul of the viewer', that is, to induce emotions by representing people experiencing them. The sight of someone suffering or grieving may prompt a comparable emotion in us. If we can truly imagine the pain of being nailed to a cross, then we will shudder with horror. In addition, such an image may arouse feelings of compassion and sympathy for the victim. Yet, is there not something paradoxical about deriving aesthetic pleasure from an image of torture? Does this not make us sadists? This issue will be discussed further later.

If Alberti is right about paintings touching the emotions, then the most enjoyable paintings should be those which show people enjoying themselves. This view seems to be confirmed by Jean-Honoré Fragonard's *The Swing* (c. 1766), an erotic scene showing a young woman on a swing with her skirts flying high being ogled from below by a male suitor. This painting has what a British politician would call 'a feel-good factor'.

In the twentieth century, Fragonard's pictorial hedonism was matched by Henri Matisse. He once remarked that his paintings should serve a soothing, therapeutic function equivalent to the comfortable armchairs enjoyed by tired businessmen after hard days at the office. Because Matisse had no wish to disturb viewers, he almost always painted positive or innocuous subjects. His paintings are doubly pleasing because they are pleasurable objects showing pleasurable things and activities. For these reasons, Matisse's art is generally regarded as amongst the most sensuous and enjoyable ever produced.

Formalism

Renaissance viewers enjoyed in art what some later critics – the formalists – came to regard as literary or illustrational. (Renaissance art was primarily a visualisation of Biblical stories and classical myths.) *Illustration* eventually became a dirty word. The American connoisseur Bernard Berenson has already been mentioned. In his writings on Italian Renaissance painting he forwarded a theory of *tactile values* to explain the appeal of so-called authentic art.[17] He condemned illustrational paintings and sculptures and argued that authentic art adds value by representing things in such a way as to 'accelerate psychical processes'. The decorative qualities of a work of art – form, line and colour – are essential, especially the sense of form which, although perceived through the eyes, arouses the sense of touch, plus other internal, physiological sensations (the sense of proportion, of space, of muscular responses).

Berenson's ideas were developed by Clive Bell and Roger Fry, two formalist critics who belonged to the Bloomsbury Group. Bell invented the term 'significant form', by which he meant lines, colours and forms combined in such a way as to move the viewer aesthetically. Significant form, Bell maintained, was a universal quality found in otherwise disparate artefacts serving different functions, produced at different times by different cultures. To make his argument clearer, Bell cited Victorian narrative paintings such as William Frith's *The Railway Station [Paddington]* (1862) and Sir Luke Fildes's *The Doctor* (1891) which, according to him, lacked significant form: *The Railway Station*, he judged, was an interesting and amusing document but not a work of art. Painting had been used to tell a story about the manners and customs of an age, not to stimulate an aesthetic emotion. Similarly, *The Doctor* was not a work of art because its forms were a means of suggesting an emotion – a highly sentimental one (a doctor cares for a child who is very ill) – but 'its forms are not the object of the emotion. To appreciate a work of art we need bring with us nothing but a sense of form and colour and a knowledge of three-dimensional space' – representational elements were thus deemed irrelevant.[18]

This appears to be a programme for a purely abstract type of art. Yet, in representational pictures, form and content can be distinguished only theoretically; even *The Doctor* is a specific combination of form and content. It may not emphasise formal properties to the extent that a painting by Cézanne does; nevertheless it has some formal qualities. It has a still life passage, for instance, that is close to Impressionist renderings of similar subjects. To enjoy Fildes's painting to the full we need to pay heed to both its narrative content and its form/style. Art lovers who think only the formal or aesthetic qualities of works of arts matter, disregard their social and historical content and referents. As Adorno has pointed out: 'Nobody can claim to be conversant with a Beethoven symphony unless he understands the so-called purely musical events in the music and at the same time hears in it the echo of the French Revolution'.[19]

Making strange, or defamiliarisation, is an aesthetic strategy identified by Russian formalist literary critics.[20] They argued that as we live from day to day the world around us becomes very familiar; consequently we lose our innocent eye and sense of wonder. One function of art was to renew our perception of the world by defamiliarising it. This is done by such means as taking photos from unusual camera angles so that at first we do not recognise what the photo depicts. (For examples, see photographs by Alexander Rodchenko.) We have to look harder and longer in order to discover what the photo represents; there is thus a *delay* in perception/recognition. By slowing down perception, and making it a more active process, art increases perceptual pleasure. Many people enjoy the challenge posed by puzzle pictures, and advertisements often use the technique of superimposition in order to make their imagery harder to decipher.

Traditional versus modern art

If we compare most Renaissance and modern paintings, then it becomes clear that a significant change in aesthetic principles has taken place – the former aimed for harmony, unity, completeness, a high degree of finish, the latter are often raw, unfinished, fragmented and dissonant. Modern consciousness is much more appreciative of lack of finish; indeed the signs of rawness, energy and spontaneity are much admired. (Contemporary viewers are likely to value John Constable's sketches more than his completed pictures.) This shift in taste may be due to the rapid change, the transitoriness of life, the sense of becoming rather than being, associated with the age of political, scientific and technological revolutions. However, admiration of modern art tends to be limited to an intellectual elite – popular taste still accords with Renaissance ideals.

Film theorists have written extensively about the form and technique of the medium, but one can be certain they would consider the formalists' idea that only these factors really matter to be absurd (although, presumably, this is the creed of some experimental/abstract film-makers). In the case of mass culture products such as Hollywood-type movies, there is a strong involvement, immersion in the film's narrative: if it is a well-made thriller, horror or Western, the story enthrals and thrills, it builds tensions and then releases them, thereby providing catharsis. The audience is encouraged to identify closely with the fates of a hero and a heroine – played by stars who may be the main reason for the visit to the cinema – and the story normally concludes with a 'closure' or happy ending in which all problems are resolved. (How different from real life!)

In the commercial cinema the arts and crafts of directing, cinematography, lighting, costume, set and prop design, scriptwriting, acting, music all combine to work on the senses and emotions of the audience. Experiencing such a movie is like taking a holiday from the cares and routines of everyday life. In the movie everything is compressed and intensified, life is speeded up – all the boring times and hard work are left out. The spectacle, immersion and escapism of popular cinema has been attacked by many intellectuals because the viewer's powers of criticism are seduced. These intellectuals think art should keep viewers at a distance so that their reflective faculties can still operate. (Bertolt Brecht's 'epic theatre', with its alienation techniques intended to instruct rather than divert, was a case in point. Arguably, both involvement and distance are required.) When such intellectuals come to make films, however, they face a dilemma: if they refuse to provide any pleasure or excitement, they are unlikely to attract an audience and hence they will not get their political point across, nor will they be able to raise funds to make more movies.

Perhaps the ultimate example of a film that refused the normal conventions and pleasures of the cinema was Guy Debord's *Howls in Favour of de Sade* (1952). It had no images: the screen was either black or white. It lasted over an hour, with twenty minutes of sound – readings of quotes taken from various sources. Debord's gesture of defiance against mainstream cinema, in this instance, involved a rejection of the visual dimension of the medium of film. In 1952 his 'film' was screened in London to a small audience at the Institute of Contemporary Arts. It is inconceivable that such a film could influence masses by gaining a general cinematic release.

According to Roland Barthes, traditional and avant-garde works of art prompted different kinds of enjoyment: first, 'plaisir' (pleasure); and second, 'jouissance' (bliss, rapture, ecstasy).[21] The former refers to those pleasures – euphoria, fulfilment, comfort – typical of 'readable' or intelligible texts (for example, traditional novels), while the latter refers to those pleasures – shock, discomfort, disruption, a sense of loss – associated with 'unreadable' or unintelligible texts (for example, experimental modern novels). Barthes also stressed the role the body plays in aesthetic experience and argued that what analysts encounter when they consider the pleasures of texts, are their own enjoying bodies.

Ugliness

Earlier, the word 'aesthetic' was defined as 'pertaining to the beautiful'. But what of beauty's opposite – ugliness? Can ugliness provide aesthetic pleasure? Is liking the ugly a perversion?[22] These questions are relevant because the charge of ugliness has been directed at many works of modern art, including Jacob Epstein's sculptures and Picasso's *Demoiselles d'Avignon* (1907). Whereas in the past, a beautiful work of art was one in which the various parts formed a unity, a harmonious composition, in modern art there is often fragmentation, disunity, dissonance, a deliberate clash of styles.

Shock effects too are part of the appeal of many images and movies – Picasso's painting was once regarded as very shocking. By now it has probably lost its shock-value but many probably still regard it as an ugly painting. Nevertheless, in spite of this – or perhaps because of it – the painting has become one of the famous and historically significant icons of twentieth-century culture. Modern art has often been taken to task for its distortions of colour and form, and especially for its deformations of the shape of the human body. Epstein's pregnant figure *Eve* (1931) provoked outrage. Even today there are those that find it repulsive. Yet, paradoxically, there are times when people take pleasure in seeing deformity; for example, when visitors to fairground side shows view themselves in distorting mirrors.

If beauty is perfection of form, then ugliness is imperfection. (To argue this in the presence of students with physical disabilities poses a problem for academics.) Ugliness can be repellent and, at the same time, fascinating – think of the desire on the part of the Victorians to see John Merrick, the Elephant Man, and the modern audience to see the film *The Elephant Man* (directed by David Lynch, 1980). The grotesque in art has always had its appeal – witness the popularity of paintings by Hieronymus Bosch (c. 1450–1516) with their weird monsters.[23]

Kitsch objects, many consider, are by definition ugly and grotesque. Yet there are millions who enjoy them without thinking their taste is bad, and there are others with camp taste who revel in their sheer awfulness (the

12 Dinos and Jake Chapman, *Zygotic Acceleration, Bio-Genetic, Desublimated Libidinal Model (Enlarged x 1000)*, (1995). Fibreglass, resin, paint, wigs and trainers, 150 × 180 × 140 cm. London, Saatchi Collection.

The British artists Dinos (b. 1962) and Jake (b. 1966) Chapman are brothers who, like Gilbert and George (for whom they once worked as assistants), operate as a duo. During the 1990s they produced a series of grotesque but memorable sculptures from readymade, stereotypical objects – shop mannequins – which they modified in various ways. Favourite tactics were to join bodies together like Siamese twins and to displace sexual organs and orifices from their normal positions to the face, and to other parts of the body. Just as they scramble body parts, the Chapmans scramble theory – they are well versed in psychoanalytic theories of scopophilia and polymorphous sexual and sado-masochistic desires. They play upon the viewer's ambivalent emotions regarding erotic scenes: a desire to see and, at the same time, feelings of guilt and shame. Like the makers of horror films, they provide a cocktail of optical delight, violence and shock-effects. They are aware that pleasure includes a sense of unpleasure.

Their use of child-like figures led to accusations of paedophilia and some sculptures were censored from exhibitions.

'they're so bad they're good' syndrome. Susan Sontag is the author of a noted essay on camp taste[24]). Furthermore, contemporary fine artists such as Jeff Koons and Mark Kostabi appropriate kitsch objects in order to exploit their saccharine, gaudy charms and their illicit appeal.

Some artists have attempted what may be called 'taste experiments' by combining repulsive content with aesthetic refinement. In the 1970s, for instance, Richard Hamilton painted a series of flower-pieces and landscapes which included piles of human excrement. During the same decade Robert Mapplethorpe became notorious because of his highly aesthetic photographs of homosexual sado-masochistic activities such as fist-fucking. When these photographs were attacked by the prosecution in an American court, their aesthetic and compositional characteristics were cited in justification by expert witnesses for the defence.

Horror and suffering in art

Let us now return to the issue of horrific subject matter and aesthetic pleasure. Artists such as Goya and Kollwitz have confronted the brutal and tragic side of human life by depicting suffering, torture and the horrors of war. How do such negative themes square with the pleasures of art? Aristotle believed art could provide *catharsis*, that emotions such as fear and pity could be *purged* by witnessing tragic plays. Centuries later Freud recast this idea by arguing that we tend to repress traumatic feelings and we enjoy tragic art because it facilitates the release of such feelings.

If we enjoy a painting or a film of a person being tortured to death does this mean we are sadists? Not necessarily: we may identify with the victim rather than the torturers; the emotions aroused by the image may be pity and sorrow rather than pleasure in someone else's pain. Furthermore, a picture of a tortured person is a representation – it is not literally an act of torture: in fictional films scenes of torture are simulated by actors. Such images can serve the positive social function of an indictment, a graphic reminder of humanity's capacity for inhumanity. And if such an image is part of a more general campaign waged by Left-wing artists like Georg Grosz and John Heartfield against Nazi fascists, then it serves a positive social value by warning against the consequences of fascists gaining power. Some European viewers of scenes of French soldiers torturing Algerian prisoners in Gillo Pontecorvo's harrowing film *Battle of Algiers* (1965) were educated about the evils of colonialism and politicised by the experience.

Of course, a minority of viewers are sadists and masochists. Such people do take pleasure in the depiction of cruelty. In addition, mass culture has a propensity to turn all viewers into sadists, at least temporarily. For example, makers of crime movies often set out to arouse righteous anger in the audience by commencing with a vicious rape or murder scene. Viewers then long for violent retribution/punishment and when it finally occurs their cruel impulses are given full rein. Violent feelings are thus aroused, legitimated and then discharged.

Given the popularity of the cinematic genres horror and science fiction, millions enjoy being shocked and frightened. Watching such films is often a test of courage, a rite of passage, among the young. Of course, the cinema is a place where danger and atrocities can be safely encountered because the fantasies are not real. However, there is a continuing debate about the social impact of 'violent' comics, films and television programmes. There are many who believe that violent media cause people to behave violently. Perhaps such media are rather a means of training people to face up to the real horrors they might meet in life. But this could also be a way of saying that exposure to violent imagery desensitises viewers and this results in them becoming more callous and therefore more likely to be cruel to others.

Aestheticisation of violence

Herbert Marcuse maintained that art could not represent human suffering 'without subjecting it to aesthetic form, and thereby to mitigating cathar- sis, to enjoyment'. He added: 'art is inexorably infested with this guilt'.[25] There are, however, degrees of aestheticisation. In films that set out to entertain rather than to enlighten, the aestheticisation of violence and suffering is often reactionary rather than progressive. In the final scenes of the gangster movie *Bonnie and Clyde* (directed by Arthur Penn, 1967) for instance, the two main characters are shot to death in a hail of machine gun bullets. The special effect of slow motion is used so that the audience can savour the moments of killing for longer than normal; the bodies, reeling under the impact of the bullets, perform a ballet-like movement in the air. The moments of pain and death become ecstatic – as they do in so many oil paintings of impaled Christian martyrs.

Similarly, in comic books and Pop art, scenes of carnage are presented in bright, cheerful colours and rendered in a highly schematic, decorative style of drawing that precludes any sense of realism – of what it would be like to be blown to pieces in a fighter plane. Some viewers find this kind of art disturbing because its pleasurable form seems at odds with its savage content. Raymond Williams identified a 'culture of distance': in American comic strips and Roy Lichtenstein's Pop paintings we are distanced, protected from the horrors of war by stylisation and aestheticism. The Japanese too delight in violent and pornographic images that are simulta- neously visually exquisite, yet, paradoxically, the vast majority of Japanese are socially well-behaved in everyday life.[26] (This suggests that the images provide emotional release in a repressed society.)

Summary

Aesthetic experiences have been discussed at great length in books and periodical articles written by philosophers and aestheticians.[27] Unfortunately, writings on aesthetics are notorious for their tedium. Ancient theoretical problems tend to be mulled over again and again without ever being resolved.

Because of the subjective character of the aesthetic experience, sciences of the mind such as psychology and psychoanalysis have been mobilised in the hope that illumination, even scientifically valid knowledge, can be obtained. Psychologists, for instance, have tried to measure aesthetic preferences by showing the same visual stimuli to groups of people under the same experimental conditions. Visual Culture Studies, it must be admitted, has made little use of the findings of such tests. There is, however, a thoughtful study by Ray Crozier of psychological responses to designed goods.[28]

Psychoanalysis has been deemed far more relevant, even though it is speculative and interpretative rather than empirical. Freud himself wrote about 'the pleasure principle' and 'the uncanny'; he psychoanalysed works of art by Leonardo and Michelangelo, and discussed how jokes and dreams work (the dreamwork of the unconscious mind was explained by reference to the ways pictures are constructed). His followers have discussed the mechanisms of scopophilia (gratification derived from looking) – and voyeurism ('a deviation in which sexual gratification is gained from viewing erotic images or sexual situations') – and they have used concepts such as narcissism, fetishism and the mirror phase in an attempt to provide highly abstract or generalised models that seek to represent the unconscious psychic experiences involved when watching visual media. Film theorists have also applied theories of sadism and masochism – deemed to have their origins in infantile sexual experiences – to the pleasures viewers derive from horror films.[29]

Among Left-wingers there are two contradictory opinions about pleasure: on the one hand, it is viewed as conservative (the pleasure supplied by the culture industries is condemned for being opium for the masses); on the other hand, it is considered subversive (the pleasure principle can undermine the reality principle; during the 1960s hedonism was imbricated in a number of liberation movements). Pleasure, it seems, can serve the ends of social control and liberation.

As this chapter has shown, certain avant-garde artists have taken a keen interest in the pleasures of visual culture. Feminist film-makers and other radical artists have sought to question or destroy dominant pleasures, while seeking alternative kinds of aesthetic experience, 'a new language of desire' (Mulvey). There is general agreement that pleasure is a crucial ingredient of the subjective experience of visual culture but, according to

social theorists, feminists and politically aware artists, it is never innocent.[30]

Notes and further reading

1   Jerrold Levinson, 'Pleasure and the Value of Works of Art', *British Journal of Aesthetics*, 32:4 (October 1992), 295–306.

2   In 1995 the anonymous author of an article about the state of critical theory claimed that radical academics are 'anti-pleasure'. See: Anon., 'Sacred Cows' Herd Instinct', *Times Higher Education Supplement*, (21 July 1995), 17. Wendy Steiner, in her illuminating book *The Scandal of Pleasure: Art in an Age of Fundamentalism*, (Chicago & London, University of Chicago Press, 1995), also castigated extremist critics (so-called 'fundamentalists') on both the Left and the Right for denigrating the pleasures of art.

3   Terry Eagleton believes there is a need 'to deconstruct that most bourgeois of all assumptions that the intellect is deadly serious and unpleasurable, and that pleasure is essentially frivolous and non-intellectual'. *The Significance of Theory*, (Oxford & Cambridge, MA, Blackwell, 1990), p. 88.

4   L. Mulvey, 'Visual Pleasure and Narrative Cinema', *Screen*, 16 (1975), 6–18. Reprinted with further commentary in *Visual and Other Pleasures*, (London, Macmillan, 1989). See also: F. Jameson and others, 'Feminist Film Practice: A discussion', *Formations of Pleasure*, (London, Routledge & Kegan Paul, 1983), pp. 156–70.

5   Men's romance with cars is celebrated in Stephen Bayley's *Sex, Drink and Fast Cars: The Creation and Consumption of Images*, (London & Boston, MA, Faber & Faber, 1986).

6   See: W. F. Haug, *Critique of Commodity Aesthetics: Appearance, Sexuality and Advertising in Capitalist Society*, (Cambridge, Polity Press, 1986), and *Commodity Aesthetics, Ideology and Culture*, (New York, International General, 1987).

7   On ornament see: E. H. Gombrich, *The Sense of Order: A Study in the Psychology of Decorative Art*, (Oxford, Phaidon Press, 1979); Stuart Durant, *Ornament*, (London, MacDonald, 1986); and Michael Snodin and Maurice Howard, *Ornament: A Social History since 1450*, (New Haven, CT & London, Yale University Press, 1996).

8   S. Kracauer, *The Mass Ornament: Weimar Essays*, (Cambridge, MA, Harvard University Press, 1995).

9   S. Sontag, 'Fascinating Fascism' (1974), *Under the Sign of Saturn*, (London, Writers & Readers, 1983), pp. 73–105.

10 S. Freud, *Jokes and their Relationship to the Unconscious*, (1905) (London, Routledge & Kegan Paul, 1960), p. 182. See also: C. P. Wilson, *Jokes: Form, Content, Use and Function*, (London, Academic Press, 1979).

11 D. Symons, 'Beauty is in the Adaptations of the Beholder: The Evolutionary Psychology of Human Female Sexual Attractiveness', *Sexual Nature, Sexual Culture*, eds P. R. Abramson and S. D. Pinkerton, (Chicago & London, University of Chicago Press, 1995), pp. 80–118.

12 Peter Abbs, an arts educationalist at the University of Sussex, undertook an informal survey in an effort to pin down the nature of the aesthetic experience. He asked arts teachers to describe in words the nature of their aesthetic experiences (even though Abbs believes such experiences resist translation into language). The characteristics listed by the teachers overlap with the account we have given. See: 'Making the Art Beat Faster', *Times Higher Education Supplement*, (18 September 1992), 18.

13 U. Eco, *A Theory of Semiotics*, (Bloomington, IN & London, Indiana University Press, 1976), p. 162.

14 P. Bourdieu, *Distinction: A Social Critique of the Judgement of Taste*, (London & New York, Routledge & Kegan Paul, 1984).

15 T. Eagleton, *The Ideology of the Aesthetic*, (Oxford, Blackwell, 1990).

16 L. B. Alberti, *On Painting*, (New Haven, CT & London, Yale University Press, rev. edn 1966), p. 75.

17 B. Berenson, *The Italian Painters of the Renaissance*, (London, Phaidon Press, 1952), p. 40, pp. 42–3.

18 C. Bell, *Art*, (London, Chatto & Windus, 1914; new edn 1949), p. 23, p. 30; R. Fry, *Vision and Design*, (London, Chatto & Windus, 1920); *Transformations*, (London, Chatto & Windus, 1926). For a Left-wing critique of Bell and Fry see: Simon Watney, 'The Connoisseur as Gourmet: The Aesthetics of Roger Fry and Clive Bell', *Formations of Pleasure*, F. Jameson and others, pp. 66–83.

19 T. W. Adorno, *Aesthetic Theory*, (London, Routledge & Kegan Paul, 1984), p. 479.

20 On Russian formalism see: L. T. Lemon and M. J. Reis (translators/introduction) V. Shklovsky and others, *Russian Formalism Criticism: Four Essays*, (Lincoln, NB, University of Nebraska Press, 1965); K. Pomorska, *Russian Formalist Theory and its Poetic Ambiance*, (The Hague & Paris, Mouton, 1968); *Twentieth Century Studies*, 7/8 (December 1972) (thematic issue); Stephen Bann and John E. Bowlt (eds), *Russian Formalism: A Collection of Articles and Texts in Translation*, (Edinburgh, Scottish Academic Press, 1973); Victor Erlich, *Russian Formalism: History – Doctrine*, (New Haven, CT & London, Yale University Press, 3rd edn 1981); Peter Steiner, *Russian Formalism*, (Ithaca, NY, Cornell University Press, 1986).

21 R. Barthes, *The Pleasure of the Text*, (London, J. Cape, 1976).

22 Karl Rosenkranz (1805–79), a follower of Hegel, wrote a book – *Ästhetik des Hässlichen*, (Königsberg, 1853) – on the aesthetics of the ugly defined as 'the self-destruction of the beautiful'. The ugly, he argued, was one of the goals of art.

23 On the grotesque see: Wolfgang Kayser, *The Grotesque in Art and Literature*, (Bloomington, IN, Indiana University Press, 1963).

24 S. Sontag, 'Notes on Camp', *Against Interpretation*, (London, Eyre & Spottiswoode, 1967), pp. 275–89.

25 H. Marcuse, *The Aesthetic Dimension: Toward a Critique of Marxist Aesthetics*, (London & Basingstoke, Macmillan, 1978), p. 55.

26 See, for example, the comic-strip illustrations reproduced in Ian Buruma's *A Japanese Mirror: Heroes and Villains of Japanese Culture*, (London, J. Cape, 1984), pp. 108–9.

27 A standard account of aesthetics is: K. E. Gilbert and H. Kuhn, *A History of Esthetics*, (London, Thames & Hudson, rev. edn 1956). See also the periodicals: *British Journal of Aesthetics* and *Journal of Aesthetics and Art Criticism* (USA).

28 R. Crozier, *Manufactured Pleasures: Psychological Responses to Design*, (Manchester & New York, Manchester University Press, 1994).

29 See, for example: Morris Dickstein, 'The Aesthetics of Fright', *Planks of Reason: Essays on the Horror Film*, ed. B. Grant, (Metuchen, NJ & London, Scarecrow Press, 1984), pp. 65–78; Gaylan Studlar, 'Masochism and the Perverse Pleasures of the Cinema', *Movies and Methods*, vol. 2, ed. B. Nichols, (Berkeley, CA, University of California Press, 1985), pp. 602–21; and Carol J. Clover, 'The Eye of Horror', *Men, Women and Chain Saws: Gender in the Modern Horror Film*, (London, British Film Institute Publishing, 1992), pp. 166–230.

30 For more on the politics of pleasure see: Stephen Regan (ed.), *The Politics of Pleasure: Aesthetics and Cultural Theory*, (Buckingham & Philadelphia, PA, Open University Press, 1992).

11   The canon and concepts of value

THIS CHAPTER considers three closely related words/concepts – value, valuation and evaluation – and also the process of ranking cultural artefacts in order to construct canons of great artists and masterpieces.

Value

A dictionary defines 'value' as 'that property of a thing which makes it desirable or useful . . . merit or importance . . . material or monetary worth . . . intrinsic excellence or desirability'. Since both material things and human desires are cited in this definition, we again encounter a subjective/objective interaction.

Several kinds of value can be distinguished. First, *artistic value*. This is the judgement that a cultural artefact is intrinsically excellent, of high aesthetic quality and significant content. Second, *use-value*: appliances fulfil practical functions – a kettle may be battered and ugly but, so long as it boils water, it has a use-value for its owner. (Some designers advocate that consumer durables should be both beautiful and functional.) Can the same be said about works of art? Yes: architecture shelters us from the weather and serves a number of other public functions; paintings and sculptures too serve a variety of purposes: decorative, symbolic, memorial, ideological and political. Third, *personal* or *sentimental value*. This kind of value is unrelated to either artistic or monetary worth because it derives from the roles possessions have played in the private, biographical and emotional life of an individual. (An album of family snapshots is a common example.) It follows that such objects are described by their owners as 'priceless' even though they could fetch prices in a sale.

Fourth, *monetary* or *exchange-value*. Many artefacts are desired by a wide range of people; consequently these people are willing to barter other goods for them, or to pay money for them. The monetary value of an artefact is extremely variable because of fluctuations in demand and the state of the economy. A house in London that cost £3,000 in the 1960s could be worth £120,000 in the 1990s despite the fact that it is three decades older. If the housing market collapsed, its value could be halved. All the while, the use-value of the house as a place to live could have remained roughly the same.

The monetary value of a new car starts to depreciate the moment it is purchased. Year by year its resale value declines until it reaches scrap-value. Exceptionally, some well-made old cars are in good working order – they have become rare and have attained the status of antiques. Their resale value is thus high despite their age and lack of modern performance.

Rubbish theory is an ingenious attempt by Michael Thompson, a social anthropologist who has taught in art and design colleges, to explain how value is created and destroyed, that is, how cultural products lose or gain in value as time passes, come to be thought of as rubbish, are then perhaps rediscovered to acquire value again.[1] Objects, he argued, fall into one of two categories: they are either *transient* (because they have finite lifespans and they decrease in value over time), or they are *durable* (they have 'infinite' lifespans and increase in value over time). What interested Thompson was the social process by which objects transferred from one category to the other. Rubbish, he considered, was an important, covert category because it was a zone of zero value upon which the whole process depended.

If a cultural artefact really does possess intrinsic artistic value, then logically – so long as the artefact remains in good physical condition – this value should remain constant over time – even if its monetary value fluctuates. Objects whose artistic value persists over long periods are often described as 'timeless' and 'classics'. There is a problem, however, because we know that tastes vary from person to person, from culture to culture and from period to period. It follows that objects and styles can go in and out of fashion.

Individuals value a range of people, things and principles. To some their love of nation is so strong that they are willing to die waging war against other patriots who are equally willing to sacrifice themselves for their father- or motherland. Our own values seem natural to us – they are largely unspoken, unexamined. Generally speaking, it is only when we encounter the values of other cultures – and find them strange – that we become aware of our set of values. Watching a foreign film or visiting an exhibition of artefacts from a distant country will prompt comparisons.

We also become more conscious of values when we wish to sell something and when we have to speak or write about something in a public situation – like reviewing an exhibition for a magazine.

Valuation and evaluation

'Estimated or assigned worth . . . to appraise carefully.' Valuation implies a conscious and deliberate process, plus the existence of experts who provide objective judgements regardless of their personal preferences – for example, the Bonhams auctioneer who estimates that a Grateful Dead skull-head belt buckle will fetch £80 in a sale of rock music memorabilia.

Experts are assumed to have had years of experience and to possess specialist knowledge of a particular set of artefacts plus a market, which makes their valuations more informed and reliable than the vendor's.

Evaluation again implies a conscious, deliberate process. It is the kind of intellectual judgement undertaken by critics/historians and is routinely manifested in comments like 'Picasso was the greatest artist of the twentieth century'; 'Martin Scorsese is one of the finest directors of his generation', etc., etc. Critics generally write in the third person, thereby conveying the false impression that their judgements are universal/shared by all their readers.

In the case of histories of art, evaluations are implicit as well as explicit. When, for example, Gombrich allocates painter A two pages in *The Story of Art* and painter B three lines, and excludes painter C altogether, the implication is that painter A is better and more important than painter B, and both are superior to painter C. When art historians observe that an artist is important or significant, this does not necessarily mean he or she is excellent from the aesthetic point of view. During the 1960s Andy Warhol was very significant and influential, while often producing paintings and films which many critics feel were poor in quality. Some artists may also be historically important because they occupied powerful, official positions. The British history and portrait painter Sir Joshua Reynolds, for instance, is not generally considered the artistic equal of Gainsborough, Constable or Turner, but he is still remembered because he was the first President of the Royal Academy, and because of the discourses or lectures on art he delivered to students of the Academy between 1769 and 1790.[2]

The question 'What correlation exists, if any, between artistic merit, art-historical importance and monetary value?' is hard to answer because not all good artists sold work and were appreciated in their lifetimes (Van Gogh is a prime example). Even so, there are cases where there does seem to be a correlation: Impressionist paintings by Claude Monet, for instance, are now generally considered to be of high artistic value and major historical importance. They are also popular with both connoisseurs and the general public. This general approbation is reflected in the high prices Monets fetch at auction.

Ranking

Since we tend to judge cultural artefacts by means of comparison, one consequence of evaluation is *ranking*. '*Stagecoach* (1939)', a film critic might well remark, 'is a superb western but it is not so profound as *The Searchers* (1956).' (Note that the comparison is within a single medium and genre, and that both films were directed by John Ford and starred John Wayne. Comparing and ranking works from different media and art forms is much more problematic.) An example of ranking is the periodic exercise of identifying 'The best ten or one hundred films ever made'. Such lists regularly appear in newspapers and film magazines. They are often based on polls in which opinions were canvassed from leading film directors, archivists and critics.

In a horse race the criterion for judging the winner is simple: the first past the post. And the ranking order of the rest of the field is equally simple. In this instance judgement is quite objective: there cannot be a disagreement about who won along the lines: 'I liked the running style of the horse who came third and so I judge it to be the winner'. In the case of beauty contests and cultural artefacts, deciding on 'winners' and 'losers' is more difficult because the criteria underpinning judgements are nothing like so straightforward and objective. For instance, it is not obvious that all fine artists are running in the same race: their work may be so disparate that comparisons seem invidious. Can a sculptor sensibly be compared to a printmaker? Mozart and Madonna are both famous names in the sphere of music but they are so different in character and belong to such different periods that there seems little point in a direct comparison.

In many cases ranking is achieved by a formal means such as *a marking scale* linked to a set of criteria (such as skill, originality, etc.). For example, a British university grades student essays according to a one-to-twenty point scale and awards degrees according to a series of classes: first, two-one, two-two, third, unclassified and fail. Presumably, students expect the tutors who mark and classify their work to be informed and discriminating, to be skilled at distinguishing good from bad work (good work being that which has met the criteria laid down). Yet many students have expressed the opinion: 'all value judgements are subjective'. A subjective element is indeed present – tutors do vary in their marking habits (some are more generous or harder than others) – but this belief tends to deny the possibility of objectivity, intersubjectivity and agreement by consensus. It is a strange belief because surely students accept that there are objective, qualitative differences between essays which receive firsts and essays which are failed? Do they really believe that the marks given are simply the consequence of the personal whim of the tutor, that they have nothing to do with the intrinsic merits of the essays themselves?

One of the earliest attempts in the history of art criticism to establish a hierarchy and ranking of artists according to explicitly formulated and rational criteria was undertaken by Roger de Piles (1635–1709). He was a seventeenth-century French diplomat and critic who, in 1708, devised 'A Balance of Painters'[3] in which he gave marks out of twenty (was he, one wonders, the originator of the university marking scheme?) to fifty-seven painters according to their performance in four categories: composition; drawing or design; colour; and expression. For example, he awarded Titian twelve for composition, fifteen for drawing, eighteen for colour and six for expression, giving him a grand total of fifty-one out of a possible eighty. Michelangelo received only thirty-seven marks.

De Piles's list includes the names of masters who are familiar to us today – Titian, Rubens, Leonardo and so on – but it also includes Albani, Lanfranco, Barocci and Diepenbeck, artists who have been completely forgotten except by specialist art historians. Some of his judgements now strike us as peculiar: he gave an artist called Daniele da Volterra forty marks, three more than Michelangelo! But how is it that judgements have changed since the seventeenth century? We may be tempted to look down on de Piles and think he was wrong in many of his judgements, but perhaps de Piles was right and it is we who are in error. How can we be sure our judgements are superior? If we have not even seen any paintings by da Volterra, how can we be certain they are of little merit?

Evaluating and ranking films and records

Today, in the sphere of mass culture, there are well-known instances of evaluation and ranking. For example, in Britain a popular television programme about new, mainstream films is written and presented by Barry Norman. He does not mark films out of twenty; rather, his assessments are delivered via adjectives of praise or blame. Clips from films are screened so that we, the viewers, have some independent evidence for making up our own minds, then the critic delivers his verdict. Norman is no theorist but he can be considered an expert in the sense that he has watched many more films than non-specialists and knows much about the movie business, so his judgements are likely to be more informed than most viewers'. However, assuming Norman's judgements are sometimes wrong, or out of line with those of his audience, would it not be better to have more than one opinion? After all, there are twelve jurors in British courts of law.

Ranking exercises take place in Norman's programmes: viewers are shown lists of the 'Top ten films in the United States' or the 'Top ten films in Britain'. In these cases the ranking criterion is box office returns: the film which attracts the most viewers is deemed to be the most popular. This is a purely quantitative measure which does not necessarily mean that the number one film is the best in terms of artistic quality released at that time, because the high attendance figures may have been due to the impact of a massive advertising campaign. (Those who were persuaded to visit the cinema but who disliked the movie unfortunately still contributed to its supposed popularity.) Clearly, the contents of 'Top ten' lists are very temporary because they change as new movies are released and older ones are forgotten or end up on video.

Moviewatch (Channel 4 television, 1993–), another British television series reviewing new films, is aimed at younger viewers and employs four judges drawn from the public rather than one professional judge. The judges are teenagers or young adults – both male and female – selected from the residents of a particular town that changes from week to week. Although the judges are amateur critics, they are likely to have seen a large number of films and so presumably they will have developed visual literacy and personal tastes.

The judges are asked to give new releases a mark out of ten. Often they disagree: one will give a film a mark of four while another will give the same film a mark of eight. Such divergences are disturbing to anyone who thinks there is something immanent about the goodness or badness of a film. When all marks have been received they are averaged. This irons out the differences and yields a consensus opinion which enables the programme's presenter to rank that week's batch of films in a final, best-to-worst order.

If we take the view of relativism based on the ideology of individualism or the diversity of cultures – which many students do take – then how do we explain the fact that sometimes a film is thought splendid by all four judges? This was the case with Spike Lee's *Malcolm X* (1993): it was given maximum marks by all *Moviewatch*'s judges. (Orson Welles's *Citizen Kane* (1941) is another film about which there is critical agreement: it appears near the top in virtually all 'greatest films of all time' lists.) Surely, in this instance, the consensus must have been prompted by the superior quality of the film compared to the others under review? (Although, we suppose, an extreme sceptic might argue that it was simply a coincidence, a freak one-off agreement.) It was so good, so wide in its appeal, that it transcended all the taste and personality differences of the judges.

Yet another British television series that ranks cultural artefacts is *Top of the Pops* (BBC-1, 1964–) Every week this popular music programme features bands and singers who are high in the record charts. Again the ranking criterion is a quantitative one: record sales. Assuming the sale figures are honestly compiled, one could argue that this is a very democratic kind of evaluation: the people choose according to what they enjoy. (Of course, they choose amongst what the record companies chose to supply and publicise.) But do the people always choose the best records from the point of view of musical quality? Sometimes no, sometimes yes. During the 1960s, the records of the Beatles and Rolling Stones were number one hits and they were of high musical quality. (Popularity, there-fore, does not always signify dross.) Whereas, in the United States, the case of the Velvet Underground – a band sponsored by Andy Warhol during the 1960s – was a different story. This group achieved little in terms of sales and chart position but it did acquire an underground reputation which developed over the decades until the band came to be regarded as one of the finest and most influential rock bands of all time. Recognition of intrin-sic worth, therefore, is not always immediate.

Another ranking exercise is the Oscar nominations/awards regarding recent movies that takes place annually in Hollywood. Most cultural industries hold similar award ceremonies in which professionals congratulate one another in public. There are also competitions with monetary prizes judged by panels of experts: the Booker (literary) Prize, the Turner (art) Prize, for example. Essentially these are publicity events (Daniel Boorstin called them 'pseudo-events'[4]) cooked up in order to promote new books and new works of art.

Masterpieces, classics and cult objects

Often, when there is uncertainty about the artistic value of a recent cultural artefact, people remark 'time will tell'. But what does 'standing the test of time' actually entail? How does a cultural artefact attain the status of a 'masterpiece', 'classic' or 'cult object'?[5] Contrary to popular opinion, time itself is no judge; mental labour – discrimination, criticism, evaluation – is involved. Several conditions need to be fulfilled: first, an artefact has to be strong and lucky enough to survive physically long after its date of production (this implies care and preservation); second, it has to be sufficiently complex and profound to bear repeated viewing and to prompt a range of interpretations over time and across cultures; third, a firm positive judgement as to its high quality based, arguably, on objective aesthetic properties, has to be given by such taste leaders as artists, critics, historians, academics, curators, archivists and fans; fourth, their judgement has to be accepted by a significant proportion of society; fifth, their judgment has to be reproduced again and again, and accepted, by subsequent generations; sixth, the artefact has to exert a powerful influence on the work of other artists down the ages and be copied and reproduced.

The contents of national galleries and standard histories of art and design are testimonies to the artistic, curatorial and critical labour of centuries. They indicate that a consensus has been reached regarding the greatness/genius of such figures as Rembrandt and Leonardo. It would be extremely difficult for a contemporary layperson, or even an acknowledged expert, to contest and overturn such entrenched judgements. In a spirit of mischief, the television series *J'Accuse* (Channel 4, *Without Walls*, 1990–) attempted just that: in one programme, Brian Sewell, a controversial British art critic, bravely took on the task of puncturing Leonardo's 'inflated' reputation.

The canon

Gradually, masters and masterpieces are identified and accumulate until they constitute a *canon*. This term derives from the Christian religion: it is a rule, law or principle enacted by a Church council establishing, for instance, who is a saint and who is not, and which books have been authorised as holy. In our context it means a body of works that have been acclaimed by people – for example, connoisseurs – who are authorities. Some students find the idea of experts elitist and repellent. They ask: 'What gives them the right to pontificate? Have not their judgements often been wrong?' Experts do indeed make errors of judgement from time to time, yet there is no gainsaying the fact that training and experience are important: someone who has tasted thousands of wines will have developed a more discriminating palate than someone who has tasted only a few. In the case of healthcare or electrical wiring, most people prefer to rely on experts and defer to their specialist knowledge. However, this does not mean that students should automatically accept the evaluations of critics and historians. They should always compare what the experts say to their own lived experience. But they should also beware negative first impressions, because some tastes are acquired.

Every established cultural form now has its canon of great artefacts and creators. In fact there are usually a number of canons for each form and for each subgenre. Their contents usually reflect national biases: a canon of great films generated by Italian critics is likely to include more Italian examples than a similar list generated by Japanese critics.

Most canons peter out before the present moment. Thousands of recently made artefacts exist, any one of which might succeed in joining the canon. How does it happen that a new work is added to the canon? Juan Bonta, an architectural historian, has considered the canonisation process of Ludwig Mies Van Der Rohe's *Barcelona Pavilion*, designed as the German entry for a 1929 exhibition held in Barcelona.[6] (See figure 13.)

According to Bonta, after a building joins a canon there are three possible outcomes: first, it can become a cultural monument beyond the reach of negative criticism – it therefore remains in the canon for centuries; second, it can suffer a decline in reputation and be forgotten altogether; third, it can be subject to re-interpretation and re-evaluation by younger generations of critics examining it from new perspectives.

Several scholars have noted that canons are not as fixed as generally imagined. First, because, as time elapses, they have to be continually revised to accommodate new masterpieces; second, because of deletions, substitutions and the phenomenon of late arrivals: little-known and little-regarded artists from the past are occasionally re-discovered and praised highly. Their works of art are then bought by national art collections and books are written about them and so they gain entry to the canon long after the creators' lifetimes. This happened to the seventeenth-century Dutch painter Jan Vermeer, who became thought of as a great master only in the nineteenth and twentieth centuries. It also happened to Piero della Francesca, an Italian painter championed by the British art historian Kenneth Clark.

In recent decades canons and canon-formation have aroused much discussion and controversy.[7] These debates are not merely of academic significance. They have economic ramifications too – for example, published lists of the type 'Best One Hundred Films to Buy on Video' serve as consumer guides to novices and collectors – and also social implications – for example, the contentious issue of which novels, plays and poems should be studied in schools in countries that impose a national curriculum. Should the syllabus equal the canon? Should it be the British 'classics' written by DWMs (Dead White Males) such as William Shakespeare and Charles Dickens? (This is the view associated with conservative thinkers and politicians.) Or should it be recent best-sellers, or avant-garde texts, or books by feminists, or by writers from ethnic minorities and from the world's developing countries?

An ideological and political debate/struggle is taking place here involving issues of political correctness and multiculturalism versus monoculturalism. Presumably, the purpose of a single, nation wide canon is to foster integration, shared values and a common culture. But ethnic minorities who wish to preserve their identities and cultural traditions will resist integration and assimilation.

Some scholars regard canons as stultifying and suffocating because they imply conformity to a set of rules and conventions, and because they tend to narrow down appreciation. Others regard them positively on the grounds that they embody collective expressions of taste in a society, connect us to the finest culture and heritage of the past and provide essential selection guides. (Given the immense quantity of literature that exists, and the limited amount a human can read in a lifetime, Harold Bloom advises us to concentrate on the best that is available.[8]) Knowledge of the great art of the past is generally assumed to be essential for those training in the arts and media.

Canons, their supporters argue, act as benchmarks against which to judge new works. Certainly, one cannot estimate the worth and originality of a new artefact without some familiarity with the highest achievements of the past. Furthermore, viewers who lack knowledge of film history will not fully appreciate post-modern movies like Quentin Tarantino's *Pulp Fiction* (1994) because they will be unaware of their intertextual references.

As already explained, the persistence of a canon over time depends upon it being reproduced by generation after generation. University lecturers are one group involved in this process. For example, Film Studies lecturers will screen certain movies as exemplars of great film-making and thus transmit a canon to their students, some of whom will become academics who will screen certain films . . . To avoid mindless transmission, some academics foreground the issue of canons and initiate seminar discussions around such questions as: 'What qualities characterise classic films? How do canons come into existence? What purposes do they serve?

13 Two views of a 1985 reconstruction of Ludwig Mies Van Der Rohe's 1929 *Barcelona Pavilion* which was originally designed as the German entry for an international exposition held in Barcelona. Plus a plan of the original building.

During 1929 this structure was erected for only a short time but it became famous and entered the canon of great modern buildings. The Pavilion was the result of the initiative of Freiherr von Schnitzler, an industrialist whose paint company I G Farben financed it. Architects and critics have hailed it as a key example of the International Style and the elemental, 'less is more' aesthetic. They have praised its simplicity, refinement and elegant proportions. They have admired the way Mies contrasted ancient and modern materials – marble, chromium and glass – and the way he created a free flow of space beneath a flat roof seemingly supported by slim, cruciform piers. (The interior walls, placed at right angles to one another, divided a rectangular space but were not load-bearing.) To soften the severe, abstract nature of the architecture, one figurative work of sculpture was included: a female dancer by Georg Kolbe. Dark areas marked on the plan were pools of water. The pavilion was furnished with chairs and tables designed by the architect which themselves later became 'classics' of modern furniture design.

Juan Bonta has identified a pre-canonical phase when the building was first described, photographed and praised by architectural critics and journals. At that stage predictions were made as to its importance and its future canonical status. Bonta contended that the first stage was the most creative in terms of interpretation because, once the building became fixed in the canon, initial insights tended to be blurred through repetition and secondary commentary. Other buildings dating from 1929 were weeded out and forgotten. Canonisation occurred when most leading critics and historians cited the Barcelona Pavilion as a key work of modern architecture. This value judgement was then disseminated more widely via books, articles and history of architecture courses. The 1985 reconstruction was confirmation of the building's 'masterpiece' status.

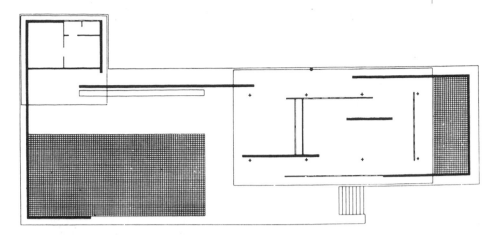

Who decides which films enter the canon? Why are documentaries, animated and experimental films normally excluded from the cinematic canon? Why do lists of the top ten films never include any female directors? Is the canon Euro/Ameri-centric and racially biased towards white film-makers? Are canons inevitable and immutable? Can they be revised or abolished?' Students are encouraged to compile their own lists of great and favourite films (the two will not necessarily be the same). The difficulty of selecting just ten or twenty films from the hundreds of possible candidates will illustrate the problems of constructing a canon from scratch.

At the risk of caricature, a spectrum of six views among politicians and academics about the existence and merit of canons can be envisaged.

First, Right-wing Ministers for Education will probably think a canon of great books or works of art is an excellent notion and so they will insist that all children in the country learn it. This will be regarded as a way to raise educational standards, impart traditional values and create a common culture. For them, the existence of a canon is unproblematic and it is the inherited one of the host/dominant culture which is to be celebrated and taught.

Second, supporters of modern art may well accept the need for a canon but think the traditional one needs revising and updating.

Third, Left-wing intellectuals and members of groups that have been discriminated against will scrutinise the canon looking for exclusions. A feminist art historian, for example, may register the lack of women artists and propose a revised canon with notable female artists added. Further additions may be suggested to make the canon more representative of a plural, multicultural society.

Fourth, more extreme Left-wingers will probably object to the existence of a single canon because it signifies cultural domination by a ruling class. They will propose alternative canons of say, great popular writers, or great African writers, or great women writers. (In David Mamet's play *Olenna* (Duke of York's Theatre, London, 1993, later made into a film), a drama about higher education and political correctness, a female student draws up a list of feminist texts for her ignorant male professor to read and teach.) Their ultimate aim would be to replace the traditional canon with a new list – or several lists – of approved, politically correct works.

Fifth, academics influenced by the anthropological attitude that all types of material culture are socially significant, and those who believe the influence of canons is baneful, will wish to dismantle canons so that they and their students can treat the whole gamut of artefacts – those from different cultures, periods and genres, the good, the bad and the mediocre – as worthy of analysis, as sources of sociological insight.

Sixth, theoretically minded scholars operating at the meta-discursive level will refuse to revise traditional canons or to compile alternatives. Instead they will attempt to understand canons by investigating how they originated and by considering what functions and whose interests they serve. From a distance they will analyse the struggles over value and canon-formation taking place within culture.

Cultural relativism

History shows that evaluations of artists and artworks have changed over time; consequently the composition of canons has altered too. Values also vary from person to person and from culture to culture. But does this mean that all values are relative, that there are no absolute or universal values?[9] Relativism is justified to the extent that understanding culture requires that the socio-historical circumstances of cultural production and consumption have to be taken into account, and also the position of both cultural consumers and those who observe them. But we should not conclude from this that there are only millions of individual subjective experiences that have nothing in common with one another. Paradoxically, human beings are both unique and very much alike – thus many characteristics, experiences and values are shared.

'Relative versus absolute' is a complex philosophical issue which is perhaps more suited to postgraduate than undergraduate study.[10] What can be said with certainty is that everyone recognises that there are qualitative differences between cultural artefacts. For instance, when shopping everyone discriminates between different designed products; everyone compares, evaluates and ranks them, if only intuitively. As the existence of canons demonstrates, agreements are also reached regarding artefacts of high aesthetic merit and some of these judgments persist for centuries.

Some scholars continue to believe in the absolute and universal nature of artistic values which, they are convinced, are objective properties of works of art just like strength is an objective property of a steel girder. The fact that some people cannot recognise them is no proof that they don't exist (people who can see and enjoy colours do not defer to those who are colour-blind). If universal human rights are deemed to exist, then why not universal artistic and cultural values?[11]

Summary

In recent decades many theorists have avoided critical evaluation.[12] One of the reasons the art critic Brian Sewell caused such consternation in the British art world in 1994 was that he continued to make value judgements and he expressed them very forcefully.[13] The refusal of evaluation on the part of theorists was partly due to the broadening of visual culture to include typical works and material of varying quality. Theorists who wished to decode a work because they were interested in the mechanics of signs and pictorial rhetoric, or in the relation of the work to ideology and social trends, felt that the artistic merit of that work was not necessarily the most important issue. If its content and impact were socially significant, then a run-of-the-mill Hollywood B movie was of as much interest as an art-cinema classic.

Critics also felt that they should put aside their own preferences and suspend their own value judgements, in order to account for the reactions of others. A critic may not have personally respected or valued the work of Jeff Koons, or the Euro-Disneyworld or the ultra-violent action films starring Arnold Schwarzenegger, but millions of people have done; consequently cultural theorists felt duty-bound to try and explain their appeal, and to analyse the pleasures they provided. However, critics and scholars do not stand outside society; they too have social responsibilities and these surely include a commitment to improving – through constructive criticism – the quality of art, design and media.

Education is one realm in which qualitative judgements continue to be made on the assumption that there are objective characteristics which distinguish good from bad work. Proof of this assertion is provided by the fact that tutors assess the work of their students at regular intervals, and dispense advice in order to improve the quality of future work. They also expect students to discriminate and to make evaluative judgements about the examples cited in their essays. Surely, therefore, it would be hypocritical if academics refused to make critical judgements of the artworks featured in their books and lectures. However, academics need to acknowledge when there are disputes about artistic value and they should distinguish between their own judgments and those of others. In the interests of learning, they should also try to explain the criteria underpinning their value judgements in precisely the same way that they make known (or should make known) the criteria by which the students' studio work and essays/dissertations are evaluated.

Notes and further reading

1   Seeking a mathematical model of change, Thompson turned to a theorem in topology – catastrophe theory – first stated by René Thom. *Rubbish Theory: The Creation and Destruction of Value*, (Oxford, Oxford University Press, 1979).

2   Sir Joshua Reynolds, *Discourses on Art*, ed. Robert R. Wark (New Haven, CT & London, Yale University Press, 1975).

3   Roger de Piles, *Cours de Peinture par Principes avec une Balance des Peintres*, (Paris, 1708). English translation published in London in 1743, extracted in E. G. Holt (ed.), *A Documentary History of Art Vol. II: Michelangelo and the Mannerists: the Baroque and the Eighteenth Century*, (New York, Doubleday Anchor Books, 1958), pp. 176–87.

4   Daniel J. Boorstin, *The Image or What Happened to the American Dream*, (Harmondsworth, Middlesex, Penguin Books, 1963), p. 21.

5   Deyan Sudjic is the author of a book entitled *Cult Objects: The Complete Guide to*

Having it All, (London, Paladin, 1985). Richard M. Blumenberg believes a classic work in any medium has the following attributes: first, permanence – it has withstood the test of time; second, it is rich and varied in meaning, third, it is unique in its vision, and fourth, it is innovative in structure, technique and style: 'The Classic Film', *Critical Focus: An Introduction to Film*, (Belmont, CA, Wadsworth, 1975), pp. 51–2. The British Film Institute is currently publishing a series of short books on individual movies called 'Film Classics'. During 1993 the magazine *Design* published as series of articles with the title 'Design Classics'. For definitions and history of the masterpiece see Walter Cahn's *Masterpieces: Chapters on the History of an Idea*, (Princeton, NJ, Princeton University Press, 1979).

6   J. P. Bonta, *Architecture and Its Interpretation*, (London, Lund Humphries, 1979).

7   For more on canons see: E. H. Gombrich and Q. Bell, 'Canons and Values in the Visual Arts: A Correspondence with Quentin Bell', *Ideas and Idols: Essays on Values in History and in Art*, (Oxford, Phaidon Press, 1979), pp. 167–83; (Various articles) *Times Higher Education Supplement*, (24 January 1992, 11 June 1993, 15 December 1995); P. Wollen, 'Films: Why Do Some Survive and Others Disappear?' *Sight & Sound*, 3:5 (May 1993), 26–8; John Guillory, 'Canonical and Non-Canonical: A Critique of the Current Debate', *ELH*, 54:3 (Fall 1987), 483–527.

8   Bloom is the author of a book celebrating the Western literary canon: *The Western Canon: The Books and Schools of the Ages*, (London, Macmillan, 1995). Bloom's advice is paradoxical: if we followed his injunction to read only the finest literature we would not bother to read his books.

9   For more on values see: J. Rosenberg, *On Quality in Art: Criteria of Excellence Past and Present*, (London, Phaidon Press, 1967); T. Eagleton and P. Fuller, 'The Question of Value: A Discussion', *New Left Review*, 142 (1984) 76–90; J. Squires (ed.), *Principled Positions: Postmodernism and the Rediscovery of Value*, (London, Lawrence & Wishart, 1993). The latter anthology was based on a conference held at the Institute of Contemporary Arts, London in December 1990 entitled 'A Question of Value'. This event indicated that value had been reinstated as a topic of importance amongst theorists.

10 For an introductory text see Louisa Buck's and Philip Dodd's *Relative Values or What's Art Worth?*, (London, BBC Books, 1991), based on a BBC–1 television series. For more sophisticated discussions see: Steve Connor's *Theory and Cultural Value*, (Oxford, Blackwell, 1992), Barbara H. Smith's *Contingencies of Value: Alternative Perspectives for Critical Theory*, (Cambridge, MA, Harvard University Press, 1989), and Joseph Margolis's *The Truth About Relativism*, (Oxford, Blackwell, 1991).

11 Ever-increasing globalisation is causing a convergence of human societies. It has already given rise to world organisations like the United Nations and the World Bank. Globalisation is also producing a common culture (though at present it mainly consists of American-dominated, commercially driven mass cultural forms). Clearly, such a development has advantages and disadvantages. If, for example, all the peoples of the world spoke one language then communication and understanding would be greatly enhanced, but the concomitant loss of other languages would drastically reduce cultural diversity.

12 For a perceptive sceptical analysis of the behaviour of literary theorists see: Raymond Tallis, 'Crisis in Criticism: The Demise of Evaluation', *In Defence of Realism*, (London, Edward Arnold, 1988), pp. 132–40.

13 In January 1994 over thirty members of the British art world signed an angry letter of protest about Sewell and posted it to the editor of the *Evening Standard*, the London paper for which Sewell regularly writes. See: B. Sewell, *The Reviews that Caused the Rumpus and Other Pieces*, (London, Bloomsbury, 1994).

12   Visual culture and commerce

> When I hear the word 'culture' I take out my checkbook.
> (Slogan in an artwork by the American artist Barbara Kruger, 1980s)

> No man but a blockhead ever wrote, except for money.
> (Samuel Johnson, 1776)

> In capitalist societies we are witnessing, on the one hand, the promotion of culture by commerce and, on the other, the promotion of commerce by culture. (Bernard Miège)[1]

> In the late twentieth century economic activity has become the principal form of human expression. Cultural engagement is perceived as cultural consumption, and indeed culture is seen more and more as a commodity like any other. Sadly, through the operation of the enterprise culture, the long front of culture has become a supermarket of styles.
> (Robert Hewison)[2]

MOST CULTURAL GOODS, once they have been made, are either given away, bartered or offered for sale. This chapter is concerned with the economic aspects of art and culture, the trade in cultural commodities, the commodification of culture, the so-called culture industries and the relationship between the arts, business and money. However, it will not be possible to treat all these topics in the detail they deserve. Examples of works of art and mass culture which self-reflexively comment upon their relation with commerce will be cited as a way of clarifying certain theoretical issues. Capital investment in, and funding of, the arts and media has been excluded because it has already been touched upon in the chapters on production and institutions.

Gifts

As the French anthropologist Marcel Mauss (1872–1950) demonstrated in his famous 1925 *Essai sur le Don*, in certain tribal societies of the past gift-exchange of such hand-made objects as decorated necklaces (which circulated in one direction) and armshells (which circulated in the opposite direction) was crucial to their social organisation.[3] In developed societies gift-exchange is not quite so important, but presents are still exchanged, most often on special occasions like birthdays, weddings and Christmas.

Children are key recipients of gifts in the form of toys. (Children are probably the group in our society who engage most in bartering via 'swapping'.) Gifts are one of the means of cementing social relationships, of creating social obligations, of saying thanks. (Van Gogh gave some of his paintings away as rewards to people like doctors who had helped him.) The vast majority of gifts are manufactured items which givers have purchased from shops; consequently before they were gifts they were commodities.

Any designed product could serve as a gift but in affluent societies a special type of object designed for giving – the gift-article – has been invented. This in turn has given rise to specialist outlets: gift-shops. Whole industries and retail chains thus rely upon the social custom of gift-giving. Gifts are clearly a topic of particular relevance to the history and practice of industrial design, and Clive Dilnot, a British design historian, has written a thoughtful theoretical paper on the subject in which he stresses the *dialogic* character of gifts – objects that mediate between people.[4]

Dilnot quotes Adorno's opinion that conditions in modern society militate against real gift-giving with the result that the act 'has degenerated to a social function exercised with rational bad grace . . . The decay of giving is mirrored in the distressing invention of gift-articles'. Dilnot comments: 'The invention of the gift-article . . . is the result both of the economic exploitation of the enforced gift relation . . . and of creating an "answer" (for the would-be gift buyer) to the "problem" of the true gift.' Hence, the gift-article becomes a substitute for the genuine gift. Often, a loss of usefulness and quality follows: 'the "gift-book" . . . is a book that is very nearly not a book'. Gifts involve 'wasteful expenditure' but 'this expenditure is nominal, not substantive: the gift-article is simply the sign of "money spent"'. The rest of Dilnot's article is an attempt to redeem industrial design as true giving. Let us turn now from gifts to commodities.

Commodities

In *Das Kapital* (vol. 1, 1867) Marx argued that commodities had a double aspect: first, they were physical things external to human beings that possessed certain properties which satisfied human wants or needs, hence they were articles of utility; in short, they had *use-values*; second, they were depositories of value which could be exchanged for other goods or for money; in short they had *exchange-values*.[5] Marx contended that the exchange-value of commodities had a purely social reality which was derived from the human labour expended in their production. While all products of human labour had use-values, only in a particular historical epoch did those products become commodities with exchange-value in terms of money, a universal medium of exchange. The epoch Marx had in mind was, of course, the era of bourgeois society, capitalism and the free-trade, market economy. Other theorists have argued that commodities existed in earlier societies.

Commodity fetishism

Marx identified a negative phenomenon called 'commodity fetishism': 'The social character of men's labour appears to them as an objective character stamped upon the product of that labour.' Social relations between people are displaced to appear as relations between things.[6] What commodities in supermarkets and advertising images hide is the labour that brought them into being. This is why John Berger, in part four of *Ways of Seeing* (1972) – an analysis of publicity – insisted on filming the non-glamorous reality of a woman on a factory assembly line manufacturing perfume. The division of labour associated with assembly lines results in a narrowing of human potential as workers become appendages of machines. They toil for money in the hope that they can fulfil themselves in leisure time. Such alienated labour is often contrasted with the greater freedom and pleasure in their work that artists enjoy.

Fetishism, a concept that merits a digression, recurs in several disciplines: economics, anthropology and psychoanalysis. It is also pertinent to Visual Culture Studies because fetish objects – objects thought to be inhabited by spirits, having magical potency, that provoke awe and blind reverence – are characteristic of tribal societies, of the public veneration for 'old masters' and some designed artefacts (so-called 'cult objects'), and also of the modern art movement Surrealism; witness the 1995 exhibition *Fetishism: Visualising Power and Desire*.[7] Fetishism in the sense of compulsive attachment to certain objects because of displaced sexual desire is clearly relevant to the erotic arts, pornography and fashion design. An understanding of fetishism will illuminate the work of artists like Allen Jones and Meret Oppenheim, and photographers like Grace Lau and Robert Mapplethorpe. It will help to clarify the appeal of pop stars like Madonna and the obsessive behaviour of fans of pop stars and groups.

Works of art as commodities

Many theorists claim that art is 'useless' and this is what distinguishes works of art from practical goods like telephones. (If they are correct, then Marx's definition of the commodity cannot apply to art.) This, we believe, is a mistaken idea. As explained in Chapter 11, works of art serve a variety of functions. The idea that art is an uneconomic, non-commercial activity is a myth. The art world has an economy: works of art are sold in private galleries every week; some fine artists accumulate fortunes. The idea that art is 'priceless' is another myth: when art objects appear in auctions they usually fetch prices. In recognition of this fact, the Southampton Institute of Higher Education has established a degree course in 'Fine Arts Valuation' intended to train students for auctioneering and the antique trade.

There are a number of reasons why so many false ideas have taken hold: art has spiritual, aesthetic dimensions that do not correlate directly with its monetary worth; many artists have had altruistic rather than money-making motives, have suffered for their ideals and failed according to purely commercial criteria (but then so have many small businessmen and women!); modern artists have generally worked independently; consequently they have enjoyed greater artistic freedom and autonomy than designers who are more subject to directives from clients and users, and to the commercial exigencies of business and the marketplace.

Often the output of an artist's studio is a series of one-off, unique artefacts; consequently, although such items are bought and sold, they are not so evidently commodities as the mass-produced goods disgorged by factories. Before the development of a fine art market, most works of art were commissioned by Royal and aristocratic patrons who retained them in their palaces and family collections. Furthermore, many of these commissions were for murals, tomb sculptures and public monuments that were designed for specific places. Such works could not become commodities unless they were detached from their physical settings. (In the 1990s tombs in Egypt are being torn apart by thieves who then sell the fragments to dealers and collectors in wealthy Western countries. Thus paintings and sculptures that the ancient Egyptians intended for sacred purposes only are forced to become art commodities.) The modern market in art depended upon the advent of portable objects such as paintings on canvas and is generally thought to have developed in seventeenth- century Holland. Markets freed artists from their dependence upon patrons but exposed them to the vagaries of market forces; they also became dependent upon dealers, collectors, curators and critics.[8]

Buildings such as houses, hotels and shops are traded like other goods but major, prestigious examples of public architecture like the White House normally remain outside the marketplace. Contemporary art still has examples of non-commodity works: community murals for instance. Artists still need to live, however: hence in these cases a fee or wage is paid. Performance art is another exception: no residue normally remains – apart from documentation – that can be bought and sold. Audiences pay entrance charges and a proportion is given to the performers. However, in the case of rock musicians, there are spin-off products – records and other merchandise – that are commodities.

Commerce and content

While the vast majority of artists have excluded money and business from the substance of their work, a few have addressed the issue head on. Andy

Warhol, the American Pop artist, for instance. Having been a successful graphic designer, he felt no guilt or qualms about the commercial aspects of art. In the early 1960s, along with commodities such as Campbell's soup cans and Coca-Cola bottles, his iconography encompassed dollar bills. Thus images of money became worth money. And since the bills depicted were of low denominations, their 'face value' inflated as Warhol's prices rose. Later, Warhol transformed his New York studio – 'The Factory' – into a business enterprise and declared: 'Business art is the step that comes after art. I started as a commercial artist, and I want to finish as a business artist . . . Being good in business is the most fascinating kind of art . . . making money is art and working is art and good business is the best art'.[9]

Warhol's lengthy professional career testified to his ability to diversify across a range of media, to exploit publicity and to market his products in ways that many business people must envy. Some Left-wing critics attacked Warhol because his work seemed to capitulate to the forces of commodification, industrialisation, standardisation and stereotyping. There was a large measure of truth in these charges but at least his art made these issues visible. Jeff Koons is Warhol's main American successor. With his self-advertisements, kitsch and porn art, Koons has carried Warhol's philosophy of business art and self-promotion to extraordinary heights. Another American follower of Warhol is J. S. G. Boggs. He has built a career out of making images from banknotes which he manages to use as a form of currency.[10] During 1986–7 the Bank of England prosecuted him but, following a court case, he was acquitted.

In 1983 the British sculptor Julian Opie constructed a painted metal relief entitled *Cash This*. It showed a cheque made out for cash (£35) being signed by Opie. What Opie was saying is that making a sculpture is equivalent to writing out a cheque to obtain money. (It also confirmed the importance of the artist's signature as a guarantee of authenticity and value.) Hans Haacke can be cited as an example of a more critical and politically committed artist who has made the issue of art as a commodity the subject of certain works. In the mid–1970s, for example, he produced photo-text 'provenance' pieces that documented the ownership-histories of paintings by Manet and Seurat and the prices paid for them whenever they changed hands.

Of course, it would be a delusion to assume that work of arts which expose their commodity character thereby transcend commodification. Unless the artist refuses to sell them and insists that they are always treated as gifts, then they too can become commodities. (In 1990–1 a travelling exhibition was organised by The Gallery, New York with the title *Art = Money?* which featured works by various contemporary artists playing with the theme of money and commodification – all items were offered for sale.[11]) Nevertheless, in their favour they can be said to provide knowledge of the capitalist nature of art under capitalism.

Evidently, there are some paradoxical products whose message or content is at odds with, or is designed to subvert, their commodity character. Some examples from the realm of rock music: John Lennon, a multi-millionaire, sold thousands of records with such radical themes as revolution, power to the people and slogans such as 'imagine no possession's. The group Bow Wow Wow's 1981 number C30, C60, C90, Go! encouraged listeners to tape-record music instead of buying it. This song, inspired by Malcolm McLaren's anarchism, was intended to embarrass the record company (EMI) that issued it. Jamie Reid, graphic designer to the Punk rock group the Sex Pistols, held an exhibition in London in 1986 which included a notice to be attached to a shop window which claimed that the shop welcomed shoplifting. Since this item was for sale, its message was contradictory. One wonders what the result of a court case would have been if a visitor had taken the instruction literally. Is it likely that someone who shoplifted a notice advocating the crime of shoplifting would be found guilty?

Objections to commodities

Various objections have been made to the art/money nexus. The enormous prices fetched by paintings by Van Gogh and others tends to interfere with the appreciation of the works themselves. Monetary value displaces artistic value. In 1988, as a comment on this state of affairs, the British artist Rose Finn-Kelcey made an installation entitled *Bureau de Change* in which Van Gogh's *Sunflowers* – recently sold for £22.5 million – was reproduced on the floor of Matt's Gallery using coins worth £1,000. This work was thus a literal demonstration of the way the Van Gogh had been transformed into money. In contrast, Finn-Kelcey's metallic image avoided commodification: when the show closed, the coins were returned to the bank from which they had been borrowed.

Millionaire collectors sometimes acquire works of art purely for investment reasons and they then hide them away in bank vaults. A frenetic, booming art market attracts greedy people whose primary interest is money rather than art. Such a market encourages art to be made for exchange and profit rather than for use. Artists compete with one another to see who can attract the most media attention. This results in what may be called 'scam' or 'stunt art' – the weirdest items are *presented* (rather than *represented*) in galleries. The British artist Damien Hirst has become notorious for his dead shark, lamb and cow 'sculptures'. In July 1995 Tony Kaye, an advertising film-director who wishes to enjoy the status of a fine artist, offered a male homeless tramp for sale as 'a living work of art'. (See Figure 14.)

One socialist objection to art commodities is that each time objects are bought and sold by a succession of dealers and collectors for higher and higher prices (of course this does not happen in every case – losses can also be made) artists do not directly benefit; they do not receive the full fruits of their labour. As those who advocate resale rights maintain, one remedy for this would be for artists to receive a proportion of any profits every time a work was re-sold.

Most fine art objects are unique. Their rarity means that they tend to become expensive, luxury goods which can be afforded only by the wealthy. Ownership of art and access to it is, therefore, difficult for the poor. The latter generally have to rely on the existence of buildings and monuments in public spaces and 'free' public galleries and museums. (Entrance charges to museums are becoming more widespread; they will discourage the poor from attending.) Some artists have been concerned about this situation and have tried to make works in editions to generate more/cheaper products: Van Gogh, for instance, attempted to have prints made that would be affordable by artisans; during the 1960s there was a vogue for so-called 'multiples' which, many thought, would democratise fine art; in the 1980s the American, graffiti-style artist Keith Haring opened Pop Shops in New York and Tokyo in order to sell various kinds of merchandise he had designed or ornamented.

Attempts to achieve a greater democratisation of art via mass-production usually fail because they contradict the restricted nature of production associated with the social institution of art as it currently exists. A fine artist who mass-produces will 'cross over' from art to mass culture. One American performance artist who achieved this to some degree was Laurie Anderson. The Pop art movement of the 1950s and 1960s had more of a popular appeal than most trends in modern art, but leading British contributors like Peter Blake and Richard Hamilton reached mass audiences not so much via their paintings as by fulfilling commissions from mass culture, that is, by designing such things as album covers for pop music groups like the Beatles.

The arts currently receive considerable subsidies from the public purse. Some commentators give the impression that culture would cease if such support was withdrawn. But, of course, what would remain are the arts and crafts that sell, plus the commercial forms of mass culture. Artists who can sell their work are probably pleased they do not need to rely on public funds and the cap-in-hand/form-filling process that obtaining such funds generally entails. Also, they can be fairly sure that their work is actually wanted and appreciated. (In the Netherlands an 'art mountain' has resulted from the over-production of art, by state-funded artists, for which there is not a sufficient public demand.) Arguably, those who pay out of their own pockets to see films or to obtain records make more of a commitment to culture than those who visit 'free' museums. Despised commercial culture, therefore, has much to recommend it, but its critics would argue (with some justice) that the mass market imposes certain limits on what can be produced: popularity and saleability are crucial. Private patronage and public arts funding are thus more likely to support experimental and critical work with a minority appeal. (Often such art depends upon self-funding by the artist.) Nevertheless, even commercial culture relies upon creativity, novelty and innovation to some degree.

Commodities are not normally thought of as works of art but as the primary or bulk products of agriculture and heavy industry – coffee, tea, wheat, gold, steel, oil, etc. – and the billions of factory-made goods that are traded in markets of different kinds. (Money, the principal medium of exchange, can also be treated as a commodity (the money markets) and

14 *Roger*, a living work of art, outside the Tate Gallery, London (June 1996).

Roger Powell, a fifty-six-year-old homeless tramp, was persuaded by Tony Kaye (b. 1953) – a wealthy and eccentric television commercials director who would like to be taken seriously by the art world – to become a living work of art. Initially Roger was offered for sale – price £1,000 – at the Saatchi Gallery, North London, in July 1995, as part of the *British Design and Art, Festival of Excellence*. Treating a tramp as a commodity seemed like a return to slavery, though in fact Powell would have kept most of the money. Since no one bought him, Kaye decided to maintain Powell until one of them dies. (A transition from slavery to wage-slavery.) A new value of £850,000 has been placed on him (should another collector wish to replace Kaye as the 'owner' of 'the exhibit'). In return for his keep, Powell has to appear in art galleries in Britain and abroad in order to discuss the issue of homelessness with gallery-goers. Kaye sees his creation *Roger* as an unusual way of calling attention to this worldwide social problem. Of course, it also generates much press publicity for Kaye himself.

even commodity markets themselves can be bought and sold.) During the last three centuries industrialisation, mass manufacture, mechanical reproduction and new communication technologies brought about an immense increase in foodstuffs, material goods, a higher standard of living, a consumer society, and a democratisation of culture. Today, virtually everyone in developed nations has access to newspapers, magazines, books, images, media, consumer durables, museums, cinemas, etc. These tremendous gains should not be forgotten when criticisms of commodification are being made.

Critics who take a global perspective argue that the consumer culture of the developed nations in the northern hemisphere is being enjoyed at the expense of the exploitation and impoverishment of countries in the southern hemisphere. Carpets from India, for example, are often woven by children employed in conditions of near-slavery. Greedy northern consumers are also accused of being mainly responsible for the Earth's ecological problems.

Another criticism often made is that the industrialisation of culture has resulted in mountains of trash: low quality, debased, ugly kitsch. In 1939 the American critic Clement Greenberg published an essay entitled 'Avant-Garde and Kitsch' in which he vilified kitsch and maintained that avant-garde art was the only worthwhile, living culture. Arguably, in developed nations, there is an enormous, wasteful over-production of artefacts that are worthless from both practical and aesthetic points of view. But some critics believe that this judgement applies to avant-garde art as well as kitsch!

The culture industry

Theodor Adorno, a leading member of the Frankfurt School of philosophy, used the disparaging term 'culture industry' to describe modern forms of mass culture. In his opinion, traditional works of art tended to be made for use whereas mass culture tended to be made for exchange and profit. Adorno remarked: 'Cultural entities of the culture industry are no longer *also* commodities, they are commodities through and through.'[12]

Commodification is regarded as negative because it alters culture's character for the worse, for example, by causing a loss of artistic integrity and quality, tending towards standardisation, pseudo-individualism, stereotyping, passive consumption, 'mere entertainment', etc. As an illustration consider a film producer's – Lawrence Bender's – view that Hollywood studios try to make movies via committees and marketing:

> The way that committees make movies is by second-guessing what the audience want to see. There isn't some person there with a passion for movies – saying what the film should be, they are usually saying 'I think we need an upbeat ending here, a bit of love interest there'. It's letting the marketing create the movie, instead of the movie creating the marketing.[13]

Bender also pointed out that test-marketing allows the public to decide the fate of a film and this presumes that everyone shares the taste of a few hundred people in a small, provincial American town.

In the case of some Hollywood movies the money spent on marketing and publicity rivals or exceeds production costs; also, the income derived from tie-in merchandise is enormous. Films as cultural experiences/commodities in their own right continue to attract customers and to make money but increasingly they are simply the basis for a host of other media and commercial ventures.

However, while it may be tempting for academics to conclude that all mass-produced goods made for sale and profit must be artistically worthless, it is surely too simplistic a response. Many such goods and popular films, records and television programmes are of high aesthetic quality and have significant content. (Intellectuals write and buy many books; consequently if they condemn cultural commodities then they should condemn their own books and their passion for book-acquisition.) Also, cultural commodities must satisfy some needs of the masses otherwise they would not sell; consequently use-values have not been dispensed with altogether. Furthermore, the content of mass culture is sometimes critical of current society and commodification.

Blanket condemnations of the culture industries do not help workers in those industries to effect change. Walter Benjamin, another thinker associated with the Frankfurt School, had some positive suggestions for Left-wing artists and writers: they should reflect upon their own position as workers within the relations of production and seek to organise with fellow workers; they should cease uncritically supplying the production apparatus – instead they should try to adapt it to the ends of proletarian revolution; their own works should 'possess an organising function' and act as a model to others.[14]

Rock and pop music

Simon Frith, a British sociologist and rock music critic, is a writer who has doubted the value of the kind of analysis which sets the arts against business:

> I don't believe that pitting art versus business . . . actually helps us in analysing a mass culture like rock. It is precisely because music, money, and adulation *can't* be separated – by musicians and audiences – that rock is so important. Rock fans and rock performers alike want their music to be powerful, to work as music *and* commodity.[15]

He went on to argue that the commercial process of rock is *essentially contradictory* because, while the music business constantly strives to control the market and public taste, it never completely succeeds because consumers are *active* not passive, and because shifts in musical taste are unpredictable. Later he adds:

> The rock industry, as a capitalist enterprise, doesn't sell some single hegemonic idea, but is, rather, a medium through which hundreds of ideas flow. Commercial logic shapes these ideas, but . . . efficient profit-making involves not the creation of 'new needs' and audience 'manipulation' but, rather, the response to existing needs and audience 'satisfaction' . . . The record industry must always try to mould its market (this is the reality of rock-as-commodity), but this must always involve a struggle (this is the reality of rock-as-leisure-commodity).[16]

Most rock bands have a love–hate relationship with their managers and record companies. Many performers have become rich but tales of exploitation are also rife. During the Punk rock era of the mid–1970s McLaren and the Sex Pistols managed to turn the tables on the record companies by exploiting them by obtaining large advances and then behaving so badly the companies felt compelled to drop them. In the following decade, new pop groups adopted a blatantly commercial, cynical attitude. Sigue Sigue Sputnik (SSS), for example, was a short-lived band devised mainly by Tony James. The band's image was consciously constructed and the marketing and publicity strategies were all revealed in interviews and in media profiles of James and SSS. Although a record and a video were eventually released, the appeal of the band was primarily the spectacle of self-promotion itself. Success was measured not in terms of musical creativity but in designing a package the record company would accept, in playing and winning against the system, manipulating it in order to obtain funds so that the game could continue.

SSS could not be accused of hiding the truth; on the contrary, the whole construction and selling process was gleefully revealed. One might have expected a negative reaction: 'This is a confidence trick, I won't buy their record', but a considerable number of the public did. James realised that the spectacle of business struggle and success was fascinating in its own right.

Another 1980s example of business as an exciting theme was the Hollywood movie *Wall Street* (directed by Oliver Stone, 1987) in which Michael Douglas played Gekko, a greedy, ruthless but rich and glamorous corporate raider and speculator. Gekko is also a collector of contemporary art. In one scene he praises art as the ideal example of how money can be profitably invested and how value can be created via a consensus reached by a group of wealthy and powerful people. In short, he celebrates art as the ultimate commodity, as the final reward for having made it. There was an echo here of a cutting remark that appeared in a 1960s' Situationist comic strip: 'Culture? Ugh! The ideal commodity – the one which helps sell all the others!'[17]

Art and economics

During the 1980s Right-wing governments and intellectuals prevailed in Britain and the United States. Economic policies favourable to business and market forces led to the selling-off and commercialisation of many public services. It became fashionable to affirm the conjunction of commerce and culture. For example, when the privately funded Design Museum opened in London in 1989 its first exhibition was entitled *Commerce and Culture*.[18] Stephen Bayley, the Museum's director, asserted that industrial design was superior to avant-garde art, indeed that it was the true 'art' of the twentieth century. He also argued that before the industrial revolution commerce and culture had been fully integrated and now they were converging again. In addition, museums were becoming more like shops, and shops more like museums. People were consuming culture (rather than contemplating it) just like they did other consumer goods.

Bayley's views were unsympathetic to the resistance and criticism of commodities and commodification which has characterised much radical, twentieth-century art. (The critical activities of Gustav Metzger are a prime example.) Of course, it is much more difficult for designers to oppose late capitalism because they would be risking their livelihoods. Even so, there are some designers with social and ecological agendas who have criticised the industrial design profession and the economic system it serves.[19]

In Britain those defending the arts and film-making against government cuts during the 1980s were compelled to resort to the economic argument. They undertook research in order to show the monetary value of the arts to the nation's economy.[20] During the same decade younger Left-wing theorists took issue with Adorno and began to use the expression 'culture industries' in a positive way. They considered that, given the decline of old, heavy industries like mining and shipbuilding, Britain could renew its economy by fostering new arts and media industries like fashion, music, publishing, film-making and television production. Tourism was also a key source of foreign earnings and the arts were one of Britain's principal attractions.

The idea that the arts could be re-categorised as 'industries' provoked a strong negative reaction in some quarters. John Pick, a professor in Arts Management at City University, London, for example, was incensed by the idea.[21] Pick might well have considered an earlier form of tourism and holiday-making – the religious pilgrimages of the Middle Ages. The huge size of medieval cathedrals was due to the crowds of pilgrims they had to accommodate, and these buildings housed fetish objects – holy relics – designed to attract visitors. The crush of people also meant that towns with cathedrals became the focus of trade fairs and business enterprises.

Intellectual property rights

Private property is the cornerstone of capitalism and therefore students who expect to function in that system after graduation need to familiarise themselves with laws relating to the ownership of such things as images. Should they ever wish to employ the cartoon image of Mickey Mouse, for instance, they need to appreciate that they will have to pay for this so-called 'character merchandising', otherwise they are likely to be prosecuted by the lawyers employed by the Disney Corporation.

Many art and design students copy images and photographs without appreciating that they might be infringing the law of copyright. Whenever images still in copyright are published for profit then the maker's (or picture agency's) permission is needed and reproduction fees are generally charged. (It is surely just that during their lifetimes photographers should receive income from the fruits of their labour but less reasonable that copyright fees should continue to be paid for decades after their deaths.) Companies and artists in many different cultural industries earn large sums from royalty payments and reproduction rights: consequently these rights are jealously guarded. (Two organisations whose purpose is to collect royalties for artists, designers and photographers are SPADEM (France, 1954–) and DACS (UK, 1983–).)

The existence of copyright has its negative effects on the production of new culture. For instance, British television producers claim that intellectual property rights are a major obstacle for those wishing to make serious programmes about the history of pop music. Jon Savage, a scriptwriter for a 1995 documentary on Punk, complained:

> The more serious brake on the programme came from . . . the labyrinth of payments and clearances that you have to have if you're going to show any non-contemporary clip – that is, outside the Pop video's promotional time-span. There are four separate deals that you may have to make: with the Musicians' Union (session fee); with the Performing Rights Society (public performance of recorded music); with the record company (ownership of recording copyright); with the publishing company (ownership of song copyright).[22]

Plagiarism

Of course, it is paradoxical that, while unauthorised copying is frowned upon, modern media companies make copying easier and easier by inventing and selling photocopying, tape- and video-recording machines. Copyright laws are thus flouted by millions of ordinary people every day as well as by criminal gangs who sell 'bootleg' copies of films and records.

Jeff Koons is an American artist who thought he could ignore copyright law and appropriate for his own use a photograph by Art Powers reproduced on a best-selling postcard. In 1988 Koons employed Italian craftsmen to carve a wooden sculpture entitled *String of Puppies* that was based on the content and composition of the Powers' photo. Powers strongly objected to the unauthorised, uncredited use of his work and took him to court. In 1991 Koons was found guilty of plagiarism and fined heavily.

Plagiarism – gaining unfair advantage by passing off as one's own the work of others – is also considered a grave offence by university authorities and students are warned against it. Paradoxically, some of the leading modern artists students are expected to study and admire have advocated plagiarism as a useful artistic tactic. Furthermore, during the 1980s, some radical artists deliberately engaged in plagiarism as an anti-capitalist, anti-commodity, subversive strategy.[23]

Summary

Whatever political system is in place, there will be an economy in which art, design and mass media play a part. As traditional manufacturing industries decline, cultural industries increase in importance. Business sponsorship of the arts and the employment of artists by advertisers mean that visual culture is increasingly being promoted by commerce and vice versa. Therefore, students should study the symbiotic relationship and tensions that exist between visual culture and commerce, visual culture and private property. They would be wise to scrutinise the business pages of newspapers as closely as the arts pages.

Notes and further reading

1 Bernard Miège, 'The Cultural Commodity', *Media, Culture & Society* 1:3 (July 1979), 297–312.

2 Robert Hewison, *Culture and Consensus: England, Art and Politics since 1940*, (London, Methuen, 1995), p. 305.

3 M. Mauss, *The Gift: Forms and Functions of Exchange in Archaic Societies*, (New York, Norton, 1976). See also: Lewis Hyde, *The Gift: Imagination and the Erotic Life of Property*, (New York, Random House, 1979); and C. A. Gregory, Gifts and *Commodities*, (London, Academic Press, 1982).

4 C. Dilnot, 'The Gift', *Design Issues*, 9:2 (Fall 1993), 51–65. For Theodor Adorno's remarks on gifts see: 'Articles May Not be Exchanged' (1944), *Minima Moralia: Reflections from Damaged Life*, (London, Verso, 1974), pp. 42–3.

5 Various explanations of commodities are given by economists, sociologists and anthropologists. See also: William Leiss, *The Limits to Satisfaction: On Needs and Commodities*, (Toronto and Buffalo, University of Toronto Press, 1976); Mary Douglas and Baron Isherwood, *The World of Goods: Towards an Anthropology of Consumption*, (London, Allen Lane, 1979); Bernard Miège, 'The Cultural Commodity', *Media, Culture & Society*, 1:3 (July 1979), 297–312; Arjun Appadurai (ed.), *The Social Life of Things: Commodities in Cultural Perspective*, (Cambridge, Cambridge University Press, 1986); Nick Rowland, *Commodities*, (London, Free Association Books, 1987).

6 K. Marx, *Capital: A Critical Analysis of Capitalist Production*, vol. 1, (London, Lawrence & Wishart, 1970), pp. 76–87.

7 An exhibition catalogue was issued: Anthony Shelton (ed.), *Fetishism: Visualising Power and Desire*, (London, South Bank Centre/Lund Humphries; Brighton, Royal Pavilion Art Gallery, 1995). See also: Donald Kuspit, 'The Modern Fetish', *Artforum*, 27:2 (October 1988), 132–40; Emily Apter and William Pietz (eds), *Fetishism as Cultural Discourse*, (Ithaca, NY, Cornell University Press, 1993); Laura Mulvey, 'Some Thoughts on Theories of Fetishism in the Context of Contemporary Culture', *October*, 65 (Summer 1993), 3–20; Lorraine Gamman and Merja Makinen, *Female Fetishism: A New Look*, (London, Lawrence & Wishart, 1994); Valerie Steele, *Fetish: Fashion, Sex, Power*, (Oxford, Oxford University Press, 1996); and Laura Mulvey, *Fetishism and Curiosity*, (London, British Film Institute, 1996).

8 There are a number of histories and studies of the art market/trade: Gerald Reitlinger, *The Economics of Taste*, 3 vols, (London, Barrie & Rockliff, 1960–70); J. Alsop, *The Rare Art Traditions: A History of Art Collecting and its Linked Phenomena*, (Princeton, NJ, Princeton University Press, 1981); William D. Grampp, *Pricing the Priceless: Art, Artists, and Economics*, (New York, Basic Books, 1989); Peter Watson, *From Manet to Manhattan: The Rise of the Modern Art Market*, (London, Hutchinson, 1992). For an account of the local and international art trade in African objects see: Christopher B. Steiner, *African Art in Transit*, (Cambridge, Cambridge University Press, 1994).

9 A. Warhol, *From A to B and Back Again*, (London, Pan Books, 1976), p. 88.

10 On Boggs see the exhibition catalogue: *J. S. G. Boggs, Smart Money, Hard Currency*, (Tampa, FL, Tampa Museum of Art, 1990), with essays by Bruce W. Chambers and Arthur C. Danto.

11 *Art = Money?* (New York, The Gallery, 1990), 16-page catalogue with introduction by Achille Bonito Oliva. The exhibition was curated by Michael McKenzie and Roberto Mitrotti.

12 T. W. Adorno, *The Culture Industry: Selected Essays on Mass Culture*, (London, Routledge, 1991).

13 Bender quoted in Lizzie Francke's article, 'Reel Rebellion', *The Observer Review*, (26 March 1995), 2–3.

14 W. Benjamin, 'The Author as Producer' (1934), *Understanding Brecht*, (London, New Left Books, 1977), pp. 85–103.

15 S. Frith, *Sound Effects: Youth, Leisure, and the Politics of Rock*, (London, Constable, 1983), p. 91.

16 *Ibid.*, p. 270.

17 The strip is reproduced in *Leaving the 20th Century: The Incomplete Work of the Situationist International*, ed. Christopher Gray, (London, Free Fall Publications, 1974), p. 16.

18 Stephen Bayley (ed.), *Commerce and Culture: From Pre-Industrial Art to Post-Industrial Value*, (London, Design Museum/Fourth Estate, 1989). See also Nigel Whiteley's essay 'High Art and the High Street: The "Commerce-and-Culture" Debate', *The Authority of the Consumer*, eds R. Keat, N. Whiteley and N. Abercrombie, (London & New York, Routledge, 1994), pp. 119–37.

19 See, for example, Victor Papanek's *Design for the Real World: Human Ecology and Social Change*, (London, Thames & Hudson, rev. edn 1985) and *The Green Imperative: Ecology and Ethics in Design and Architecture*, (London, Thames & Hudson, 1995).

20 See: John Myerscough, *The Economic Importance of the Arts in Britain*, (London, Policy Studies Institute, 1988). This report revealed that the arts had an annual turnover of £10b, that £4b was generated from overseas earnings, and £3b from tourists. Total attendances by people at art events in 1984–5 reached 251 billion. Consumer spending on admission charges to arts events was estimated as £433m

during 1985–6. However, another report — Ruth Towes's *The Economics of Artists' Labour Markets*, (London, Arts Council of England, 1996) – showed that there is an oversupply of arts graduates and artists; consequently the majority experience poverty.

21 J. Pick, 'Perspective: Arts under the Hammer', *Times Higher Education Supplement*, (20 January 1989), 13, 17.

22 J. Savage, 'Never Mind the Bollocks', *The Guardian*, (11 August 1995), p. 20.

23 For more on plagiarism see: Stewart Home (ed.), *Plagiarism: Art as Commodity and Strategies for its Negation*, (London, Aporia Press, 1987); John A. Walker, 'Perspective: Living in Borrowed Time', *Times Higher Education Supplement*, (26 February 1988), 13, and his book *Art in the Age of Mass Media*, (London, Pluto Press, 2nd edn 1994).

13 New technologies

> Most people are accustomed to asking the question 'What will the new technology do?' very few are inclined to ask 'What will it *undo*?' Then I think we have to ask the question 'Who will be the winners and who the losers in any new technology?' because all technological innovation is a Faustian bargain – it giveth and it taketh away, but not in equal measure.
> (Neil Postman)[1]

THIS CHAPTER considers some of the ways in which new technologies – often called 'New Media' or 'Computer-Mediated Communication' (CMC) or 'Electronic Arts/Media'[2] – are imbricated in the production, distribution and consumption of contemporary visual culture. It also examines, briefly, the educational implications of 'the age of information' for the study of visual culture.

Defining technology

The word element 'techno', which derives from the Greek term 'techne' meaning art or skill, gave rise to modern words like 'technical' and 'technique'. In one sense 'technology' means 'knowledge of applied science and engineering'; in another it means 'systematic treatment'. Yet what most often comes to mind when we hear the word 'technology' are images of the powerful machines, engines, instruments, weapons and complex, organisational systems that made such things as cars, aircraft, nuclear bombs and space travel possible. In terms of visual culture, we think of a succession of waves of new media: photography, the cinema, television, video, computer graphics, communication satellites, multimedia, the Internet, virtual reality. To this list can be added: lasers, holography, photocopiers and FAX (facsimile) machines.

Those responsible for the development of 'the hardware' – mechanics, scientists, engineers and inventors – are not usually artists or designers (there are some exceptions). Designers adapt it to suit practical human needs; architects employ it to construct new kinds of structure; artists rely upon it to produce and deliver 'the software', that is, the art or communication itself (after all, no one would buy television sets if there were no programmes to watch). The 'hardware/software' distinction indicates a significant difference between contemporary media dependent upon machines and the older, craft-based arts.

Technological 'progress' appears to be relentless. It is driven by various factors: human curiosity; the desires to reduce human labour and to solve problems (paradoxically, the solution to a problem caused by technology may itself be technological); profit (thousands of researchers are employed by large companies for the purpose of inventing new materials, machines and products). Commercial imperatives often result in products performing similar functions which, for some time at least, are incompatible. Competition between rival firms also fuels the spate of new inventions and gadgets which in turn results in rapid obsolescence. The impulse for technological innovation is especially strong in the sphere of mass entertainment.

Past and present

There is nothing recent about the relationship between technology and visual culture. The first person to make a flint axe in order to shape a stone figure employed basic technology. All the arts − except perhaps the Conceptual − rely upon technologies of various sorts and degrees of sophistication. Technology extends globally across all cultural groups and underpins the whole evolution of visual culture from prehistoric cave paintings to the work of living artists such as Laurie Anderson, Bill Viola and Stelarc. Volumes would be needed to describe the history of the tools, invented materials, machines and industrial manufacturing plants that eventually evolved into the systems of mass media/communications and designed products familiar to us today.[3] For this reason, our focus is new rather than old technologies.

Some key historical breakthroughs do need to be acknowledged, however − for example, the technologies of die-casting metal coins stamped with the same image of an emperor and the printing of books by means of metal type that yielded editions or batchs of identical objects. These were the origin of our modern world of billions of products/commodities enjoyed by vast numbers of people. During the industrial revolution and the era of Fordism (that is, the innovations of the motor car entrepreneur Henry Ford), the invention of engines and machine-tools, the specialisation of tasks/division of labour, standardisation of parts, and the organisation of factories into moving assembly lines, and, later still, the augmentation or replacement of human labourers with robots and automated, computer-controlled systems, made possible enormous increases in productivity which have resulted in the affluent but profligate consumer societies typical of today's developed nations.

During the second half of the twentieth century technology developed beyond the industrial or machine age into what is now known as the post-industrial or *information age*[4] (cynics would say 'the age of disinformation'). To mechanical means of image reproduction and dissemination were added electronic forms. Systems of transport, trade and communication proliferated, accelerated and became ever more globalised.

As producers, humans have shifted from a world of hand-held tools requiring manual dexterity to a world of mechanical tools requiring a combination of manual skill and operational know-how. And shifted again to a world of electronic equipment demanding little in terms of manual effort but considerable operational knowledge. Beyond the equipment itself, new visual aids have had to be designed to facilitate its use; for instance, illustrated instruction manuals and the layout of the operating information on the machines themselves – the physical manifestation of a graphical user interface (GUI). Visual literacy, therefore, now encompasses the ability to assimilate the instructions on the lid of a photocopier and the set-up diagrams in a hi-fi manual.

Mechanical reproduction

This subject, one of the most discussed in the literature on art and technology, requires further attention. At one time most artworks were unique and therefore could be seen only in one place. According to Walter Benjamin, author of the famous 1936 essay 'The Work of Art in the Age of Mechanical Reproduction', the presence of the original object and its physical location endowed it with an 'aura' or halo of significance. Mechanical reproduction via photography, he thought, shattered that aura. Now we mostly encounter visual works for the first time in a reproduced form: in a book, a magazine or on television. Inevitably, transformations of scale, colour, texture and context occur. But there are many gains as well as losses. Benjamin and John Berger perceived revolutionary potential in the reproducibility of images through such means as film- and photo-montage.[5]

Today, many types of visual culture exist only in reproduced form, indeed they have been designed for mass replication; for instance, photographs, posters, multiples and music videos. Artefacts produced in large editions are widely available and cheap, thus mechanical reproduction has resulted in a significant democratisation of culture.

Technological determination and determinism

A recurring issue in technology's relation to art is the extent to which the nature of the technology in question *determines* form, content and style. Berger, in the section of *Ways of Seeing* dealing with private property, perceived a connection between the advent of the new technology of oil painting in Europe and the worldview and lifestyle of the upper/middle-class patrons of this artform. Oil painting, Berger argued, made possible an unprecedented verisimilitude in the depiction of reality: 'What distinguishes oil painting from any other form of painting is its special ability to render the tangibility, the texture, the lustre, the solidity of what it depicts. It defines the real as that which you can put your hands on.'[6] Patrons commissioned pictures of themselves, their food, livestock, houses and estates. Oil painting reflected back to them, and thereby affirmed, their way of life. The subsequent history of the medium indicates, however, that its iconographic and stylistic potentials were much wider.

According to Raymond Williams, technology is a *precondition* for the existence of a modern medium such as television, but he thinks television is really 'a cultural form' or 'art' involving human imagination and creativity; consequently, its content, style and quality cannot be explained by reference to technology alone.[7] (Excellent and poor programmes can be made with the same equipment.)

Film theorists such as Jean-Louis Baudry, Jean-Louis Comolli, Raymond Fielding, Barry Salt and Steve Neale have written at length on the subject of the technology of cinema.[8] Neale comments:

> Technology is a basic component of cinema, a condition of its existence and a continuing factor in its development (as witness . . . special effects technology in . . . science fiction films . . .). It has its own specificity, its own history . . . [which] cannot be reduced simply to the status of an effect produced by economic, psychological or aesthetic factors . . . The history and current state of cinema rather involve an uneven and often complex interweaving of all these elements, each conditioning, but not fully determining or explaining, the others.[9]

Despite the complexity of cinematic technology, all those studying film need to learn as much as they can about it because such knowledge will deepen their understanding of the construction of films.[10] Furthermore, new technical developments in the cinema – the advent of sound, colour and film formats like CinemaScope – have repeatedly been used by film studios as publicity and selling points.

The expression 'technological determinism' refers to the belief that technological revolutions are inevitable: 'The atom bomb would have been invented sooner or later and, once in existence, it was bound to be used at some time or another.' Baudrillard, according to Sean Cubbitt, provided 'the most extreme version of the technological determinist thesis' when he contended that 'whole societies can be envisioned as effects of their characteristic media technologies'.[11]

Such fatalism puts technology in the driving seat, and leaves humanity feeling helpless in spite of the fact that it is we who are responsible for it. A disturbing future scenario, prompted by the quest for artificial intelligence, is that one day machines that can think, sense and replicate will rule the world. Another scenario, based on developments such as genetic engineering, is that humans will merge with biological machines to produce a 'neo-biological civilisation'.[12] What is certain – historical examples prove it – is that successful new technologies transform the world and thereby the ways humans think, feel and behave.

Technology's social impact can be considered further via the example of photocopying machines. Such machines are indifferent to the content of what they copy: they will reproduce a racist tract as well as a statement of human rights. However, in the Soviet Union photocopiers were rare and kept under lock and key, because their copying ability (plus their ability to generate many copies of the same document), was itself a threat to the regime. Photocopying facilitated the flow of more information of all kinds and thereby fostered a freedom of expression that undermined centralised, totalitarian control. It is clear from this example that the impact of technology has to be considered in relation to the particular social context in which it is introduced.

Television is similarly a neutral channel as far as the transmission of content is concerned. Some critics argue that, in the West, the key social impact of television is not the disparate nature of its programmes but the fact that it is an entertainment and information medium millions watch at home for hours each evening – it is thus a self-policing form of social control, an 'opium for the people', because of its fascination and the manner in which it is viewed.

One perennial question is particularly relevant to artists and designers, namely, 'Is technology ethically and politically neutral?' Those who enjoy shooting guns point out that it is the person who pulls the trigger who kills not the gun by itself. However, a gun is *designed* to wound or kill and an automatic pistol enables a deranged individual to murder many more people faster and at a greater distance than a person armed with a club. Since contemporary nuclear and chemical weaponry can destroy all human life, weapons designers carry an awesome moral responsibility.

It is symptomatic of the present epoch that most cultural producers are critically aware of how technology affects their work (either for good or ill). Indeed, many have a clearly articulated theory and method whereby they seek to control and turn technology to their advantage, rather than allowing it to dominate them. The London fashion designers Angel Biotek and Aki Sony have remarked: 'You don't need to fear or respect technology. It's better to abuse it.'[13]

McLuhan and the mass media

After a period of neglect, interest has revived in the ideas of the 1960s' guru of the mass media Marshall McLuhan, author of the seminal texts The *Gutenberg Galaxy* (Toronto, Toronto University Press, 1962) and *Understanding Media* (London, Routledge & Kegan Paul, 1964). He declared the mass media to be 'extensions of Man'. This is one of the key characteristics of technology: it increases human labour power both physical and mental; it augments human artistic capacities both quantitatively and qualitatively. The tremendous *magnifying power* of modern media technology is best illustrated by the example of actors and singers who, as a consequence of mass media exposure, become 'stars', quasi-mythical beings worshipped by millions of fans around the world.

However, as the British Luddites discovered, the automation associated with machines can also replace human labour and result in de-skilling and mass unemployment. But new technologies can also ameliorate human drudgery and give rise to whole new industries.

One of McLuhan's key slogans was 'the medium is the message', by which he meant that the medium or delivery system was more important than the content delivered by it. Writers in *Wired* magazine deem this idea relevant to new developments such as the Internet. By distinguishing between hot (e.g. movies) and cool (e.g. television) media, McLuhan provided a fresh way of classifying our relationship with culture. But it now needs to be revised in the light of a medium such as the Internet which is both participatory and vivid, both situation and spectacle, that is, a mixture of hot and cool.

In spite of McLuhan's slogan, the contents of visual media remain important as far as viewers are concerned. Examples of, and news about, the traditional arts are often relayed by television; even new technology is discussed in the media.[14] Furthermore, technology is the subject matter of many horror and science-fiction movies which play upon our feelings of euphoria or anxiety in regard to robots, computers, and so on.

Artists and technology

All artists depend on technology but the extent varies according to the period and the individual. There is clearly a difference of magnitude between a painter of 1600 who could make pictures with pigments, brushes and canvas, and a 1990 team of movie-makers who require masses of expensive and complex equipment before they can produce, edit and project a major feature film. (Of course, at any one time, various technologies – some ancient and some modern – co-exist. The advent of a new medium does not necessarily totally replace the old ones.) Artists have differed markedly in their reactions to new media: when photography appeared in the 1840s some painters welcomed it as a visual aide-memoire while others concluded 'Painting is dead'.

One strand of twentieth-century art which had an intimate relationship with technology and machines was Kinetic art.[15] (For example, metal sculptures that moved via the agency of electric motors.) Also, during the 1960s, particularly in the United States, there was a vogue for so-called 'Technological' or 'Techno art', that is, work that foregrounded technology and deliberately tried to take advantage of the latest machines and inventions.[16] Since the latter were associated with industry and big business, the artists were compelled to seek sponsorship and technical help from those sources.

In the sphere of architecture there was an equivalent, namely, the 'high-tech' buildings designed by such figures as Buckminster Fuller, Richard Rogers, Norman Foster and Michael Hopkins. An opposite tendency was called, of course, 'low-tech'.

Many artists and designers not only use such technology as part or all of the creative process, but have made it the focus of their work, whether celebrating, exploring, critiquing or subverting available means. Today, there are a number of visual artists – Mark Pauline and Stelarc, for instance – whose involvement with machines is extraordinarily intimate. Pauline constructs robots and weapons of various kinds from discarded technology and then, by means of remote control, he makes them fight battles as a form of public spectacle. Stelarc seeks to become a 'cyborg', that is, 'a human with technologically-enhanced capabilities'.[17] (See figure 15.)

Stelarc's work reveals a general truth: we are all partly mechanised; we

---

15 [facing page] Stelarc, *The Third Hand*, Tokyo, Nagoya, Yokohama (1976–81). Stelarc is a remarkable Australian performance artist and cyborg philosopher who has explored the body's relationship to technology in public for two decades by means of biocompatible inventions, multimedia events and by risking his own body. The robotic third hand augments the body's abilities; it is controlled via EMG signals from abdominal and leg muscles. Stelarc has mounted numerous events in which his body has been suspended from hooks piercing his flesh in order to test the body's physical limits. He has also filmed the insides of his stomach, colon and lungs by inserting mini-robotic sculptures equipped with lights and endoscopic cameras. Internal rhythms such as brainwaves and heartbeats have been externalised and amplified by attaching electrodes and other sensors to his body linked to light and sound, and interactive video systems.

Stelarc has also enabled his muscles to be stimulated by a pre-programmed computer and by other people so that some of his movements become involuntary. In other words, he has relinquished control of his body to a machine and to strangers. Also, via the Internet, it has become possible for his body to be activated by people who live far away. If the body is linked to robots via electronic communication systems its operational abilities would be improved so that actions could be performed at extraterrestrial locations.

Most people think technology should become more user-friendly, more adapted to human needs, but Stelarc takes the opposite view: he thinks humans should become 'more compatible to their machines'. Stelarc believes the human body is now obsolete and very limited, especially in regard to the demands of space travel, and that therefore evolution should continue by *redesigning* the body. His own experiments anticipate the day when the body's performance is enhanced by mechanical additions and micro-minaturised implants, and worn-out body parts are replaced by plug-in mechanical units. Assuming the latter happens, Stelarc sees no reason why humans should not live for ever. Extending the human life-span, Stelarc argues, is essential for long-distance space travel.

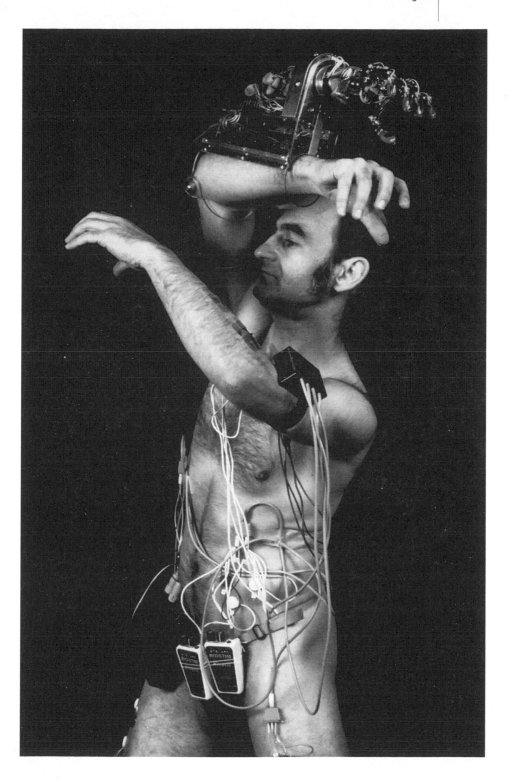

are all relying upon and interacting with machines such as cars, hairdriers, mobile phones, heart pacemakers and computers. Indeed, the amount of time children now spend in front of computer screens has become a matter of social concern.

Artists, indeed non-artists, can now afford a wide range of technological aids: personal computers, camcorders, video-cassette recorders, image scanners and modern-day software equivalents of brush and canvas: Photoshop and Freehand. Increasingly, machines can be connected or used in combination, so that a convergence of media is discernible.

In one chapter it is impossible to survey all the new media technologies that have come into being since the emergence of photography and the uses artists and others have made of them: therefore, one – computers – will be considered as a case study.

Computer art/graphics

Computers date from the middle of the twentieth century. Initially they were huge machines used by scientists, the military and large corporations to perform mathematical calculations. Today, they are owned by millions of individuals and organisations; their computing power has increased dramatically and they are used for a multitude of purposes.

Computer art has been produced internationally since about 1956 by people belonging to a variety of professions – in fact, anyone with access to computer time. Since many computer images were generated by scientists and commercial designers, the distinction between computer graphics and computer art was often hard to discern. If the latter served no immediate utilitarian purpose, was aesthetically pleasing and was exhibited in an art gallery then it counted as art rather than design.

The relevance of computers to the visual arts was not fully recognised until 1965 when a computer graphics show took place at the Howard Wise Gallery, New York, and 1968 when the *Cybernetic Serendipity* exhibition was held at the ICA, London.[18] Artists who have contributed to computer art shows include Simon Biggs, Harold Cohen, Jonathan Inglis, Alyce Kaprow, Scott Daly, William Latham, Manfred Mohr, Brian Reffin, Brian Smith, Barbara Sykes and John Whitney. Most professional fine artists were not specialists in the medium; in 1988 the American David Em (b. 1949) declared himself to be the first full-time computer artist.

Initially the 'art' produced via computers was mostly drawings and graphics. Computers linked to printers and plotters were programmed to print out specified geometric shapes in random combinations or to transform images by a series of discrete steps, for example, the image of a man into a bottle and then into a map of Africa. However, as Robert Mallary and David Morris demonstrated, sculpture could also be produced with the help of punched tape and milling machines. More recently the British artist William Latham has used computers with evolutionary-type programmes to generate designs for weird, complex, organic forms which mutate over time.[19] He calls them 'computer sculptures' even though they exist only in two-dimensional form on screens thus far. (Of course, they have also been photographed – Cibachrome prints – and filmed.)

In the 1980s highly expensive and sophisticated computer graphics machines became available – such as the Quantel Paintbox – which enabled artists and designers to 'paint' directly with light. Colour photography and printing enabled such images to be fixed permanently. Alternatively, video recordings of computer art patterns could be replayed on television monitors.

Computer art was similar to photography in the sense that a single programme could be used to generate many copies and thus enable a democratisation of visual culture to occur. The advent of personal computers, with graphics tablets and dot matrix printers, made it possible for millions of ordinary people to create computer images if they so desired.

Computer-aided design

Computers have transformed the production of graphics, cartoon animation, feature films, video games, television logos and adverts, and rock music videos. During the 1970s and 1980s computers were increasingly employed in the fields of architectural, engineering, industrial and graphic design. Complex, three-dimensional objects such as buildings, oil-rigs, cars and aircraft could be represented by mathematical models stored in the computer's memory. Images of these models could be studied on VDUs (visual display units) from all angles and transformed at will. It was obviously cheaper and quicker to alter and test computer simulations rather than actual prototypes.

Computer-control systems

Computers can use feedback information to monitor and control other machines and systems. In various countries architects have been experimenting for some years with such control systems in order to link together all the machines found in modern homes to design an 'intelligent house' capable of responding automatically to the needs and wishes of the inhabitants,[20] for instance, turning down the volume of the television when the telephone is picked up. Le Corbusier's famous definition of a house as 'a machine for living in' seems likely to become literally true.

Digital imagery

As a result of the development of copying and scanning machines, mechanical reproduction has been joined by electronic reproduction. It is now possible to download a movie clip from the Internet, or load an image on to a computer from a CD-rom, and even scan a three-dimensional object. With the aid of a sophisticated range of filters and functions, the object can be manipulated by the reader/user. Its hue, shape, contrast and so on can be altered. This enables the consumer to become a producer and much of the debate about multimedia and interactivity is concerned with a shift from passive to active modes of engagement.

This has become possible only because of a significant change in technology from *analogue* to *digital* means of recording and storing information. Digital images consist of a mosaic of small pixels (picture elements) which are machine-readable. Once in the memory bank of a computer, images can be altered via image-processor software. In 1992 Kodak introduced the Photo CDS camera, the first digital camera, with a hard disk instead of film. Once they are full, disks can be inserted into computers and images appear on their screens. Media companies such as Philips, Sony and the SD Alliance are currently introducing the DVD (Digital Video Disk), a new format intended to provide high-definition images and to bring the one-stop home entertainment centre closer.

Digitalisation is happening across most visual media giving rise to new aesthetic experiences. Digital animation techniques have led to the film *Toy Story* (1995), which has a greater sense of depth and motion than any hand-drawn Disney cartoon before it.

The degree of manipulation which is now possible using digital imaging software makes the cliché 'the camera never lies' outmoded. According to William J. Mitchell, we have entered a 'post-photographic' age in which 'morphing' (a term derived from 'metamorphosis'), retouching and cloning in both still and animated imagery render photographs untrustworthy.[21] Knowledge of this situation provokes questions like 'Did the American Astronauts really land on the moon in 1969?' and 'Did the Gulf war take place?' Jean Baudrillard has written on the latter subject.[22]

Telematics or informatic art

This term was devised by Simon Nora and Alain Minc to describe the new electronic technology derived from the convergence of computers and telecommunication systems. Their 1978 report to the French government – *L'Informatisation de la Société* – led to the establishment of the 'Programme Télématique'.[23] The term was subsequently adopted by the British artist and art educator Roy Ascott who with others around the globe has used international computer-telecommunication systems to generate interactive artworks. (The first live two-way satellite video transmission by artists took place between the East and West Coasts of the USA in 1977.) Such networking had implications for traditional conceptions of authorship because 'in telematic networking, authorship of images can be dispersed throughout the system'. Besides Ascott, artists involved in this kind of activity included Eric Gidney (Australian), Tom Sherman (Canadian) and Robert Adrian X (Austrian).[24]

Without participating in these networks it is difficult to judge the nature and quality of the art produced. However, it has been claimed that a new, collaborative type of art was produced which involved 'many individuals in the creation of meaning', art that dealt 'with the flux and flow of images and forms within shifting creative strategies'.

The Internet and virtual reality

Once computers were linked together in networks so that they could 'talk' to one another, then the 'Internet' or 'Net' and 'World Wide Web' (a point-and-click graphical interface for the Internet) became possible.[25] Millions around the globe with computers, modems and telephones now have access to this 'information superhighway' and use it to transmit texts and still and moving images. The opportunities for artists and designers are legion. Art 'magazines' are now published on the Internet. Fashion designers can now show their work in real time, and creative collaborations can take place involving people who are thousands of miles apart. By using a groupware product like Lotus Notes, participants can conduct a brainstorming session, or review a design in virtual reality.

Virtual reality is one by-product of ever-increasing computer power.[26] To experience virtual realities – computer-generated artificial or simulated, three-dimensional worlds – viewers don headsets with display screens and wear datagloves/suits. People have the power to move within and alter the simulated environment. Kevin Atherton is a British artist who has created a fictional art gallery in which all kinds of magical effects occur: as a viewer moves towards or away from objects their sizes change; the viewer can walk through walls and disregard normal social conventions (women can enter men's toilets).

The future of virtual reality is still uncertain but already there is much published speculation. At present VR is used by the medical profession and the military for training purposes. Clearly, it is beneficial for novice surgeons to perform operations on simulated bodies before they perform them on patients. War-game simulations, in contrast, can distance soldiers from the horrors of real wars. Currently, the most publicly available virtual reality is arcade-type entertainment for the young: violent games in which several participants seek to zap one another. Once tactile as well as visual dimensions are more fully developed, the appeal to the pornography industry of 'cybersex' is obvious. VR may eventually replace cinema and television. It has also been proposed that virtual architecture could supplement real architecture. A university library, for example, that has no more space for books could decide to fund a virtual rather than a real extension by scanning images and printed matter into a series of databases. At University College, London, a virtual reality centre for the built environment was founded in 1996 for the purpose of generating VR models of cities in order to evaluate the impact of new buildings and developments.

Max Frisch once observed that technology was 'the knack of so arranging the world that we don't have to experience it'. Some writers on VR fear that society may disintegrate if people retreat from RL (real life) into artificial worlds. (But this concern also applies to people who 'lose themselves' in paintings, novels and television soaps.) There are two safeguards: VR has to be paid for, hence work will still have to be performed; simulated food will not keep VR addicts alive.

Invisibility

The desire to visualise is fundamental to the way we think and experience, and is one aspect of our inheritance from the Enlightenment, which emphasised sight over the other senses. It is a paradox of visual culture that some theorists believe that recent technological innovations such as miniaturisation – so-called 'nanotechnology' – have caused 'a crisis of visibility'.[27] Today, a range of electronic tools inhabit grey plastic boxes and we have no means of visualising what is happening inside them. If something goes wrong most of us cannot 'look under the bonnet' and figure out a way of fixing it.

There are significant implications of such a crisis for designers and the design process. Some designers wonder if it is necessary any longer to design things that are visually and materially apparent. Certain writers now prefer to discuss design in terms of an experience, such as a package holiday, where from start to finish each aspect of the experience has been designed. Victor Margolin, an American design historian and theorist, has argued that what is important now is the whole *product environment* rather than the product in isolation.[28] As far as consumers are concerned, the 'environment' includes selecting and acquiring the product, learning to use/maintain/repair it and developing an emotional attachment to it. This implies that different criteria will be applied during the genesis of a new product, which in turn will influence its final 'look'. Margolin believes that the purchasing decisions of consumers will increasingly depend on blind faith and brand reputation rather than upon visual inspection.

Redundancy and obsolescence

In recent decades, the speed of technological development has accustomed us to the fact that products quickly become redundant. Those who work with computers constantly face new learning curves. Extraordinary demands are made on visual artists and critics alike: instead of perfecting an art or technique over a lifetime using the same medium, artists must master new software in a matter of months, and critics must often acquire a basic understanding of what the new technology does in order to be able to interpret and evaluate the artists' work.

A further problem arising within visual culture, as a result of technology's ability to increase output, is the current deluge of visual imagery. In this situation, fine artists find it harder and harder to make any kind of public impact. This may help to explain the prevalence of extreme behaviour designed to generate media headlines. A few artists have even advocated 'going on strike' (that is, ceasing to produce for a time) as if this futile gesture would make any significant difference.[29] Of course, the massive reservoir of imagery has also, for some artists, become nature, that is, their primary subject matter.

In the near future artists themselves may be made redundant by artificial intelligence technology. Analyses of creativity gradually reduce its mystery. Any human activity that can be precisely formulated and reduced to a set of instructions can be automated. In the past, automation first affected physical labour, then it affected clerical and administrative work. The next logical step – the automation of creative activity – is already happening (witness computer-animation), but for the moment we appear to be in a transitional phase in which artists enhance their creative capacity by interacting with machines.

Reactions to new technology

People respond to new technology in different ways: there are technophiliacs and technophobes. In fact, four categories can be distinguished: first, enthusiasts like the Italian Futurists (who celebrated the power of machines) and those contemporary artists who try to master new technology, regarding it as a challenge and an opportunity. Second, supporters of 'appropriate' and 'alternative' technologies, a group who, while critical of existing technology, do not reject its potential altogether.[30] What they seek are new forms of technology which are more user-friendly and ecologically friendly. Third, 'Modern Primitivists', a group who prefer to resist the advance of new technology in order to preserve ancient, craft-based skills. Fourth, 'New Luddites', people who are so critical of technology that they seek to end humanity's dependence on it. One such advocate – Kirkpatrick Sale – once opened a public debate by smashing a computer.[31]

A headline in a 1996 advert for a British university seeking to recruit students for its Faculty of Technology stated: 'Control your future with technology!' This we regard as over-optimistic because the problem is to control technology. Our advice to students is: be sceptical of the beneficial effects claimed for new technology by those with an interest in its success, because there are usually negative or 'revenge' effects too. But, given the ever-increasing presence of technology in our lives, ignoring and rejecting it are not viable options for most of us. Somehow we have to get to grips with new technology. We need to develop a historical and critical under-standing of it because only an informed populace/electorate will be able to be more discriminating and will stand a chance of influencing the future.

Gender and technology

The differential impact of technology is illustrated by the ways the two sexes respond to it. Although women have traditionally used various kinds of machines in factories, offices, hospitals and homes – typewriters, tele-phones, sewing and washing machines for example – there is a widespread impression that technology is more masculine than feminine, that men invent and design machines with themselves rather than women in mind, that men are more at ease using and mending machines than women, and that some men use new technologies in order to commit familiar crimes against women (sexual harassment via the Internet, for instance). In short, a 'toys for the boys' culture dominates and visual media are permeated by macho values (think of all the violent video games enjoyed by young males).

As the liberation of women proceeds (in fits and starts), the situation is changing: more and more women drive cars and make use of computers, become designers, animators and film-makers. In the meantime, however, considerable research and analysis is being undertaken by feminist design historians and theorists concerning the issue of gender in relation to products and technology, and by other writers like Dale Spender and Sherry Turkle concerning women's relationship to new technologies such as computers and the Internet.[32] (The term 'cyberfeminism' has been invented.) On the Net, people can adopt false personae if they wish, so 'gender-bending' can occur.

Impact on mental life

Through new media technologies more images and more aesthetic experi-ences engage our attention but, arguably, our ability to apprehend them and to concentrate has been gradually reduced by the daily bombardment of ephemeral visual material. We are in danger of losing the quality of *firstness* in an aesthetic experience – a heightened sense which is both memorable and unrepeatable – which Berger stressed in *Ways of Seeing*. Simmel, in a 1903 essay 'The Metropolis and Mental Life', identified a new state of mind – blasé – caused by the multiple impressions of modern cities.[33] This blaséness has blunted our sense of wonder towards our sur-roundings and our encounters with everyday life. New technologies have made us impatient so that we crave speed; hence, fast food, the soundbite, the thirty-second commercial, instant celebrities. Contemporary youth television programmes and commercials saturate the senses by delivering several kinds information simultaneously.

Some commentators think that there are now signs of a slackening of our powers of visual competence, an increasing shallowness of perception. They feel we are becoming visually lazier because of information overload and that our inattentiveness is rendering the subtleties of a well-crafted artwork unnoticed and unappreciated. Others disagree and suggest that we have developed the ability to appreciate faster flows of imagery and information which make earlier examples of visual culture seem antiquated in comparison. (McLuhan thought our response to 'information overload' was 'pattern recognition'.)

Such divergent views show that new technology is raising unprecedented analytical problems. Theoretical speculation has resulted in a spate of neologisms – 'technoculture', 'cyberspace' and 'televisual'[34] – and a series of questions: 'Who owns and controls the technology? Who has access to the media? Who owns the copyright? Do we really need all this new technology? What are its psychological and social effects? How can we enhance visual perception? After virtual reality, what is reality?'

The fact that humans are now exposed to so many simulations has led to the feeling that reality itself has been devalued, or that the distinction between the real and the simulated has become blurred. Arthur and Marielouise Kroker contend that *panic* is a now a widespread response to a sense of the loss of the real. In an encyclopedia they provide entries for panic art, architecture, fashion and so on.[35] Panic, the authors claim, is a key psychological mood of post-modern times as people oscillate between feelings of ecstasy and dread.

Implications for analysis and education

New technology is not only altering the ways visual culture is produced: it is also impacting upon the ways in which that culture is analysed and studied. For example, CD-roms are published by such cultural institutions as the National Gallery, London, which are visual-text catalogues and guides to the whole collection which art lovers with a multimedia personal computer can explore at home. In addition, some British art historians have formed a group called CHArt (Computers and the History of Art), for the purpose of using computing power to help solve problems arising in the practice of Art History.[36]

In the near future what may be of value to theorists of visual culture will be the visual programming languages and databases which utilise fuzzy logic to retrieve files for users who have only a vague visual memory of the image they wish to retrieve. This will prompt new research into cognitive and associative patterns, and this in turn will lead to new semiotic analyses of visual forms and their connotations.

Given the present speed of change, many universities struggle to keep pace and to envisage the impact new technology will have on the future lives of their graduates. They are slow, therefore, to incorporate sufficient discussion of technology-related issues in the curriculum. At the conceptual level, more thought needs to be given to processes and implications. Furthermore, in general, they are not equipping all students with the skills necessary to operate machines and software. Degree programmes and modules in such subjects as interactive multimedia are rare. Exceptions to the above criticisms include: The Centre for Art and Media Technologies at Karlsruhe, The Centre for Electronic Arts at Middlesex University, and The Centre for Inquiry in the Interactive Arts, Gwent College of Higher Education.[37]

However, it seems probable that new technology will eventually transform university teaching and learning. Indeed, the most extreme scenarios for the future imply the disintegration and disappearance of universities as physical campuses altogether.[38] As numbers of students expand and numbers of teaching staff reduce, and financial resources decline, students may be compelled to rely more on texts, slide/film/video archives, and data stored on CD-roms. More distance learning along the lines of the Open University is likely to occur and students working from home may soon 'attend' lectures, seminars and tutorials in virtual space rather than real space.

Multimedia encyclopedias and the Internet are already being heralded as stimulating alternatives to face-to-face teaching. Advertising rhetoric already extols the multicultural imaging of 'Windows 95' and the hyper-real world of computers with 'Pentium (processor) inside'. They appear to offer compelling substitutes for the old, chalk-and-talk mode of teaching.

Such developments pose particular problems for practical, studio-based subjects like fine art and graphic design: the time available for hands-on teaching over the drawing board or in the workshop, where skills are honed and questions arise through doing, is increasingly being regarded as a luxury which higher education can no longer afford. Simultaneously, however, design studios are increasingly being filled with rows of computer workstations.

Summary

This chapter has touched upon several of the established and recent themes raised by both old and new technologies, found within the present discourse on visual culture. Many issues have been left unresolved but we hope that some insights have been communicated and avenues for further thought and research opened up.

In every epoch humans face the problem of reconciling the culture of the past with the culture of the present and future. At the moment electronic visual media foreground optical experiences at the expense of tactile and visceral experiences. Wandering in the artificial environments of cyberspace, viewers enjoy new freedoms – like the ability to pass through walls – but they lack the sense of bodies situated in real space interacting with real human beings. But does this mean we should reject such new technologies? Let the last word be that of Pat Califia, a Modern Primitivist, who has argued for hybrid forms and experiences: 'We need a world where we can have both computers and campfires.'[39]

Notes and further reading

1 Neil Postman, speaking during Mark Harrison's *Visions of Heaven and Hell,* Part 1 (London, Channel 4 television, 1994).

2 For an illustrated survey of electronic arts see Frank Popper's *Art of the Electronic Age,* (London, Thames & Hudson, 1993). See also: Bob Cotton and Richard Oliver, *Understanding Hypermedia: From Multimedia to Virtual Reality,* (London, Phaidon Press, 1993); Simon Penny (ed.) *Critical Issues in Electronic Media,* (New York, State University of New York Press, 1995).

3 The existing literature on technology in general is extensive: Charles Singer and others (eds), *A History of Technology,* 5 vols, (Oxford, Clarendon Press, 1954–8); T. K. Dewey and T. I. Williams, *A Short History of Technology from the Earliest Times to A.D. 1900,* (Oxford, Clarendon Press, 1960); M. Daumas (ed.), *A History of Technology and Invention: Progress Through the Ages,* 3 vols, (London, John Murray, 1980); D. Birdsall and C. M. Cipolla, *The Technology of Man: A Visual History,* (London, Wildwood House, 1980).

Martin Heidegger is a modern philosopher who has reflected much on technology and human life; see: *The Question Concerning Technology and Other Essays,* (New York, Harper & Row, 1977). See also: L. Mumford, *Technics and Civilisation,* (London, Routledge & Kegan Paul, 1934); S. Giedion, *Mechanisation Takes Command: A Contribution to Anonymous History,* (New York, Oxford University Press, 1948); Phil Slater (ed.), *Outlines of a Critique of Technology,* (London, Ink Links, 1980); Rosalind Williams, *Notes on the Underground: An Essay on Technology, Society and the Imagination,* (Cambridge, MA & London, MIT Press, 1990); David Nye, *American Technological Sublime,* (Cambridge, MA & London, MIT Press, 1994). The contents of the academic journal *Technology and Culture,* (1958–), International Quarterly of SHOT: the Society for the History of Technology, are relevant.

On new technology see: Stephen Hill, *The Tragedy of Technology: Human Liberation versus Domination in the Late Twentieth Century,* (London, Pluto Press, 1988); Andrew Feenberg, *Critical Theory of Technology,* (Oxford, Oxford University Press, 1991); Verena A. Conley (ed.), *Rethinking Technologies,* (Minneapolis, University of Minnesota Press, 1993); Gretchen Bender and Timothy Druckery (eds), *Culture on the Brink,* (Seattle, WA, Bay Press, 1994); Edward Barrett and Marie Redmond (eds), *Contextual Media and Interpretation,* (Cambridge, MA & London, MIT Press, 1995); A. R. Stone, *The War of Desire and Technology at the Close of the Mechanical Age,* (Cambridge, MA & London, MIT Press, 1995); Nicholas Negroponte, *Being Digital,* (New York, Knopf/London, Hodder & Stoughton, 1995); Derek Leebaert (ed.) *The Future of Software,*

(Cambridge, MA & London, MIT Press, 1995); James Brook and Iain Boal (eds), *Resisting the Virtual Life*, (San Francisco, CA, City Lights, 1995); Edward Tenner, *Why Things Bite Back: New Technology and the Revenge Effect*, (London: Fourth Estate, 1996); Francis Babbage (ed.), *Cultural Babbage: Technology, Time and Invention*, (London, Faber & Faber, 1996); Anthony Smith, *Software for the Self: Culture and Technology*, (London, Faber & Faber, 1996).

For visual culture and science/technology, see P. Hayward (ed.), *Culture, Technology and Creativity in the Late Twentieth Century*, (London, Paris, Rome, John Libbey, 1990); P. Hayward and T. Wollen (eds), *Future Visions: New Technologies of the Screen*, (London, Arts Council & BFI Publishing, 1993), and the journals *Leonardo* and *Art Technology* (official journal of the British Computer Arts Society).

4   See: T. Forester (ed.), *The Information Technology Revolution*, (Oxford, Blackwell, 1985); D. Lyon, *The Information Society: Issues and Illusions*, (Cambridge, Polity Press, 1988); Mark Poster, *The Mode of Information: Poststructuralism and the Social Context*, (Cambridge, Polity Press/Oxford, Blackwell, 1990); Theodore Roszak, *The Cult of Information: A Neo-Luddite Treatise on High-Tech, Artificial Intelligence, and the True Art of Thinking*, (Berkeley, CA, University of California Press, 2nd edn 1994); Mark Poster, *The Second Media Age*, (Cambridge, Polity Press, 1995); and *The Information Society: An International Journal*, (London, Taylor & Francis).

5   See: W. Benjamin, *Illuminations*, (London, J. Cape, 1970); J. Berger, *Ways of Seeing*, (London, BBC/Harmondsworth, Middlesex, Penguin Books, 1972); and J. A. Walker, *Art in the Age of Mass Media*, (London, Pluto Press, 2nd edn 1994).

6   Berger, *Ways of Seeing*, p. 88.

7   See: R. Williams, *Television: Technology and Cultural Form*, (London, Fontana/Collins, 1974).

8   J-L. Baudry, 'Ideological Effects of the Basic Cinematographic Apparatus', *Film Quarterly*, 28:2 (Winter 1974–5), 39–47; J.-L. Comolli, 'Technique and Ideology: Camera, Perspective, Depth of Field', *Movies and Methods*, ed. Bill Nichols, (Berkeley, CA, University of California Press, 1985); R. Fielding (ed.), *A Technological History of Motion Pictures and Television*, (Berkeley, CA, University of California Press, 1967); B. Salt, *Film Style and Technology: History and Analysis*, (London, Starword, 1983); S. Neale, *Cinema and Technology: Image, Sound, Colour*, (London & Basingstoke, Macmillan Educational, 1985).

9   Neale, *Cinema and Technology*, p. 2.

10 Besides theoretical and review journals like *Screen*, *Premiere*, *Film Comment* and *Sight and Sound*, film students should read more technical magazines such as *American Cinematographer*.

11 S. Cubitt, *Timeshift: On Video Culture*, (London & New York, Comedia/Routledge, 1991), p. 24.

12 See: Kevin Kelly, *Out of Control: The New Biology of Machines*, (London, Fourth Estate, 1994).

13 Biotek and Sony were quoted in *The Guardian*, (17 February 1992), 35.

14 New technology is regularly featured in the television strand *Equinox* (Channel 4, 1988–). See also the 1994 BBC-2 eight-part television series entitled *White Heat*. A tie-in book was published: Carroll Pursell, *White Heat: People and Technology*, (London, BBC Books, 1994).

15 For a noted survey of Kinetic art see: Frank Popper, *Origins and Development of Kinetic Art*, (London, Studio Vista, 1968).

16 For further details see entry 657 'Technological Art' in John A. Walker's *Glossary of Art, Architecture and Design Since 1945*, (London, Library Association/Boston, MA, G. K. Hall, 3rd edn 1992).

17 On cyborgs see: Donna J. Haraway, *Simians, Cyborgs and Women: The Reinvention*

of Nature, (London, Free Association, 1991). See also the 1989 film *Cyborg* directed by Albert Pyum and starring Jean-Claude van Damme. For more on Stelarc's ideas see his article: 'Prosthetics, Robotics and Remote Existence: Postevolutionary Strategies', *Leonardo*, 24:5 (1991), 591–5.

18   Jasia Reichardt (ed.), *Cybernetic Serendipity: The Computer and the Arts*, (London, Studio International, 1968). For a well-illustrated survey of computer art see: Cynthia Goodman, *Digital Visions: Computers and Art*, (New York, Abrams/Syracuse, Everson Museum of Art, 1987).

19   Stephen Todd and William Latham, *Evolutionary Art and Computers*, (London, Academic Press, 1992).

20   One such automated dwelling is called the Tron House and is being designed by Professor Ken Sakamura of Tokyo University. See: Neal Morris, 'Windows of Opportunity in a Dream House', *The Guardian*, (10 January 1991), 31.

21   W. J. Mitchell, *The Reconfigured Eye: Visual Truth in the Post-Photographic Era*, (Cambridge, MA & London, MIT Press, 1992). Digital photography is also discussed in: 'Digital Dialogues: Photography in the Age of Cyberspace', *Ten 8*, 2:2 (Autumn 1991) and Martin Lister (ed.), *The Photographic Image in Digital Culture*, (London & New York, Routledge, 1995).

22   J. Baudrillard, *La Guerre du Golfe n'a pas eu Lieu*, (Paris, Galilée, 1991), and 'The Reality Gulf', *The Guardian*, (11 January 1991), 25.

23   S. Nora and A. Minc, *L'Informatisation de la Société*, (Paris, La Documentation Française, 1978).

24   On telematics and art see: H. Grundmann (ed.), *Art Telecommunication*, (Vancouver, Western Front/Vienna, Blix, 1984); R. Ascott, 'Arte, tecnologia e computer', *Arte e Scienza, Biologia, Tecnologia e Informatica*, (Venice, Edizioni La Biennale, 1986); *Beuys, Warhol, Higashiyama: Global-Art-Fusion*, (Bern, Art-Fusion-Edition, 1986); R. Ascott, 'On Networking', *Leonardo*, 21:3 (1988), 231–2; R. Ascott, 'Art Education in the Telematic Culture', *Synthesis: Visual Arts in the Electronic Culture*, eds M. Eisenbeis and H. Hagebölling (Offenbach am Main, Hochschule für Gestaltung, 1989), pp. 184–203; R. Ascott and C. Loeffler (eds), 'Connectivity: Art and Interactive Communications', *Leonardo*, 24:2 (1991), thematic issue.

25   On the Internet see: S. R. Hiltz and M. Turoff, *The Network Nation: Human Communication via Computer*, (Cambridge, MA, MIT Press, rev. edn 1993); J. C. Herz, *Surfing on the Internet*, (London, Abacus, 1995); Clifford Stoll, *Silicon Snake Oil*, (London, Macmillan, 1995); Dale Spender, *Nattering on the Net: Women, Power and Cyberspace*, (Melbourne, Spinifex, 1995); Rob Shields (ed.), *Cultures of the Internet: Virtual Spaces, Real Histories, Living Bodies*, (London, Sage, 1996); and the magazines *Wired, Internet, Internet World* and *.Net*. On art sites and the Internet see: M. L. McLaughlin, 'The Art Site on the World Wide Web', *Journal of Communication*, 46:1 (Winter 1996), 51–79.

26   On VR see: Myron W. Krueger, *Artificial Reality II*, (Reading, MA, Addison-Wesley, 1991); Steve Aukstankalnis and David Blatner, *Silicon Mirage: The Art and Science of Virtual Reality*, (Berkeley, CA, Peachtree Press, 1992); Barrie Sherman and Phil Judkins, *Glimpses of Heaven, Visions of Hell: Virtual Reality and its Implications*, (London, Hodder & Stoughton, 1992); Benjamin Woolley, *Virtual Worlds: A Journey in Hype and Hyperreality*, (Oxford & Cambridge, MA, Blackwell, 1992); *Virtual Reality: An Emerging Medium*, (New York, Guggenheim Museum Soho, 1993), leaflet; Howard Rheingold, *The Virtual Community: Finding a Connection in a Computerised World*, (London, Secker & Warburg, 1994); Steven R. Holtzmann, *Digital Mantras: The Languages of Abstract and Virtual Worlds*, (Cambridge, MA & London, MIT Press, 1994); Mary Eagle and Christopher Chapman (eds), *Virtual Reality*, (Canberra, National Gallery of Australia, 1995);

Mary Anne Moser and Douglas MacLeod (eds), *Immersed in Technology: Art and Virtual Environments*, (Cambridge, MA & London, MIT Press, 1996); Ralph Schroeder, *Possible Worlds: The Social Dynamics of Virtual Reality Technology*, (Boulder, CO, Westview Press, 1996).

27 On nanotechnology see: K. E. Drexler, *Engines of Creation: The Coming Era of Nanotechnology*, (London, Fourth Estate, 1996).

28 V. Margolin, 'Expanding the Boundaries of Design: The Product Environment and the New User', *Design Issues*, 4:1/2 (1988), 59–64.

29 Two art strikers were Gustav Metzger and Stewart Home. See: James Mannox and others, *The Art Strike Papers: The Years Without Art 1990–93*, bound with S. Home, *Neoist Manifestos*, (Stirling, Scotland, A. K. Press, 1991).

30 D. Dickson, *Alternative Technology and the Politics of Technical Change*, (London, Fontana, 1974).

31 Kirkpatrick Sale is the author of *Rebels Against the Future: The Luddites and their War on the Industrial Revolution*, (Reading, MA, Addison-Wesley, 1995).

32 Wendy Faulkner and others, *Smothered by Invention: Technology in Women's Lives*, (London, Pluto Press, 1985); Cheris Kramarae (ed.), *Technology and Women's Lives*, (New York, Routledge, 1988); Michele Martin, *'Hello Central?': Gender, Technology and Culture in the Formation of Telephone Systems*, (Montreal, McGill-Queens University Press, 1991); Ann Gray, *Video Playtime: The Gendering of a Leisure Technology*, (London & New York, Comedia/Routledge, 1992); Gill Kirkup and Laurie S. Keller (eds), *Inventing Women: Science, Technology and Gender*, (Cambridge, Polity Press/Open University Press, 1992); Eileen Green and others (eds), *Gendered by Design? Information Systems and Office Systems*, (London, Taylor & Francis, 1993); Ellen Lupton, *Mechanical Brides: Women and Machines from Home to Office*, (New York, Cooper-Hewitt National Museum of Design/Princeton Architectural Press, 1993); Carol A. Stabile, *Feminism and the Technological Fix*, (Manchester & New York, Manchester University Press, 1994); Spender, *Nattering on the Net*.

33 Georg Simmel, 'The Metropolis and Mental Life', *The Sociology of Georg Simmel*, ed. K. Wolff (Columbus, Ohio State University Press, 1959), pp. 409–24.

34 Constance Penley and Andrew Ross (eds), *Technoculture*, (Minneapolis, MN, University of Minnesota Press, 1991). The word 'cyberspace' was invented by sci-fi writer William Gibson; see also: Michael Benedikt (ed.), *Cyberspace – First Steps*, (Cambridge, MA & London, MIT Press, 1991); Douglas Rushkoff, *Cyberia: Life in the Trenches of Cyberspace*, (San Francisco, CA, Harper/London, Flamingo, 1994); Mark Slouka, *War of the Worlds: Cyberspace and the High-Tech Assault on Reality*, (London, Abacus, 1996).

35 A. and M. Kroker and David Cook, *Panic Encyclopedia: The Definitive Guide to the Post-Modern Scene*, (Basingstoke, Macmillan Education, 1994).

36 William Vaughan and Anthony Hamber, *Computers and Art History*, (London, Mansell, 1988) and CHArt's journal: *Computers and the History of Art*, (Reading, Berkshire, Harwood Academic, 1989–).

37 Roy Ascott is the director of the Gwent centre. He is an artist/art educator who is also an advocate and enthusiast for new technology. He believes that 'Connectivity, interaction and emergence are the watchwords of cyberculture'. See: 'Aesthetics argued on a Phone Extension', *Times Higher Education Supplement: Multimedia Features*, (10 November 1995), vi–vii.

38 Chris Hutchinson, 'Snares in the Charmed Circle', *Times Higher Education Supplement, Multimedia Features*, (12 April 1996), iv–v.

39 Pat Califia, quoted in David Toop, *Ocean of Sound: Aether Talk, Ambient Sound and Imaginary Worlds*, (London, Serpent's Tail, 1995), p. 167.

Appendix: Modular schemes

To understand how the subject of visual culture is actually taught in universities, organisational arrangements need to be outlined. Since the authors of this book both lecture at Middlesex University, North London, it will serve as the principal example.

Many universities now divide the teaching year into two semesters and deliver the content of teaching via discrete units called 'modules' (most of which are one semester long). The modular system was borrowed from the United States by the new British polytechnics formed during the 1970s. Many of the latter absorbed art and design colleges with long histories. (The colleges became faculties of the polytechnics.) The polytechnics awarded degrees so it was only just that, in 1992, they were permitted to call themselves universities.

At Middlesex University (which incorporated Hornsey College of Art), first year students select modules from a catalogue listing hundreds. The modules are grouped into 'sets' according to subject matter – for example, an Art and Design History set, a Film Studies set. Sets are the responsibility of schools which are principally groups of staff knowledgeable about the same subject. The schools in turn are grouped into faculties such as the Faculty of Art, Design and Performing Arts.

Students at Middlesex are encouraged to take modules from different sets (at least two) and to plan a programme of related modules, to be taken over three years (by full-timers; part-time students take longer). The modules selected will cover a variety of subjects but the total programme ought to make intellectual sense. Most sets have introductory modules taught in the first year designed to orientate students and to provide guidance as to sensible pathways through the thicket of second and third year modules.

Supporters of modular schemes argue that their advantage over traditional, single-strand, specialist degree courses is that they provide a broader education and a wider variety of subjects and give students greater freedom of choice and flexibility. Modules are given credit ratings (for example, 20 credits) and students accumulate credits by passing modules until they reach an agreed total for a degree with honours. (Marks given for the student's work are thus different from the credit numbers associated with each module.) Another reason modular schemes are favoured is that they allow students to discontinue at certain points – at which time they may qualify for a lower award – and/or to resume later, or to transfer to other institutions.

Given the range of subjects that can be studied, there is greater breadth but, by the same token, less depth than in traditional degree courses. Modularity encourages multi- and inter-disciplinary because students can cross traditional departmental boundaries and combine disparate topics. For example, a student undertaking a 'combined studies programme' could take modules from three sets, say, American Studies, Art and Design History, and Writing and Publishing. Cross-disciplinarity also occurs within modules: for example, a module entitled *Art in the Age of Mass Media* could include examples drawn from contemporary fine art, advertising, rock music and videos, and films/television programmes about art and artists.

Students can also construct a degree by taking an equal number of modules from two sets (a joint major) or they can take more from one set and fewer from another (a major/minor). Furthermore, after the first year of study, most schools offer a

'Specialised Award Programme' which enables students to prioritise a particular subject. Certain modules are exclusive to such award programmes.

The teaching within schools of art and design, that is, schools whose students engage in studio practice, proved difficult to modularise and resistant to the inter-disciplinary thrust of modular schemes. In some schools they have reached a half-way house: they have converted their three-year courses into a sequence of modules but they have retained pathways that result in a specialist award in their main subject. The history and theory of visual culture is generally taught to art and design students as a compulsory minor making up about one-third of their total degree. Thus the long-standing problem of the full integration of theory/history and studio practice remains unresolved.

In those universities where schools of the History and Theory of Visual Culture have been established as independent entities, the theory/practice division has been institutionalised. (In some surviving art colleges the opposite happened: Art History Departments were abolished and their staff dispersed to the studio areas.) Visual Culture lecturers in such schools face the demanding task of teaching two groups of students with rather different interests, abilities and needs: first, the studio-based students whose priority is their studio specialism (architecture, fine art, fashion, graphics, product design, etc.); and, second, the academic-stream students who study and analyse Visual Culture rather than produce it.

Some of the latter students, having acquired a degree in Visual Culture, may wish to undertake research at a more advanced level. There are taught Master of Arts programmes that enable them to do this. At the time of writing, Bath College of Higher Education and Middlesex University offer courses that lead to postgraduate diplomas and MAs in Visual Culture.

Index

Note: 'n' after a page reference indicates the number of a note on that page.